India Tomorrow

'Pradeep Chhibber and Harsh Shah's *India Tomorrow* gives the reader a synoptic glimpse into the minds of a carefully curated list of young leaders from the Indian political class, the nuances of their leadership styles and the principles and values they claim animate them. Through a series of frank interviews and candid admissions, the book offers compelling insights into a wide range of topics from questions of dynastic politics, anecdotes of personal tragedy and stories of challenges overcome and, ultimately, an engaging account of what drives the next-generation leaders who will make India tick tomorrow.'

—Shashi Tharoor
Member of Parliament (Lok Sabha) and author

'A fascinating book that stands out for the sheer diversity of voices it brings together. In a country where half the population is under 25, we finally hear first hand from the 'young' politicians who will lead India into a 'new' tomorrow. Breaking stereotypes, offering hope, *India Tomorrow* is a must read for any observer of Indian political life.'

—Rajdeep Sardesai
Indian news anchor and author; consulting editor at India Today Group

'What drives the next generation of Indian politicians? *India Tomorrow* helps answer this and many other questions by bringing together a diverse set of well-known leaders to discuss vital issues about their political life and India's future. Having worked and interacted with many of these outstanding politicians, I can assure you that our future is in safe hands. Their forward-looking ideas and deep understanding of grassroots politics is a testament to the vibrancy of India's political process. An easy read, the book promises to be a real bestseller that will stand the test of time. It should be read by everyone interested in India and its development.'

—Jayant Sinha
Member of Parliament (Lok Sabha)

India Tomorrow

Conversations with the
Next Generation of Political Leaders

Pradeep Chhibber
Harsh Shah

OXFORD
UNIVERSITY PRESS

OXFORD
UNIVERSITY PRESS

Oxford University Press is a department of the University of Oxford.
It furthers the University's objective of excellence in research, scholarship,
and education by publishing worldwide. Oxford is a registered trademark of
Oxford University Press in the UK and in certain other countries.

Published in India by
Oxford University Press
22 Workspace, 2nd Floor, 1/22 Asaf Ali Road, New Delhi 110002, India

© Oxford University Press 2020

The moral rights of the authors have been asserted.

First Edition published in 2020

ISBN-13 (print edition): 978-0-19-012583-7
ISBN-10 (print edition): 0-19-012583-7

ISBN-13 (eBook): 978-0-19-099144-9
ISBN-10 (eBook): 0-19-099144-5

Typeset in Goudy Oldstyle Std 11/14
by The Graphics Solution, New Delhi 110 092
Printed in India by Rakmo Press, New Delhi 110 020

To our families

Contents

CONTENTS

Acknowledgements

I ndian party politics is undergoing a generational transformation. The younger politicians who will inherit India have no personal memory of the struggle for independence. They came to age in an era of competitive party politics, robust democratic exchange, while representing the largest youth population in the world. While most of the young leaders we interviewed come from political families they have, over the years, developed their own distinct voices. These interviews capture these voices.

We have accumulated multiple debts while writing this book. The task of interviewing politicians is daunting and our largest debt is to the 20 young politicians who took time out of their very busy schedules to speak with us, some of them at short notice. Some took time out on more than one occasion to answer our questions. Many of the politicians we interviewed not only gave us suggestions for whom to interview, but also helped arrange meetings with their colleagues across party lines. A large network of well-wishers either helped arrange the interviews for us or gave us the appropriate contacts.

The idea of the book, whom to interview, and the questions we should pose to the politicians was a collective enterprise and we owe a special thank you to Shankkar Aiyar, Rajdeep Sardesai,

ACKNOWLEDGEMENTS

Pranav Gupta, Rahul Verma, and Munjaal Kapadia for their helpful suggestions and comments along the way. Amit Ahuja and Adnan Naseemullah read the manuscript once we had completed the interviews and encouraged us to publish them quickly and as is. We are also grateful to Dolly Jaitley and the late Arun Jaitley, Vijay Parekh, and Ravi Raheja for their support in different ways.

We would like to thank Moutushi Mukherjee and Ranjini Majumdar at Oxford University Press for being instrumental through the publication process and in bringing the book to the shelves. The work has also benefited enormously from the editorial inputs by Shikhar Vyas and Swarnima Narayan.

Finally, we owe a special thank you to Kaja, Anuka, and Neela for their forbearance, and to Suchita, Jayesh, Maniti, and the rest of the Shah and Kapadia families for their unwavering support.

Introduction

For most of its life as a nation-state, India has been led by politicians who grew up either in the nationalist movement or in its shadow, when Jawaharlal Nehru was prime minister. Those who grew up in the movement had a calling for politics that was deeply influenced by the anti-colonial struggles. This was a time of unhindered imagination: the possibilities of a united and prosperous India seemed limitless. Politics was richly pluralist and accommodative. Yet, India was poor, the population was mostly uneducated, food insecurity was pervasive, and the state power faced real limits, both domestically and internationally. India was a young country.

The death of Nehru—and Lal Bahadur Shastri shortly after—changed the face of Indian politics. The unanimity and idealism which had been the hallmarks of the post-Independence years soon withered to give rise to an era of political fragmentation and conflict. The Congress party underwent a split and various state parties and caste parties emerged to challenge the behemoth. The consensus of the 1950s and the early 1960s dissipated under the onslaught of multiple protest movements. These movements were fanned by linguistic identities, farmers concerns, religious fundamentalisms, caste politics, and genuine social concerns. The politics of consensus led by the Congress party no longer defined Indian politics.

In a bid to robustly face these challenges and consolidate itself, the state accumulated more power. This was led by an unprecedented centralization of power in the office of the prime minister. In the name of socialism, the state's tentacles reached everywhere. State governments followed suit, and the well-known and much-derided permit-license raj flourished in earnest. The culmination of this unabashed use of power was heralded by the National Emergency in 1975. The end of the Emergency changed the nature of Indian politics forever: a politics could now be imagined without the Congress Party at the centre and in every state.

The idea that the Congress could be defeated truly took hold, opening up opportunities for politics of all kinds. The tumult that followed was powerful in its scope. The separatist movement in Punjab and the subsequent anti-Sikh riots in 1984 (till now the single largest religious riot in the history of India) were punctuated briefly by the spectacular success of the Congress Party in the 1985 elections. The period that followed was no less turbulent with the civil war in Sri Lanka, the Shah Bano case and its aftermath, the opening of the locks in the Babri Masjid, and the defeat of the Congress in the 1989 elections, with the decade being capped by the anti-Mandal agitations. The decade or so that followed saw a more prominent manifestation of religious tensions, seen in the destruction of the Babri Masjid and the 2002 Gujarat riots. This period also marked the beginning of the ascent of the Bharatiya Janata Party (BJP) and its muscular nationalism, a version of which we continue to see today reflected in the party's moves on citizenship and Article 370.

Most of the prominent next-generation leaders who currently dominate India's political landscape came of age in this period of turmoil. Their political memories are not of pan-Indian solidarity under the leadership of leaders like Nehru, but rather of widespread ferment. By the time they entered the political arena, the idea of consensus had been relegated to the history books. Indian politics had been singularly transformed, with an explosion of vigorous democratic oppositions to any ruling government, dotted with periods of violence and unstable coalitional politics and accompanied by an unrelenting focus on caste and religion as the singular sites of identity formation in India.

The model of development so cherished by Nehru and spurred by a global consensus of the 1950s, lay in tatters, marked by the sluggish Hindu rate of growth which defined the country's economy until the liberalization reforms of 1991.

Today, Indian politics is undergoing an ideological and generational transformation. A new generation of leaders is poised to take the reins of power in the coming decade. The aspirations and beliefs of these leaders are more reflective of contemporary India, which is now a nation struggling to redefine its identity. Its body politic cares less about consensus than power: the Indian state, in effect, is growing up. India is not as poor as it used to be, its youth are more educated, food insecurity has been reduced for a large share of the population, and the state is more potent than ever before. Amid this new political environment stand India's youth—on one hand a demographic dividend waiting to be realized, on the other a time bomb waiting to explode. India is the youngest nation in the world. More than half of the country's population—a staggering 600 million people—is below the age of 25, and more than two-thirds below the age of 35. It has the largest youth population, by considerable distance, of any country in the world. And yet, the youth are grossly under-represented in politics. Political veterans occupy most of the political landscape, with barely a handful of parliamentarians below the age of 35. In fact, in the 15th Lok Sabha, the average Member of Parliament (MP) was 30 years older than the average Indian. Competing in electoral politics in contemporary India requires money and resources. Family connections and wealth are therefore necessary to enter politics and become a leader. All the politicians we interviewed for this book, except one, were far wealthier than the average Indian.

India's future, in some senses, will be determined by its political leadership. While it is easy to exaggerate the role of politicians in a vast and complex society and economy, it must be noted that India's political leaders have been responsible for some of the country's most significant successes and failures. While we have many biographies and assessments of the leaders who led India from Independence through the first 50 years or so of its nationhood, we do not know enough of those who are now inheriting the role of the torchbearer. We know their names, but not what lies behind the political facades that many of them have carefully built. For instance, what moves them? Who inspires them? What are the causes they truly care about? What are their passions and interests outside of politics? Do they have any regrets about their political careers? How do they explain some of the inconsistencies in their words and actions? Have their career choices come with big personal costs?

Our first attempt at interviewing such leaders started in 2014 when we began inviting prominent politicians to the University of California, Berkeley, to engage with Berkeley students, faculty, and interested residents of the San Francisco Bay Area. Shashi Tharoor, Arun Jaitley, Milind Deora, and Omar Abdullah candidly fielded questions from the diverse groups at Berkeley that had gathered on the campus. Each event was met with a surprising level of interest and excitement. In September 2017, on learning that Rahul Gandhi was visiting California, we grabbed at the opportunity to interview him. One of India's most famous yet most polarizing political leaders, this turned out to be his first such interaction on the international stage.

Given that Rahul Gandhi had essentially shunned the media for years, we were aware that such an interview would generate some interest. However, we were taken aback by the scale of its impact—on the Berkeley campus, the event was so heavily oversubscribed, additional viewing rooms adjacent to the main hall needed to be reserved to accommodate the overflowing audience. Hundreds of students stood for hours in the rain as Special Protection Group (SPG) officers (who flew in overnight from New Delhi due to security threats from certain Sikh groups based in California) ran thorough security checks. In India, the interview became the topic of debate on almost all the prime-time news channels, with senior cabinet ministers in the Modi government even holding press conferences to respond to Rahul's responses. Years later, people still recall the significance of the event. Indeed, Rahul's party colleague, Milind Deora, and journalists like Priya Sahgal, have gone on record to say that the event was the 'turning point' in Rahul Gandhi's political fortunes. Whether this is an accurate assessment or not is debatable, particularly after the Congress party's dismal performance in the 2019 elections. However, the response to the event demonstrated that there is a large and growing body of people in India that is interested in learning more about their political leaders and their stories. After extensive deliberations, we set out to write a book that would give readers a snapshot of contemporary Indian politics, and its future, through the stories of 20 of the country's most prominent next-generation politicians, each of whom we would interview in person. The goal was simple—to understand their personalities and ideologies, and offer readers unique insights. This book does not focus much on the quotidian aspects of politics, but rather attempts to unravel the personalities, aspirations, ideologies, interests, passions, and motivations of the leaders featured. In doing so, it explores issues and tensions that lie at the heart of contemporary India's politics, including but not limited to divisions of caste and religion, institutional decline, federalism and centre–state relations, integration of Jammu & Kashmir, dynastic politics, and women empowerment.

Of course, the production of a project such as this hinges in large part on the individuals featured. Finalizing this list involved a painstaking, iterative process. At first, we drew up a list of India's most prominent next-generation politicians. Keeping in mind the paucity of bright young leaders holding important positions in political parties or government, and the need to feature those having the right blend of youth and experience, we decided to set an age cut-off of 50 years. Hence, anybody of the age 49 or below at the time of the interview was eligible. We then embarked on a wide consultation process, having the list vetted and modified by leading journalists, academics, and politicians. We also shared the list with each politician that we interviewed, and often ended up adding more names on their recommendations.

The list is by no means exhaustive—there are countless young leaders across the country making significant impact on the ground who have not been profiled in this book. In fact, many political changemakers who are important voices in their communities are not even featured in the media at all. However, we have tried to make the list fairly representative—bringing in diversity in terms of age, experience, region, political party, gender, and most significantly, viewpoints, and ideologies. For instance, you might notice a stark contrast between the philosophy, language, and attitude of the independent Gujarat Member of the Legislative Assembly (MLA), Jignesh Mevani, and somebody like a Jyotiraditya Scindia, who has been schooled in politics since an early age. Similarly, there may be numerous differences between the 29-year-old Aaditya Thackeray, leader of the right-wing Shiv Sena, and an Asaduddin Owaisi. However, you might find that Aaditya is more liberal than most others on many issues. And that despite being in the BJP, Varun Gandhi's economic and social outlook is not very far from that of his cousin, Rahul Gandhi.

The single most significant limiting factor for us was whether a politician was willing to make time to sit down with two strangers who are writing a book for an academic press. Thankfully, we were eventually able to meet almost everyone we had hoped to.

INTRODUCTION

Anyone who has interviewed Indian politicians will appreciate the enormity of the task—the lack of formal channels for outreach, the endless hours of waiting, and the constant juggling and re-juggling of schedules. By the end of it, we grew accustomed to last-minute cancellations. We travelled to different parts of the country for the interviews, from a village in rural Uttar Pradesh to big cities like Ahmedabad and Delhi, sometimes showing up in the city only to learn that the interview has been rescheduled. Yet, to say that the journey has been exhilarating would be an understatement.

In this book, we present the interviews in the voices of the politicians, while lending our own perspective at the start of each chapter. While we had some common questions that we felt were pertinent to ask across the board, we largely allowed each interview to chart its own course. All the interviews were conducted in person, in order to allow for the necessary follow-up questions and also get a better sense of the individual. The conversations were recorded and transcribed. We have not rewritten the answers to conform to any linguistic convention or style. We want you to read the interviews as we heard them. Indian politicians have their own unique perspectives on issues that many Indian citizens care about. As you read these interviews, we hope that you listen to their voices, their unique idioms, and their viewpoints. We also hope that you, the reader, will hear them for who they are in their own authentic assertions and relish these conversations as much as we did.

Aaditya Thackeray

The roads leading to Shiv Sena Bhavan—the head office of the Mumbai-based nationalist party, the Shiv Sena—are strewn with the party's signature orange-coloured flags and posters of its founding leader, Bal Thackeray. On the top floor of the building, there is a large room with a high, arched glass ceiling which lets in plenty of sunlight. This room, we are told by party workers, is often used to conduct party meetings. In one corner sits a tall, cushioned chair—resembling a throne—that was once used by Bal Thackeray. Nobody has sat on the chair since his death over seven years ago. Even his son, party chief and current Chief Minister of Maharashtra, Uddhav Thackeray, chooses to sit on an ordinary chair while conducting meetings.

Shiv Sena has always had traditional stands on most social-conservative concerns, including issues like nationalism and Hindutva. Over the last couple of decades, this has earned it the image of a hardline right-wing party. But today the party faces significant challenges. First, its old alliance partner, the Bharatiya Janata Party (BJP), has achieved tremendous success in recent elections in Maharashtra while advocating similar positions on such issues. By deciding to contest alone in the 2014 assembly elections, the BJP showed that it was no longer willing to treat the Sena as the big brother of the alliance in the state. The BJP is, by all measures, a larger and more financially powerful organization. Second, the perspectives of young urban voters on many of these social issues are changing, and they are often less conservative than their parents' generation. By sticking with its traditional positions, the Shiv Sena may risk losing the support of this large constituency.

In the room adjoining the main conference hall in Shiv Sena Bhavan, we sit down with Bal Thackeray's grandson and Maharashtra's current Cabinet Minister for Tourism and Environment, Aaditya Thackeray, to discuss, among other things, these important challenges. At 29, Aaditya has already spent 10 years in active politics. Many of those who have closely followed his political career have been left wondering whether the young leader subscribes to the firebrand style of politics that has become synonymous with his party over time. Almost a decade ago, soon after he entered politics, he led a campaign to ban Rohinton Mistry's novel *Such a Long Journey* from the Mumbai University syllabus, allegedly because it described the Shiv Sena and Bal Thackeray in unflattering language. A few years later, he found himself in another row after he publicly defended Sena's ink attack on journalist and politician Sudheendra Kulkarni, who had organized an event to launch the book of Pakistan's former foreign minister.

In our interaction with Aaditya, we are pleasantly surprised. He is candid and straightforward, and remarkably clear about the vision Shiv Sena advocates, as well as the principles that he and the party will not compromise on. What takes us back the most, however, is his open-mindedness about the issues on which the Sena has traditionally upheld a hardline stand. This notion has been demonstrated by some of his recent actions as well, where he has distinctly departed from the Sena's traditional conservative position on many sociopolitical issues. For instance, he put an end to the Sena workers' infamous practice of harassing Mumbai couples on Valentine's Day and also campaigned for bars and restaurants in parts of the city to be open 24×7. As the Minister for Tourism, he has already taken steps to implement this policy across the city.

Does he find it challenging to advocate such modern, liberal positions in a conservative and traditional party? Aaditya insists it has been easy, partly because in the party, 'there is a hardcore discipline that the boss is always right,' implying that the party wouldn't tolerate much opposition to such ideas once he has voiced them. When prodded on how he reconciles his modern approach with the Sena's history of using strong-arm tactics and violence to get its way, Aaditya argues that the party no longer deploys these strategies. He attributes this to the changing needs of the new generation, of both the voters and the party cadre. He is a big believer in the idea that politics is evolutionary and argues that parties should continuously adapt to the changing times. 'We don't want to be a rigid party. For us to remain relevant, we must remain fluid,' he says. He goes on to provide examples of how, despite being considered a right-wing party, the Shiv Sena is left-wing on many issues. In fact, one of his biggest political inspirations is Tony Blair, whom he happened to meet recently in Mumbai and who has always identified himself as left-of-centre.

Aaditya has a far more liberal outlook than one would imagine the leader of the Shiv Sena to have. However, he makes it clear that he will not concede on issues of patriotism. He identifies three principles core to the Shiv Sena's ideology which the party holds with steadfast loyalty. The first is Hindutva, but he insists it's different from the Hindutva of the BJP, in that it speaks up for Hindus but not against any other religion. The second is 'bhumiputra', the idea of standing up for the rights of the locals in any area. And finally, the third is nationalism, but he's quick to add—in a thinly veiled dig at the BJP—'not the type that is about

3

giving certificates to people saying you're speaking against me, so you're anti-national.'

It appears that the scion of the Thackeray dynasty is trying hard to strike a balance between expanding the party's base by embracing a more modern and liberal outlook, while also appeasing Sena's traditional supporters. Only time will tell whether he and the party will reap electoral dividends for walking this ideological tightrope. What is clear, however, is that the Shiv Sena of the future, with Aaditya at the helm, will look very different from the Shiv Sena of the past.

Interview

Q. In the ten years that you have been in politics how have you changed? And what are the major changes that you have experienced?

The biggest example is just before I entered politics, I was writing my CV and I was writing something for college admissions. Then, for me politics was about winning, it was about power, and now over a span of a decade it has become something completely different, it is a medium to reach out to the people. Now we are helping drought-affected people in Marathwada or Vidarbha; we are creating alternative jobs for farmers who are trapped in a vicious cycle, and we are going behind single-use disposable plastic. For me, it is not about elections anymore. Of course, elections matter to us because you have to win elections and once you win you can do a lot of good. But the whole transformation for me in terms of politics as a concept has been from focusing only on elections to those five years between elections, I think that is crucial. That the last person in the rank who doesn't have a voice has to be voiced, the last person who doesn't have access to healthcare, you have to reach out to him. So when we partner with local non-governmental organizations (NGOs) and we go out to malnourished areas and we are trying to treat them, I think that is more satisfying to me than anything else. So that as a concept has evolved over the last 10 years. Of course, victories are important, I am not one who says that you learn from defeats and be humble in victories. You always have to be humble in victory or defeat, and learn from both.

Q. What have been the two or three things that have been most fulfilling for you, and also a couple of things that have been very frustrating and were challenging to face?

So when I speak with my friends who are not in politics, this topic obviously comes up because we are all looking back at the last 10 years—back then we used to chill in college and hang around, we still do that. But every day is different, every day you have something which you have accomplished and something which is frustrating because everywhere around the world, be it the States, be it the UK, be it India, you have a certain system that you have to bang your head against, you have certain slow processes. For example, if you want to make a toilet somewhere along the beach and it is for people's good it is not for your own self, you have to take a 1,000 permissions right from Coastal Regulation Zone (CRZ) to Maritime Board to the roads, footpaths to the traffic department, and that takes time. You see people are walking around here and they want to use the washroom but you cannot do it within a month's time. So that is frustrating. But of course, you have to understand the other side. This system is in place so that there is no bad happening, or that there are no loopholes. As many as loopholes we do have, there are also plugs to it. But looking at the good side of politics, I have come to believe that the more power you gain the more humble you need to be and the more responsible you need to be, you can't just unleash power anywhere you want to. I am loving what I am doing. I love Mondays and many people don't really love Mondays. In terms of policies, electric mobility is something that I am really looking forward to. Banning single-use disposable plastic is another thing I have pursued passionately. In the Brihanamumbai Municipal Corporation (BMC), we're digitizing education, and education has been my focus. Each day is a victory in that sense.

Q. *If you are sitting with a group of people trying to work together, what are the principles you would not compromise on?*

There is a set of ideologies, and there is a set of principles. And of course, the ideologies are out there. The principles that my father and my grandfather have set in the party are to never lie to

6

the people and don't give promises that you can't fulfil. Because unfortunately, what I have come to believe is politicians are the most innovative and creative people in the world. We create ideas, we create dreams for the masses, we sell them to the masses during elections and after winning when we don't fulfil those dreams, we create reasons for not fulfilling those dreams, and that is something I want to avoid. That is something I would not like to compromise on. If I have made a promise, I will follow that through.

Q. *But there are various promises that you can make right? When you had the letter exchange with Rajdeep Sardesai, for example, on the ink attack against Sudheendra Kulkarni, it seemed like there were some principles that you were willing to stand on ...*

Absolutely. For example, if someone is standing up against the nation, or if someone is standing up against my city, or against the people I represent or the people who trust in me, or the state, you have to voice out against that. That will happen the world over. That is a principle I think every one of us will take. If you are leading a team and someone speaks out against that team, you will stand for your team. Of course, your team has to be on the right path. You cannot in any which way defend something which is not logical or not true.

Q. *From the kind of issues that you have advocated and championed over the last ten years, some would say that you have a modern, open-minded, and perhaps even a liberal stance on many issues. Would that be a correct assessment? For instance, you have advocated for 24/7 nightlife in malls and restaurants in Mumbai. You have stopped some of your party workers from harassing couples on Valentine's Day. Have you found it difficult to advocate such positions in otherwise what people would consider a traditional and conservative party?*

This is a question that I get asked by many friends, and especially now as we speak about a lot more issues that are radically different from what we are thought to be. It has been easy for me and the reason is in our party there is a hardcore discipline that the boss—the party president—is always right. It was my grandfather first and then, of course, my father and these ideas are a part of upbringing. Had it not been so open in the family, or these ideas not seeping or percolating through the family, I don't think I would have ever thought of them or voiced them. But for me to take a go-ahead from the party and voice it out in the open, pursue it with conviction, there has to be complete support from the party. For all our MLAs, MPs, and for all of us as colleagues to toe the line that the party has taken, it is necessary that there is a unanimous decision in the party. And as long as you know that you are not doing anything wrong, not hitting out at anything, or maybe not damaging your city, your state, or the country, then there is no harm in evolving some ideas. As I said, the whole idea of politics is that it has to be evolutionary. If you see my grandfather's politics, in each decade he has been very pertinent to the time and its demands, be it the 1960s, 1970s, or even the 2000s. So when I proposed a couple of these ideas, he gave his 'OK' back then in 2012 or 2011. And some of the ideas, say Mumbai 24/7 that I propped up after he had passed away, someone sent me a video of his from 1996–7 where he is speaking about Mumbai 24/7 and that blew my mind because I hadn't seen that video. He was actually more modern than me. I remember in 2011 when we were having our first gathering of the *Yuva Sena* and I had recorded a small video on his behalf giving compliments to everyone. In that video, he is speaking of Mark Zuckerberg and Julian Assange, Facebook and Wikileaks. For someone who is over the age of 80 to be so in tune with what today's demands are, I think that is very difficult for anyone and that's what made it easier for me.

Q. *In an interview with* The Guardian *you had said that 'These are changing times. My grandfather's generation, my generation, all have different needs. We are keeping our core values the same. But with time priorities change.' What are the core values that the Shiv Sena stands for? And how much of the movement is tactical whereby you adjust to new circumstances?*

The core for the Sena is, of course, Hindutva, but not the Hindutva that is professed by the BJP. For us, we speak for the Hindus, but of course, we are not against any religion. The other day when I was speaking, there was *azaan* going on, and I stopped for it as a mark of respect and it became a huge thing in the media. It was natural for me to stop because my grandfather always taught me to respect other religions. But if someone speaks against you, you have to stand up for that. The second thing is the concept of *bhumiputras*, which we have voiced since the 1960s, which is whichever state you are in, be it Punjab, be it Uttar Pradesh, be it Bihar, for us it is Maharashtra, you have to stand up for the rights of locals. And that is what is being seen in Brexit right now and in the United States as well. What we say is—we don't mind skilled labour coming from anywhere else, but if there is skilled labour in your locality, why look around the world. Give jobs where you are first, in your locality, and then look for things around the world. And the third principle is nationalism, but not the type which is about giving certificates to people saying, 'You are speaking against me, you are anti-national.' Our nationalism is simple. If you respect the country you are a nationalist, you are a patriot, and that is it. Respect the soldiers, respect the county, don't do anything that is damaging the country or its image across the world. These are the core values, but of course, as I said politics personally for me is about aspirations of the people in each generation. The needs of my father's generation or my grandfather's generation would be different from my generation. And that is why if you see in the *Yuva Sena*, we have got every office-bearer who is under-30 because if you are going to voice the youth, you cannot have someone away from the youth voicing the youth. You have to be in the age bracket to understand what is relevant to youth.

Q. *In terms of the ideology, the only thing the BJP may perhaps disagree with you is the* bhumiputras *piece. Other than that, a BJP politician would also say, 'We are for Hindutva and we are for national pride.' What distinguishes the Shiv Sena from the BJP?*

For us, speaking out against the government would not be anti-national. Lynching someone on what he eats or what he drinks is not Hindutva. Saying that eating at a certain altitude, or eating on the terrace is against the culture is not something that is Hindutva for us. So our principle is very simple—we believe that everyone can live together in harmony, except that the locals have the first right to the vicinity and Hindutva is speaking out about your own religion and not imposing it on anyone else.

Q. *Isn't that what the Congress is also saying now? How's your Hindutva different from that of the BJP or the Congress? Where do you think the Sena's ideology is different from all other parties?*

There has been quite a blur on that. In fact, if you see the Sena's politics, as such we are taken to be right-wing, but on many issues we are centrist, be it Mumbai 24/7, be it being liberal on food habits, and again we are the only party which is a right-wing party with unions in all hotels, hospitals, schools, airlines, and airports across Maharashtra and a couple of them outside Maharashtra as well. So essentially we are both right-wing and left-wing, we promote the industries as well as voice the labour. And again the basic rule for us is, whatever said and done even for the unions, you will never go on a strike in a hotel or a hospital or a school because only if the hotel or the hospital or an

10

industry works will you get your salaries and we'll both benefit. So it is always a balance. That has been the ground rule for us and hence, in the best hotels which have the best service. If you see the person who is serving you there, it is likely to be a Shiv Sainik. Wherever we have focused on employment and giving jobs to locals, we have made sure that the locals are skilled for the job requirement. If you go down right now to the second floor of this building, you'll have a lot of classes going on for the railways examination, UPSC examination, banking sector examination, whichever it is, or just English language classes because you have to be the best in your profession. So we impart them skills.

Q. *Shiv Sena has a history of using some strong-arm tactics, what is often called direct action, often including violence. How do you reconcile your more modern approach with that? And do you think that it is necessary to have those kind of measures?*

Things were like that 15–20 years ago. When things were that way, they probably needed to be that way. In the last 10 years that I have worked, of course, the Sena has a considerable presence not only in Maharashtra but across India. Today we take up issues like the Land Acquisition Bill in the Parliament which was a draconian act coming into the Parliament and they had to roll it back. So now we have come to a place where we really don't need to focus on those direct action issues. The whole dynamic of the Sena cadre is changing. The next generation of the Sena cadre is something different from probably what the earlier one would have been. Again, each generation, as I said, or each decade has its own needs and requirements and so we have moulded ourselves as per that.

Q. *What are the conditions in which you think direct action becomes necessary?*

See honestly, today if you see it is not just about parties, but the polarization that is happening in our country; it is on a very edgy place because of demonetization, Goods and Services Tax (GST), job losses, religion, and caste. The way we are headed, we'll need Band-Aids very soon. Around the world if you see, Paris had riots, there was demonetization in a South American country and people were out on the streets. The Arab spring, they came out on the streets against the armed forces, they faced tanks. So these sporadic events can always happen because finally, it is human nature, it is dynamic, and frustration will take a toll. But will it be necessarily organized, or in an organized manner by saying an organization or an agency or a party? I don't know. It is human nature and you never know what will happen.

Q. *As you look at expanding your party beyond Maharashtra, you will have to reach out to different communities. How do you strike a balance as you try and reach out to more groups but still want to retain your traditional support base?*

The core values will always be the same, which is nationalism, Hindutva, and *bhumiputras*. If we go to Rajasthan, we will speak about *bhumiputras*, speak about their rights. For us, India is all about different states, about different cultures, and you cannot impose one culture onto another by force. And that is where the rights of the locals come in. For example, we campaigned in Rajasthan and we got great support there. We contested in UP, we contested in Bihar. In Bihar, we got about 2,86,000 votes campaigning in a span of one month. It was the first time I went to campaign out of the state. And there have been times we have spoken about Kashmiri Pandits, we have spoken about Kashmir, we have spoken about Bengal and the point is we are probably the only regional party right now which is speaking about national issues in the Parliament and that is why we think we can really step out and voice those aspirations as well.

Q. In Mumbai, the data shows that you did not get many votes from Muslims, Dalits, North Indians (loosely defined). If you want to expand your base in Mumbai, what do you think you will have to do?

Thankfully because of social media, we have broken those biases that were created by the regular media. And you would be surprised to know that Bahrampada is one seat which has traditionally not been with the Sena because it has a Muslim majority and this is the first time that the Sena has won there. And again, those biases were broken and that is what we said that this is the ideology, this is what we follow, this is what we have done over the years and if you accept us it is great and we don't have to impose anything on you or onto ourselves, we have to work for the society. And we are making better roads there, we are creating systems where water will reach their houses, we are creating better waste management systems there and they are liking it so we have got votes, we have won there. Imamwada Dongri for that matter, this is the second time that we have lost by a very narrow margin. We would have never imagined winning there.

Q. Whenever a party that has deep ideological views tries to expand, they run into trouble with their base. Thinking forward, if you want to do this, how do you reconcile? Where do you see the Sena going in the future?

So the thing is, we can absorb many more people than we already have, and the core base understands that and the core base wants to help people. And thankfully, if you see, the Shiv Sena runs the largest ambulance network for any political party across India. Forty years ago we had almost 300 ambulances, I can't even remember how many we have currently. But when we go out to help people, when we go out, say with an ambulance, or to pick up garbage from somewhere and to pick up some issue and voice it, we don't ask whether you are a Hindu, or a Muslim, or a Christian, we don't ask your caste or what creed you belong to. You are a citizen, it is your right to get your problem resolved and that is our duty. So it is as simple as that. Voting is finally by choice, and every time there are elections, I keep saying this to all our cooperators, to all our MLAs that there have been people who have voted for us and that is why we won, and there are people who haven't voted us, let us prove to them that we are worth voting for. And it is our job as political parties to reach out to them and to convince them that we are here for the greater good.

Q. *What, according to you, should be the role of the government? What do you think the government should be? Do you think that the bureaucracy, the courts, the elected politicians, and the representative processes should actually determine things like religious practices, customary norms, or should they stay out of it?*

So where the government is needed according to me is in things like, for example, the BEST Bus Service. You have to run the best public transport, be it the metro, be it the bus, be it the railways, or say something like Air India so that everyone can afford to travel very easily, or be it healthcare, or access to education, or be it clean water. But according to me, the government shouldn't determine what you wear, what you eat, where you go and pray, what comes into your bedroom, who you are married to. I don't think that should be the role of the government. Yes, by and large, you can have policies which are helping you make things better in life, create a better environment around you, but not intrude into your private life as long as your private life doesn't intrude on anyone else.

Q. *But some people would see a contradiction between that and let's say Hindutva policies. Do you not see that?*

14

That is why I told you. On the grid, where do we stand? Are we centrist right-wing, centrist left-wing, centrist? And we prefer to be that way because, see, we don't want to be a rigid party. We always want to voice what is more relevant, we always want to solve issues and issues are not going to come as right-wing or left-wing. You will always have issues that are coming up permanently. If there is a pipeline that is burst out here, am going to go and say that you are right-wing or not? No. Which is why we have to be more fluid for us to remain relevant. For example, the reason the Sena has been relevant over the last 50 years to each and every decade, to each and every state or national issue, is because we remain fluid and take up the issues which are supposed to be solved right now.

Akhilesh Yadav

Saifai, a large village in rural Uttar Pradesh, is where we meet Akhilesh Yadav, president of the Samajwadi Party (SP). Saifai is Mulayam Singh Yadav's birthplace and the regular site of the Yadav family's retreats. Akhilesh did not grow up here but spends a lot of time in the village. The contrast between the village and his political career so far encapsulates the contradictions that lie at the heart of contemporary Indian politics.

The Agra–Lucknow Expressway, with excellent signage and construction, has definitely made travel from Delhi to Saifai easier. The project was started and completed when Akhilesh was the Chief Minister of Uttar Pradesh. The Expressway was built in record time and under the projected cost. The road from the Expressway to Saifai, however, meanders through some villages before we pass a world-class cricket stadium that has so far hosted just one cricket tournament. The stadium is part of a complex that includes, among other amenities, an indoor all-weather swimming pool. We meet Ashish Yadav who handles the media for Akhilesh at Café Saifai—a café whose design and aesthetics would be at place anywhere in the world. At 4 pm, five men sit eating an aromatic, wholesome lunch of *roti*, rice, and various north Indian curries. The place itself is part of an oval-shaped shopping centre anchored by a clock tower at one end. When we arrive there that Sunday evening, the mall is deserted except for some idle young men revving their motorcycles.

It becomes clear that Akhilesh has invested energy and resources in developing this area. However, his major initiatives as chief minister—whether it is the Expressway, the disbursement of millions of laptops by his government, or the allocation of pensions—were not enough to ensure a return to power in the 2017 elections. The Samajwadi Party was washed aside by a Bharatiya Janata Party (BJP) tsunami, with its vote share tumbling by over 12 per cent. Akhilesh concedes that the election results made him realize that development and doles alone do not guarantee victory, and social coalitions are still important.

While we wait for Akhilesh to arrive at his house in Saifai, the surroundings are peaceful. There is hardly anyone save for a few policemen, milling around with the staff. Akhilesh's arrival springs everyone into action. The lawn outside the home fills up and National Security Guard (NSG) commandos are seemingly everywhere. While we sit with Akhilesh, the crowd waits patiently outside. The weather takes a turn for the worse and looms ominously, so Akhilesh steps outside to talk to some journalists and to meet the local *netas*. What follows is organized bedlam—everyone wanted to get a word in and be noticed by him. For many of the *netas*, just the perception of being close to the president of the SP is enough for them to cement their own power and authority in the party. Akhilesh is acutely aware of this dynamic and the perils of chasing political goodwill and clout at the expense of meaningful service. He berates one of them in front of us for spending more time trying to meet him rather than working at his polling booth like other local Samajwadi *netas* (who are sending Akhilesh photos of their local campaigns). As the local *neta* leaves, he touches

Akhilesh's feet. Despite his personal aversion to people touching his feet as a sign of respect, Akhilesh has resigned himself to the fact that this will not change despite his best efforts. As the room empties, he remarks, almost ruefully, that most of the local *netas* who had gathered outside were Yadavs. It's palpable that he has found it difficult to expand the party's core social base beyond just Yadav-Muslims.

Akhilesh became the youngest Chief Minister of Uttar Pradesh at the age of 38. Over the next few years, he managed to take over the party from its founder and his father, Mulayam Singh Yadav. He even succeeded in wresting control from his powerful uncle, Shivpal Yadav, who was eventually forced out of the party and left to forge an independent political career. The Samajwadi Party has all the trappings of a family-run political party with power resting within a small kin group. However, the party's dynastic nature does not prevent the politics from being any less cut-throat. To ensure his political career and the longevity of the party, Akhilesh took on his father and his uncle. We wondered how he felt about this! In a country which places great emphasis on family values, did he feel morally torn while going through with a public dispute with his family? Is there any lingering regret today?

To our surprise, Akhilesh is remarkably clear-headed and at peace with how the situation unfolded. He argues that the changes made were necessary for the good of the party—indeed, to uphold his father's vision for it. When pushed, he does concede that he needed to have a '*mazboot dil*' (strong heart) to take some of these decisions but insists that the restructuring was imperative. Our conversation with him on these family struggles highlighted the fact that robust decisiveness and the ability to de-emphasize one's emotions may be central to the making of a successful politician.

Our dialogue with Akhilesh is wide-ranging, covering everything from his relationship with his father to the challenge of running India's largest state to his audacious move to ally with his party's historical bête noire, Mayawati, for the 2019 elections, one that proved to be a disaster. He comes across as amiable and nonchalant, yet has political acuity, making him a fierce critic of the central government. He is also full of jokes. However, over the course of our conversation, it becomes clear to us that there is a thick-skinned and shrewd politician beneath the surface, with the courage and conviction to take bold and risky political decisions. Regardless of his long-term electoral success or failure, that might just be his enduring legacy.

Interview

Q. Who is an inspirational figure for you in politics?

I would say that I was fortunate enough to have been born in a family with a political background. I derived my understanding of politics and its workings from my family, Netaji (Mulayam Singh Yadav), leaders talking about Mahatma Gandhi. Janeshwar Mishra ji influenced my life in a major way. Former Samajwadi leaders like Dr Ram Manohar Lohiya and Jaiprakashji are a part of daily conversations amongst party members and I learnt a lot about politics and its ways from their philosophies. I was fortunate enough to have gotten the chance to contest from the same constituency from which both Netaji and Dr Ram Manohar Lohia did. Also, my wife Dimple is a Member of Parliament (MP) from the same constituency. So, being elected from a socialist constituency, meeting the people there, my father Netaji, Janeshwar Mishra ji, who also filed my nomination, these people and experiences taught me a lot of important lessons.

Q. In India, the people, and especially the youth feel that Indian politics has a ceiling because the leading posts in almost all the major parties—including the Samajwadi Party—have members belonging to one particular family. What are your thoughts about this?

This is not only unique to politics, this happens in every field and profession. Yes, because BJP runs on propaganda, family politics has become the most important topic to be hammered upon. Every country and every profession in the world is like this. Currently, in our party, I'm the only one who fits the family narrative. But if you look at other people in our party, we have given a chance to people with no background in politics. People are not wrong when they say that Samajwadi Party and Samajwadi ideology is like a factory of leaders. If you talk about young leaders, the maximum number of young people in the house belong to the Samajwadi Party. Even Janeshwar Mishra ji was posed with this question during the time of my nomination. He was called out for critiquing the Congress for family politics and while playing an active role while he filed my nomination. I remember he said that he was against dynasty politics but he was not against struggle in politics. Indeed, that time was a very difficult time for me because I was in the opposition. While other people in politics were just given seats, I had to go to the people, fight the election, and struggle my way to the top, and that has not been an easy task.

Q. *Politics is a 24×7 job. You are a politician and so is your wife, Dimple. Has this posed any difficulties in your personal life? How do you manage your personal, public, and political life?*

If you would have asked this question two years ago, I would have said that it was difficult. Currently, we are in the opposition so we are a bit relaxed. You should have asked this question two years ago when I was the chief minister and administering various things, for example, improving the quality of roads so that travel time reduces from 5 hours to 1 hour 50 minutes. Apart from celebrating festivals together, I try to take my family along whenever I travel so that we can spend some time on the way. But it is very difficult when both of us are in politics, we miss the growing years of our children. But in life, you win some, you lose some.

Q. *You had to face a lot of criticism, from within the family. Your family criticized your policies and alliances. How do you deal with it considering it's your family? Is it just the give and take of politics? Is it healthy criticism?*

I've grown used to it now. But in the beginning, it was difficult. But after a lot of deliberation with party workers and leaders, I realized that this was the best path for the future of the party.

Q. *In a county where family is very important, you took a bold step and chose to take the party under your wings, which meant that your father and your uncle were sidelined. Although you say you did it for a better cause, when the process started, were you a little apprehensive and/or morally torn between right and wrong? After all, it is difficult to choose between family and politics.*

See, every generation has a mindset and beliefs that are different from the previous generation. Every generation works in a different way. Netaji also believed that it is very important for the new generation to be at the forefront. I remember that our social leaders would iterate the importance of youth in a party and that a youth party always goes forward and lasts longer. Also, it was Netaji who revived the socialist ideas of our party. Everyone had forgotten the names of Lohia ji and Jaiprakash ji, but Netaji revived their ideology in Indian politics. Thus, if Netaji has kept the flame alive for the last 50 to 60 years, then it is only our responsibility that we should work in such a way that we keep it alive for the next 100 years. My mindset has never been to sideline the old generation but to give the new generation an impetus to work harder with the blessings of the older generation. I felt that there were people who were not working for the party but for their own selfish needs and they did not care about party's ideology and principles. That's why I tried to understand how this works. And after all, who will respect Netaji if not me. I knew Netaji's respect and image depended on how I perform in politics and with that alliance we won 50 MPs and Netaji was the happiest.

Q. *A lot of people remark that the rule of the party was really 'goondaraj'. How are you trying to shift that image? There has been a considerably more reserved approach towards direct action from your party. Why is that?*

Try to understand my point, when I went to Mumbai a lot of questions were raised and my only answer to the people was that whatever they know about me, they know through television and the image that news has created of me. The other day I was watching a news channel and they were talking about the Expressway. My whole family was sitting together and I was expecting them to mention that it was my initiative and execution that led to the building of the Expressway, but not a single news channel mentioned my name. That is why no one knows about us and the Samajwadi Party. Today, there are lakhs of success stories of students who have benefitted from the laptops that I distributed. I can give you examples of students who have offers from Harvard, and they come to me and thank me for our policies. However, even though our work is not highlighted enough, whether it be the Expressway or laptop distribution, we are not mindlessly campaigning to claim goodwill for what we have done. Such problems are a part of the politics of our country.

Q. The state witnessed development during your term in power. However, the results were not in your favour. What do you think happened? What did you learn from the defeat? Are Indian elections not about development?

During the elections, I met a senior journalist while travelling. I had a conversation with her over tea and she said that if I win the election, the narrative will be always about development. But if I don't, then elections will be based on caste and religion. When I lost the election, people failed to understand my Expressway, they were enamoured by the promise of a bullet train. I persuaded them as much as I could, but they were misled by some people. This election, we were trying to take the narrative towards development; however, others deemed it fit to direct the attention of the voters towards *Diwali/ Ramzan, Kabristan/ Shamshan,* and sold them fake stories. I have now understood some of the harsh realities of Indian politics. I will surely bring development, my agenda is development, but I will work on development only when I am in government. If I am not in government, how will I bring about development? Thus. this is the compromise that I have struck. I had forgotten the truth of our nation, which is that I am a Yadav and you are a Punjabi. That is the truth.

Q. *Since you want to bind communities together, won't all communities then demand that their interests be fulfilled? Does that not create barriers in the path of development?*

Even in the US, someone had to fight for black people's right to vote. Even there affirmative action has a role to play. Similarly, I want preference to be given to minorities and groups of people who have been made backward castes. This approach exists around the world.

So, development would take its time. Perhaps next time our voters will look for leaders who will bring development. It is possible that they have not been able to find one because they haven't walked on the Expressway or travelled on the Lucknow metro. The metro was under construction in five places in UP and all of them were sanctioned by Samajwadi Party, while the prime minister could not manage a single metro line in Ahmedabad when he was the chief minister of the state. Now, the Congress is proposing to launch a scheme promising people INR 6,000, and BJP has some similar scheme as well. But in Uttar Pradesh, I had already introduced the Samajwadi Pension and provided people with INR 500 by directly transferring the money to their accounts. Even women benefitted from my scheme. My scheme is inspired by a similar scheme in Brazil. I just modified it according to the Indian context and our people's needs and implemented it here for three years. This year I had already planned to increase the amount to INR 2,000. If the UP government with its minimal budget can aim to provide INR 2,000 to 55 lakh women, can't the enormous budget of the central government give INR 6,000? We can surely give more than that. That is why, I emphasize studying and helping out with the real needs of the poor: a house, free electricity, and pension, these three are a must.

Q. *You were the youngest Chief Minister of UP. Most politicians in India are in their 50s, 60s, or 70s. In India, even a 60- or 70-year-old politician is considered young. As a youngster, how do you feel dealing with older politicians who are set in their methods and ways?*

Socialism is evident when it comes to diseases and medication. Diseases don't differentiate between poor and rich, which means it is socialist in nature. The medication for these diseases is also socialist as both the rich and the poor will have to take, say, a paracetamol. Nowadays, information has also become socialist in nature. Today, nobody can stop information. And because there is a general equality amongst people as recipients and consumers of information, people are demanding the truth. Most fake news are called out. It is because of information that terms such as 'jumla party', 'feku party' have come into existence. Had it not been for the internet, this would not have been possible. So now, traditional politics will have to coexist with the modern policies of change.

Q. *One of Uttar Pradesh's biggest difficulties is that it is a huge state geographically and population-wise. Many people suggest that the state should be divided into two or three parts. What is your opinion on this matter?*

The people who say so are mostly slackers and are lazy. If dividing was the solution to size and population, then why hasn't a huge nation like the US divided its 50 states? This is not a legitimate demand that can be asked for and fulfilled. During my term, I promised to provide infrastructure so that Lucknow is not more than four hours away for anyone in any corner of the state. Thus, good infrastructure, hospitals, quality education, and the like, are what we aim to render. This is what other developed nations have done as well.

Whenever I have talked about the Expressway, I have mentioned several times how America made roads and roads made America. Another thing that I often said was that if you can double the speed, we can triple the economy. When I visited Paris, I was inspired by the *mandis* (market places) that I saw there, and I made such *mandis* alongside the Expressway in UP. I initiated hundreds of acres of *mandis* for potatoes, onions, garlic, etc. Baba Ramdev was allotted 500 acres land for a mango *mandi*. All of this is because the motive of this Expressway was not limited to just increasing connectivity, but to boost our rural agriculture and economy too. For example, during Diwali last year, I was heading to Lucknow when I saw 10 trucks being loaded with cabbage. I had always seen and known cabbage to be transported to markets in Delhi, Agra, and Firozabad, and so I was amused to see it go in the opposite direction that day. On enquiring I learnt that it has more value in Lucknow and which was why all the 10 trucks of cabbage were headed there. The prime minister chants with ease 'gati aur pragati' (speed and development). But this, here, is real development, this is 'gati aur pragati' in its truest sense.

Q. *Another problem that Uttar Pradesh faces is its severe social divisions and diversity. How can that be managed?*

Social diversity and division exists all over the world, and if not in the world, then all across India at least. It exists in almost every state—in the south, in Mysore, Karnataka, and even in Punjab in the north. But Uttar Pradesh is a very political state, for it decides the PM. The division becomes more crucial. Moreover, Uttar Pradesh is the birthplace of three Gods, which makes the divisions more salient. But it is fine, it'll all be okay.

Q. *Why is the state of UP so political?*

I can't tell the reason for it, maybe it's because all the three rivers, Ganga, Yamuna, Saraswati flow here, or perhaps it's Chambal river water. Nothing else I think of as the cause of it.

Q. *What are some of the major challenges you have faced?*

Look, barriers and challenges are inevitable, especially when you are involved in politics. Regardless, one has to go on. I believe if your intentions are pure and clear, if you can work hard, and you have courage in yourself, then you can take these decisions. I made this decision because people wanted change. Who would have brought the change if not me, for only I had the opportunity then and it would not have passed it to someone else. That is why I tried my best to clean the Samajwadi *andolan* as much as possible and carry it forward in the best direction. It was my responsibility as Netaji had entrusted me with the position of the president, and I got the opportunity to work even more as a chief minister. All my efforts were devoted towards the path of development so that we can give something to the young generation. The roads, the Expressway, and all the other opportunities were created for this purpose. Take the case of the Lucknow metro, for example. If my son does not do well in politics, then at least his son will be able to proudly say that his grandfather was behind the metro. So, see this is the socialist legacy that we want to preserve as well as continue.

Q. *Your alliance with Mayawati was a very interesting experiment. This alliance was very difficult to pull off in Uttar Pradesh. Why was an alliance between the other backward classes (OBCs) and the Dalits so difficult?*

I have learnt one of the most important lessons from BJP. In 2014, BJP made a backward-caste person the state president and then during the 2017 elections, the prime minister himself became backward-caste, and brought up the usual things about how he is an uneducated tea seller from a lower caste, to support his claim. During the 2017 elections in Uttar Pradesh, which I lost, the BJP staged an apparently backward-caste candidate for state president, said that he is a Baghel and that will be made the chief minister. Through this, they gained the electoral support of the backward-caste voters, but ultimately did not make a backward-caste person the chief minister. Such people just use the tag of being backward-caste for power games.

To fight the evils of the society, Dr Bhim Rao Ambedkar Ji and Ram Manohar Lohia Ji got along to fight together, Netaji and Kanshi Ram Ji carried forward this legacy. But the BJP broke it. Hence, I understood that probably these people are in greater need of constitutional security and so I struck this compromise.

Q. *Currently, there are debates on federalism, cooperative federalism, and centralism. In your opinion, which direction is Indian federalism heading towards?*

Indian federalism needs to be strengthened. Initially, the prime minister wanted to dissolve Yojana Aayog (Planning Commission), and now, the Congress wants to dissolve NITI Aayog. But have the states benefitted because of this? Earlier, Yojana Aayog used to make policies, now NITI Aayog does. But how has this federal system benefitted from either? The toilets that Congress constructed on lesser land, the BJP, through NITI Aayog, constructed the same using more land. But neither party has done anything about water supply. So what good is your policymaking? You just want the states to rely on these institutions that don't care for the state. The centre made the Shiksha Mitra Yojana, but the state bears the brunt of protest. The national parties, especially the Congress and the BJP, would never want the regional parties to become stronger. Thus, certain policies are launched just to subdue us regional parties. But now, the regional forces have awakened with power. In fact, it is a regional party today that is hindering BJP's reach. Moreover, paying attention to and understanding the problems of different states strengthens our country as a federal nation. They proclaim 'sabka saath, sabka vikaas', but how is that possible without engaging the states and regional parties? Their slogan is bound to fail because they don't want different people to come together. The BJP should read Rabindranath Tagore's *Nationalism* to truly understand the meaning of the word, but they don't read.

Q. *India is a very religious country and almost everyone has faith in religion. But why and how can BJP win elections through religious propaganda? Most other parties have religious members, then why are they lagging behind?*

Around seven to eight years ago, the Expressway wasn't there and I was travelling from Agra when I started counting all the temples from a village 6 kms away. I could count around 32–34 temples whose peaks were visible to me. So yes, God does exist in this country, but I wouldn't argue about which God.

The BJP government prefers those people who have pledged allegiance to them and try to have them recruited into such institutions. The BJP is spreading hatred in the society, and so are the RSS and the Sangh Parivaar who support the BJP. It is our nation's misfortune that the educated people of our country are also communal. This is the problem of our country, and that is why I was not appreciated on national television for the expressway. This expressway is not for me, it is for the country. Approximately INR 1.5 crores worth of toll is collected per day through this Expressway, and this figure is bound to increase. These people who used to rant about UP's roadways have gone ahead and given this money to the people of Maharashtra. We don't mind that, but when someone from Uttar Pradesh goes to Mumbai they are looked down upon. Thus, the people are not religious in the least, they are only working for their own vested interests. Everyone has faith in religion, but no one has the will to actually understand it.

Q. Do you have any passions or interests outside of politics?

I have spent my entire life playing sports. I've switched between football, cricket, and tennis. When I was the chief minister, I used to play tennis and cricket with the officers. I remember an IAS association once came to me with a request to celebrate IAS week with them. IAS week was a tradition in UP wherein all the IAS officers working across UP would come together. My condition was that I would grant them permission if they would play a match with CM's 11, and they happily agreed. This match was one of its kind across the country. And after my departure from the government, this tradition also stopped. Prayers and rituals might have replaced this system now.

Q. Do you find time to watch movies or read books?

I watch films. I have watched *Gravity* several times.

Q. Why do you like Gravity *so much?*

I don't know. There is emotion. But I do watch it alone. *Gravity* is the sort of movie one should watch alone. Like, I've watched it twice while travelling on plane. And now I feel like watching it again after the 300 km target. I don't even know if it's true or not. And now they'll call me traitor if I ask any question.

Q. *What about politics is most satisfying for you? And what frustrates you the most?*

Some workers assume that if instead of working, they make themselves visible, talk about work, and make contacts, they will impress the leader. That kind of attitude is difficult to deal with.

But, mostly politics results in great things, and there is nothing more satisfying. A significant decision, say a hospital, changes the lives of many people, and that gives me immense happiness. It doesn't matter if these people vote for us or not. But earlier, the people who had to sell their farms and travel to Delhi and Mumbai for their treatment can now avail free treatment in this one-of-a-kind medical facility.

Q. *You seem to suggest that in politics somebody is capable of taking credit for things that is either actually not real or not done by them? But it could be that the BJP's media strategy is great while other parties' need to up their game. What do you think are the some of the constraints for parties like yours?*

Our party is a regional party. We cannot become a national party. To become one, you need to have leaders and resources. The BJP doesn't have any leaders after the current ones. Only two or three people are running the country. They know they need to gather resources to work, and so, they have collected resources. I don't think I have that kind of access to resources. If I enter in a room with two televisions sets, both of them will have people from BJP on it. Today, when I was watching TV, Yogi Adityanath had occupied one window while Amit Shah was on the next one. They had occupied two subsequent slots by themselves without any advertisement in between, because when they are on TV, no advertisements can play. I don't have the power to distract the minds, but they do and they have the resources for it. They continue to spend massive amounts of money on TV. Today, I cannot have my advertisement on TV because I have limited resources. What I indirectly mean is that the PM and BJP have given boost to corruption in the country. Political parties in the future will follow their footsteps, collect resources and manipulate people like them. It is ironic that the people who were going to bring back black money from abroad and end corruption have themselves paved the way for a political party to stay on TV. I am also a part of a political party, even I want to send out a message, but I am not on TV. My face is only there on the *mahagathbandhan* posters. Otherwise I am not in the news. All of what I do, be it rallies or anything, none of it is documented and shown on TV or even in the newspaper. I am there only on social media.

Q. *What would you want your gravestone to read about you?*

This is interesting. A man like me would not want anything, not even my name to be written. I would want it to be mentioned that I like speed in everything. Who wants to wait?

Asaduddin Owaisi

O n a warm afternoon in Hyderabad, we find ourselves in the waiting area of a huge, well-guarded house on top of a hill in the historic and crowded Old City area. The house belongs to Asaduddin Owaisi, who is currently serving his fourth term as MP from Hyderabad and is the president of the All India Majlis-e-Ittehad-ul-Muslimeen (AIMIM). We are eager to meet Owaisi: many of the other politicians we had met—particularly (and remarkably) those from the Bharatiya Janata Party (BJP)— had praised his brilliant legal mind and exceptional oratorical skills. They all seemed to draw a distinction between the Owaisi seen in rallies or on news channels and the one seen in private, or even in Parliament. We wait patiently for Owaisi's convoy of cars to arrive. Instead, we are surprised to see Owaisi arrive riding a motorcycle. He reveals to us that he often ditches his car for the motorcycle because it allows him to better navigate Hyderabad's heavy traffic and cover more areas and events in a day.

Owaisi is followed into his house by a TV crew from the news channel, Republic TV. We are hardly surprised. He has become nothing short of a media personality in recent years. 'Presently in India, a bearded politician with a cap on his head is very popular on TV channels,' he later says with a smile. In reality, Owaisi has become one of the most prominent Muslim politicians in contemporary India. What makes him so noticeable? How did the leader of a small, regional party with a minimal presence outside Hyderabad become so visible across the country? In our long and wide-ranging conversation with him, we realize that his prominence is attributable to three factors: his remarkable clarity of thought on legal and political issues, his nuanced advocacy of secular Muslim interests, and his defiant, truculent approach to dealing with political confrontations.

Owaisi is singularly clear-headed and makes succinct and sophisticated political arguments. For instance, his opposition to the BJP government's Triple Talaq bill is rooted in a carefully calibrated deliberation. He is quite explicit in his view that Triple Talaq is a sin and a social evil, but he maintains that the criminalization of Triple Talaq, as proposed in the bill, is a deliberate and cynical political move. It singles out the Muslim community for a practice that should be dealt with in a civil, not criminal court. He points out that child marriage, still rampant in India, does not carry penal provisions but a far more rare event, the Triple Talaq, has been criminalized.

Owaisi is a fierce advocate of Muslim political interests. The interests he seeks to represent are basic needs—education, employment, and economic welfare for Muslims—which he feels need to be given more priority than the community's religious practices. A good example is his vociferous opposition to what he calls 'the stupid Haj subsidy'. He insists that the money may be better utilized in the form of scholarships to Muslim girls. The secular parties, in his view, have failed Muslims because they have stereotyped the community as just a religious group, a vote bank whose patronage could be secured by supporting their religious practices. With the rise of the BJP, Muslim interests have been marginalized even further. The Congress—which he refers to as 'BJP 1.5'—has simply adopted a lighter version of Hindutva, instead of fighting the BJP ideologically. He truly believes that secularism, at least as the mainstream parties practice it, has failed the Muslim community. To address this, he pushes for greater political representation for parties that vociferously advocate for the community's economic needs.

Finally, Owaisi wears his political beliefs on his sleeve and is not afraid to call a spade a spade: this is what galvanizes his supporters and riles up his opponents. He is defiant and combative, particularly during debates and confrontations with people from the BJP and other right-wing outfits. In 2016, when RSS chief Mohan Bhagwat declared that those who do not chant 'Bharat Mata ki Jai' should not live in India, Owaisi publicly refused to chant the slogan, knowing fully well that it would 'lead to a lot of commotion'. He tells us that he has no issue with the slogan itself but is concerned with it being imposed as a 'test of loyalty' to India. He rues that he constantly faces this trial despite his love for the country and the work he has done. It is this trademark confrontational style of Owaisi which often lands him in controversies, yet he remains unbothered. Indeed, he almost seems to relish these ideological battles.

What is notable about Owaisi is his single-minded focus on his job—to build a party that represents Muslims and asks tough questions of the government. He has the unique ability to drown out the noise around him and work on the task at hand. Much to the chagrin of other secular parties which often accuse the AIMIM of cutting anti-BJP votes, Owaisi is determined to take his party to other states and has already achieved some success. However, the lonely warrior strategy has its limits. Owaisi's success will depend a lot on the goodwill of larger parties (like his ally, the Telangana Rashtra Samiti) and on his ability to mobilize significant sections of the population and keep himself relevant in the public eye.

Owaisi cares deeply about the Indian Constitution and believes that it is vital to guarantee social justice for all Indians. He hopes to eventually be remembered as somebody who, above all else, fought bravely to defend the ideals and principles enshrined in the document. 'Apart from just the hate speeches and controversies, of course,' he laughs.

Interview

Q. Can you tell us a little bit about some of your passions outside of politics?

It is difficult because usually for me if I can get an hour's worth of exercise, either walking, some freehand exercise or some stretching, and then if I am able to read 15–20 pages of any book, that really helps, because presently in India a bearded politician with a cap on his head is very popular on TV channels, so you have to read up on various topics. Politics itself is a very passionate thing for me. To realize a different passion is a problem because this itself is a huge thing for me. I get quite surprised when people say—what is your passion? Politics itself is so self-consuming. Unless and until one has a passion for politics one should not be in politics. This work itself is like a jealous mistress; the moment you blink, it is gone. Having a law degree, I have realized how the constitution and law-making plays an important role in everyday politics. That is very important and that makes me read the constitution many times. But that is again related to my work.

Q. What are the political causes that you care deeply about?

There is definitely a great burning desire that the party should do well, the party should progress, win more elections, that the party should spread to different states, that is very important work for me. Apart from that, in Parliament my primary responsibility as an MP is to raise people's issues, to ask more questions, to participate in each and every debate so that my voice and criticism is heard. And third, giving public speeches is again a responsibility. It is not easy to give a speech of 70–80 minutes extempore, so you have to keep your mind ready, think and absorb. I would be failing in my duty if I don't say that I definitely want political empowerment of the Dalits and the Muslims in particular. That is where I feel political empowerment is a key which opens many locks. Some political scientists might not agree but the crass reality of our democracy is that if you have a political voice then you progress. And one of the reasons why Muslims have not progressed, and there is empirical data for this across social, educational, and economic health indicators, is because they don't have a political voice. So the reality is that you need more political representation, more empowerment. That is the most important. Education of Muslims is very important to me. We try our utmost to achieve this. For example, in Telangana, we played a very important role and the chief minister should be given the credit for what we could do. He opened minority residential schools in Telangana wherein from class 6 to 12 the medium of instruction is English, and on each student, the government is spending a lakh a year. You will be happy to know and also surprised that 50,000 Muslim children are studying now—25,000 boys and 25,000 girls. That is a very satisfactory thing. Another thing that we are consistently demanding from the various governments in the centre is to remove this stupid Haj subsidy which is not being used and give it to Muslim girls as scholarships. My innermost desire is that these scholarships which are given to minorities are made demand-driven. The expenditure is only a 1,000 crores. By not making it demand-driven, there is data which shows that 82 lakh Muslims are being denied scholarship. So this contradicts the allegation of all the communal parties which say that we are not interested in studies. And of course, the most important thing is to preserve the great ethos of this country which if destroyed in the process will put the minorities at a loss.

Q. *Why is it that you are having difficulty in expanding your political party? Every region has its own particular Muslim leaders and parties. What are your difficulties on the ground?*

I have deliberately not gone to Assam and Kerala because I am of the opinion Indian Union Muslim League and the All India

United Democratic Front (AIUDF) should not be disturbed. That is why we are concentrating on Uttar Pradesh, Bihar, Maharashtra, and Karnataka. In terms of the issues that stop us— our Muslim mind has been trained over the last 50–55 years that you must ensure that secularism wins. We have been trained in such a way that every election for us is a matter of life and death, and then after elections, we die every day. No one cares about it after elections. So when it comes to elections, at a subconscious level we are trained in the way of '*Aap* secularism *ko zinda rakhna, yeh aapki zimmedaari hai*' (you keep secularism alive, it is your responsibility). Muslims feel very proud of this. We don't realize that this is a burden that needs to be shared by everyone. But we become the torchbearers for that election period of 20 days and then people forget us. So that is why it is my constant struggle to tell them that this is a burden which everyone has to share, it is not only you. But the people sitting in Delhi, who are the 'merchants of our destinies', have trained us in such a way that it becomes a matter of life and death for us. So when Akhlaq happens, when Pehlu Khan happens, when National Security Act (NSA) is applied to three Muslim boys in Madhya Pradesh despite the Cow Slaughter Act being in place, no one talks about it. So once we come out of this bonded labour of secularism, I feel Muslims will do much better.

Q. Secularism is a complicated philosophical concept. Is it secularism or is it your version of Muslim politics that is not as acceptable to people in UP or Maharashtra?

In Maharashtra now we have an alliance with Prakash Ambedkar because the argument was put forward to me—'*Aap kya khaali Muslim votes jeetenge?*' (Will you win on Muslim votes alone?) That question is asked by the trained mind, not by a person who believes in Muslim empowerment. Then that trained Muslim mind then says, '*Arrey bhai aap kya sirf do vote se jeet jaayenge?*' (Will you be able to win with just two votes?) Then we had a huge meeting in Shivaji Park which broke all the records. Even Bal Thackeray in his heyday could not have had that kind of gathering. Again people said, 'Arrey aapne toh kamaal kar diya' (You have done wonders). If I have done wonders, then you should support us. And the response we get is, 'Nahi nahi aise kaise aa jaaye, BJP jeet jaayegi' (How can we support you, BJP will win). What we don't realize is that even despite you not voting for BJP, BJP has won. Now god knows what will happen. So that mind has to be broken. But we don't aspire to be the chief minister of Madhya Pradesh or Maharashtra. My concern is that you have your representative, and we give them the example of Telangana. We have only seven MLAs, but here the minority ministry budget is 2,500 crores. In the Government of India, it is 4,300 crores. You wouldn't believe that on our representation, the government is giving scholarship to boys who are studying in universities in the USA, UK, and Australia. Their demands are even more than Dalits. They get their full scholarship. We tell them that this is what you can do. You have to have your political representation. We are not saying don't vote for a secular party, but we are in a certain constituency where you can win, so you win those seats. Because there have to be checks and balances, your diversity has to be represented which will take some time. But I am sure that, over a period of time, among the Muslim youth there will be a realization that it doesn't matter if we only have 2–3 MLAs, we must have them. I want this change in the Muslim mentality that you must have political representation and your own voice and you fight for it and you see what happens. So that is what we try to make them understand—get at least 2–3 people, get them elected, work hard, let them represent and see the difference because that will also keep a check on these parties.

Q. *Why did you oppose the Triple Talaq bill? Under the pretext of religious and cultural practice, one could ask for Sati, in Hinduism, to be allowed. How does one strike a balance?*

Triple Talaq is a sin. Even in Hanafi school of thought, which majority of Indian Muslims follow, if a man divorces his wife to Triple Talaq, it is a sin, you are committing a grievous sin. Even the Supreme Court did not call it unconstitutional. They simply said that they'll set it aside. In fact, Chief Justice Khaher and Justice Nazeer said that yes the divorce happens. It was Justice Nariman who said that it fails the test of arbitrariness. Justice Joseph took a very different position. Now the Supreme Court has given a judgement that even after Triple Talaq the marriage is not dissolved. The Constitution says that whatever be the judgement of the Supreme Court it is the law. So what is the harm now? My question is what is the point of you making a law when the marriage is not dissolved and I am also accepting the same thing. So why have a penal provision when the Supreme Court judgement is there? For example, we made laws on child marriage which is a social evil that needed to be eradicated. But the 2011 census says that out of some 1 crore odd child marriages that happened, 80 lakhs were non-Muslims. I mean if you are really interested in women empowerment we have 2.4 million married women who are deserted, or married like the prime minister's wife—no one talks about her. What about her empowerment? We have empirical data in Hyderabad collected from all the Khazis appointed by the government that Triple Talaq is minuscule and what is high is a woman asking for a divorce from her husband. That is in large numbers. Yes, there are instances of Triple Talaq, I am not denying that, and it is a social evil. But why do you want to interfere in my religious practice? How do you know that by doing this it will stop?

Q. *As a legislator, you have spent time and effort thinking about the law. What is happening in the legislature? Do you think we are seeing a legislative decline in India?*

Yes, absolutely. Firstly, the government is making such lousy and pathetic legislations. I had told (Law Minister) Ravishankar

Prasad in the Parliament that you may be good lawyer but you are a pathetic draftsman. How can you make such laws like the one on Triple Talaq? That man cannot even differentiate. He said Supreme Court had made it unconstitutional. I challenged him to show me the proof. And why is the quality of debate in declining? Because MPs don't read and come. That's the second reason. We don't read. We don't go behind the subject, speak to experts. Like if you are a political scientist, I should speak to you. We don't do that. We have this PA who is now an Einstein for us. He prepares all stupid things and we stand up and read them. So that is why the standard of debate is very low. And third, the government is not interested in debates, the government wants to finish everything. How can a legislation like Triple Talaq be given three hours? Why three hours? Why not six hours? Why not eight hours? Aadhaar got two hours. Why two hours? Have six hours. The government has a group majority so one gets only three hours.

Q. *It is said about you that you are very different in private than on the news channels and in the rallies. And of course, the controversial things that you have said in the rallies are pointed out ...*

What is controversial? So, for example, I said I refuse to say *Bharat Mata ki Jai*. I said that because seven days before I made the speech, RSS Chief Mohan Bhagwat had said that people who do not say that slogan have no right to live in India. My reaction to that was, who the hell are you? Who are you to say that I should say this? I will not say this. That is why I said what I said. I knew very well that this will lead to a lot of commotion, but I was fine with that. Is that the test of my loyalty? I am not stopping you from saying it. I will definitely respect your right to say whatever you want. But you cannot superimpose your views on me. That is the beauty of democracy. So I said that I will not say it. So they raised a hue and cry. I'll tell you about an interesting incident. I had lunch with some of my friends at Le Meridien Hotel in Delhi. After that, we came out and we were waiting for the car. There were some 20 people wearing fantastic suits and shoes. You could tell they were very learned by their dress. They approached me and said, 'How are you Owaisi ji?' 'I am fine.' 'All of us are doctors and have come to attend a conference.' 'That's very good,' I said. Suddenly they raised the slogan, 'Bharat Mata Ki...!' So I started laughing. They said, 'Are you laughing?' 'Yes I am laughing.' They said, 'Are you not ashamed?' 'No. I am not at all ashamed. I am shameless,' I said. Again they raised the slogan, 'Bharat mata...!' 'Beat me up, not once but ten times', I said. They said, 'What kind of a man are you?' I said, 'I am a human being.' They asked, 'Are you not feeling anything? Will you beat us?' I said, 'I will not beat you. Will you beat me? Then you would also have to treat me since you are all doctors.' What can I do if this is the thinking? Unfortunately, it has become the test of loyalty. If you don't say it then you are anti-national and you don't have the right to live in this country. If I go to the Congress party they say that I am communal and not secular. So where do I go? You do this you are damned, you do that you are damned, everyone wants to damn you. So I said damn you, I'll do whatever I want to do. So you see, it is not controversial, it is my right. This is how you fight them. Ideological fights are done like this. Scholars might have a different method, but as a politician, these are my methods. But Javed Akhtar took offence to it. He said that he is proud so he'll say it. I am not stopping you. I am saying don't impose it on me. I'll say *Jai Hind!* This was a slogan which was used during the War of Independence. Everyone used it. Our nationalism cannot be one size fits all.

Q. *So according to you, on one hand, we have this ideological fight that has been reduced to sloganeering and on the other hand we have a legislature which is not doing its work. Where do you think we are headed?*

Disaster, I am telling you. Because ideologically we are losing that battle. And whether you like it or not, the Congress party is not willing to take them on ideologically. And that is why I have come to the opinion that in India we have only one national party that is the BJP, and the second is BJP 1.5. And because you are not taking them on ideologically, you are losing that battle in the legislature because the executive is becoming stronger and stronger. The more debates you have in the legislature, that shows that the legislature is independent. It is a check on the executive. We have no debates in legislature. Everyone wants to just stomp out. How can you expect a man who wants to become the Prime Minister of India to go and hug the prime minister of the day? Is that the level of the legislature? That is not your stand there to go and embrace someone. You are there to provoke him, expose him, and take him on. That is your work. You are not there as Munnabhai. That is why Munnabhai is in a film, not on the floor of the Parliament. You expose the government, you bitterly criticize them. Can we remove a prime minister if we had a war in India by moving a No Confidence motion? Everyone will be like 'Are you crazy? The nation has been attacked!' But the beauty of democracy is that it can be done even in a state of war. Churchill had to face it. Here you cannot do it because you have lost the ideological battle.

Q. Why has Congress lost this ideological battle?

I feel that they lost it long back. And Rahul Gandhi says in Madhya Pradesh that Congress is a party of Hinduism. If I had made the statement that 'My party is for Muslims or Islam' that will cause controversy, but when Rahul said it that was not a controversy. Why? Simply because it appealed to the majoritarian ideology. He is falling in line. They say he is a *janeu-dhari* Hindu. So where does that leave me? I am not in the Varna system.

Then Manish Tiwari goes and says that 'We have the DNA of Brahmins.' Where does that leave me? Maybe I don't have DNA at all now. So where are you heading? What I was taught by my father during my initial days in politics about taking on a political opponent—*Mukhaled ke ghar pe jaake nahi laarna. Usko ghar se nikaalo. Ghar pe jaake ladenge toh chaaro khaane chit ho jaayenge.* This is the basic thing he taught me—Never fight your opponent on his strong points. If you fight him on his strong points, how will you win?

Q. What is the position of so-called secularism in India?

Where is secularism in India? There is secularism only in the constitution. On paper. But the constitution has to be a living document which we as Indians have failed to make. The responsibility also lies with me. The constitution has to be a living document, it can't be a mere paper which it has become now. People say that it was incorporated by Mrs Gandhi. No, it was there since the constituent assembly. We are heading towards bad days. Everyone only wants to win the election actually. Now secularism is the dirtiest word to use in India, no one uses it now. You should do a google search and see how many times Rahul Gandhi has used the word secularism. You'll be shocked to know that he has never used it. Why? What is wrong with that? If it has been incorporated by his grandmother, at least live up to her legacy. Tell me, if India was not secular, would Sheikh Abdullah have agreed to join India? If what is happening today happened in 1947, would Sheikh Abdullah have joined? Would we have got Sikkim? Or the Northeast? That is what I am saying. These are things that you will have to live up to. And I am not saying that secularism means that you pander to me and pamper me. I am saying that secularism means that you do not impose majoritarian views. Now it is the majoritarian religion that is ruling India.

Q. You have spoken about how the Muslim population has been in a rut, not being able to achieve the upliftment that they would like. What are some of the issues on which you think you have been able to personally have a good, big impact? And where have your party's efforts failed?

I am sorry but I cannot judge myself. Maybe when I die scholars can write my obituary in some newspaper. It is a constant struggle. I was at Harvard University some time ago for a conference. After the event, Madhu Trehan, a very famous journalist, asked me, 'I've heard from the others about what work they've done. What have you done?' I said, 'Madam I have not done anything. The only thing that I am doing right now is to create confidence in democracy. This is the most important thing that I am doing.' This is what I do. I go around India, I give speeches, people come and listen and they like what I say. But at the end of the day when they listen to what I say there are some bitter truths. It has to be definitely against Congress and BJP because you have to start talking about how we have been deceived by these political parties. And when you ask the Congress questions like why is it that you don't have a Muslim MP in Maharashtra for two terms, they have no answer. In Karnataka there hasn't been a Muslim MP for two terms, you have no answer. You have no Muslim MP in UP now, you have no answer. Who is responsible for the most populous state? The reality is that the non-Muslims are not ready to vote for Muslim candidates, that is the reality. We have Muslims because our mind has been trained for 50 years that we have to vote for a 'secular' candidate. So it is like we are a machine and we have been programmed in such a way. But people don't want to vote for their own candidates. That is why I go and give these speeches because I have to say the reality. And then it becomes controversial and this and that. In Shivaji Park I criticized Imran Khan (post-Pulwama), I called Jaish-e-Mohammed, Jaish-e-Shayateen, and Lashkar-e-Shayateen. My MLA was telling me from Maharashtra that Shiv Sena MP told him that 'Boss, what a speech! We cannot criticise him now.' After 70 years, the test of my loyalty is how much I speak about Pakistan, so what can I do? This is what it is. Congress and BJP, they are no different. Simply because their ideologies are the same. The Congress Party, from Nehru to Rahul Gandhi, we have come a long way. A man in jail without a laptop, without Google writes *Discovery of India*, Nehru was Nehru.

Q. *Do you feel you are carrying the burden of responsibility because Congress and BJP are not doing enough and there are not many other Muslim parties out there? Do you feel like you are carrying a torch for other Muslims?*

No. It is not like I am carrying a torch or I am being burdened. Just like everyone, I have limited time in my life, so I am doing the best I can. As long as my health and age permit I'll do it. Once my eyes are closed desire for things left undone should not be there. At the end of the day whatever I do, and I am being very honest with you, I don't have any personal ambitions of having that blue-red light on my car. I think people have realized that this man has no personal ambitions. But I want this discourse to change. I definitely want Dalits and Muslims to get justice, and what is wrong in that? How can the prime minister wash their feet? I would love to go and ask them how many times their feet were washed before the prime minister washed them. In Hyderabad and Delhi, I still see people going into the sewers. And the prime minister wrote in his book that cleaning shit is a spiritual experience, and then he washes the feet of these people. The prime minister stands up in 2014 in the Lok Sabha and says, '*Humko satta milli hai 1200 saal ke ghulaami ke baad*' (We have gained power after 1200 years of slavery). As an Indian, I know 200 years of British rule, what is 1,200 years? But that is the mindset! In 1,200, 600 years are of Mughal rule and god knows where my forefathers came from. I am still answerable for them. They say I am an offspring of Babur. How do I know who was Babur? The most I can go to is my grandfather's father who came from Nandiad, I can't go beyond that. But still, they will call me Babur's offspring.

Q. Other parties, particularly the so-called 'secular' ones, say that instead of joining hands with us to consolidate the vote, Mr Owaisi is cutting our votes ...

You see, I have become the 'Umrao Jaan' of Indian politics and all of them say I have taken money from Amit Shah, from Modi, and all that. I was supporting the Congress party for eight years from 2004–12. I said to one Congress leader you are absolutely right that I have taken money from BJP. He said, 'What are you saying!' I said, 'Yes. In 8 years, you gave me less money. Now I am getting more.' He said, 'But we didn't give you anything.' I said, 'Yes, that is where you went wrong.' So this is nonsense you see. They say that I should not contest elections. When I ask why, they say that they are losing. Good! Then you win! Who is stopping you from winning? I didn't contest in Maharashtra—no Muslim MPs, I didn't contest Karnataka—no Muslim MPs, I didn't contest UP—no Muslim MPs. This is a very lame and arrogant attitude that says, 'You should not contest! Why should you stand in front of us?'

Q. They would prefer that you become allies ...

Basically, if you cannot defeat, join them. It's like Chinese democracy. Let us hope that we don't come to that stage. Why shouldn't I contest? I want to contest. The beauty of democracy is to fight elections, the beauty of democracy is not to hold a seminar and have beliefs on paper. The beauty of democracy is contesting elections and putting forward my views. I may not succeed today, I may succeed tomorrow or maybe after my lifetime. But that I should not contest elections is a wrong argument to put forward. Then you do not believe in democracy at all. You believe in selection, you don't believe in election. You give candidates and then ensure that your candidates win. There is serious talk in the Congress on how many Muslims can we give tickets to? Quota system *thodi hai?* (As if there is a quota system?)

Q. *For India as a country, if you marginalize such a large proportion of your population and not give them a political voice, that is a bad sign.*

If I wanted to go and join *jihad*, the easiest way for me was Kashmir. In the last 50 years, only 20 people have gone from India and joined *jihad* in Kashmir. I can take a bus from Azamgarh and go to Kashmir, I have not gone. Geographically, Al-Qaeda is nearer to me, I have not joined. Some 25 people joined ISIS out of which some 19 were studying abroad, some were from Hyderabad and Bombay, the rest have not joined. What more do you want us to do, boss? What more? No one appreciates this. When I state these facts, people say, 'Are you threatening?' I am not threatening, I am telling you this is how much we love this country. This is how much we care for this country. What I am asking is when we love and care, where is my share? Give us something. If you will eat the cream and the curd, drink the milk and then run away with the utensils, what will I do? Will I keep waiting in the queue with my hunger? That can't happen. Till how long can I wait hungrily with the hope that my stomach will be filled? This has to end. That is why I want to contest elections. Whether I win or I lose, that is different. But still, I hear, 'You don't contest, BJP will benefit from it.' But you are also benefitting BJP by not letting Muslims win. The moment Rahul Gandhi started going to the temple, Arun Jaitley made a statement saying why would people choose a clone when they have the original? He is right! And it is not only the Congress but other secular parties as well.

Q. *We are a young nation and people have aspirations. Let us move away from Muslim politics. What, in your view, should the Indian government be doing to ensure a better life and a better future for India's youth?*

Fifty per cent of India's population is below the age of 25. But in Indian politics, no leader ever becomes old. Even a grandfather is considered a 'Youth Leader'. That is our concept. I'll tell you Indian democracy will never help the youth unless and until the youth have enough money to spend on elections, to win elections. How many young people have money? You need a minimum of 4–5 crores. Even if they work very hard for 10 years, 4–5 crores is difficult to accumulate. I have a friend in Congress who was looking for a seat and was told, 'How can that seat be given to you, we are getting more money for it'. You're selling seats! How can a young person win an election? And all these youth faces that you see in Parliament, 90 per cent are family-oriented, only 10 per cent are green shoots. If you don't have money, how will you contest? A similar argument is there for women. The prime minister says there are so many women in the Parliament. Look closely, they have a political background, they have money. There might be eight or 10 who are not from such a background, but they are an exception, not the norm. So how will the youth come into politics? Who will give them the ticket? Unless and until a party gives financial support to a youth candidate they cannot win. All this 'youth power' is nonsense. They are lying to the people of India. What power are they giving to the youth of India? A person of 55–60 years becomes a 'youth leader' in India and at 40 years one can become a prime minister in the UK. This demographic dividend will not last beyond 2030–40.

Q. Are you predicting a demographic disaster?

Yes, and so is our democracy. Because earlier it was 'Hum do humaare do'. Then everyone started saying that now demographic dividend has come. What is the demographic dividend? If you don't invest in education and infrastructure, what will the youth do? Will they sit and play carrom or join the anti-cow slaughter squad? The population in the south is ageing now. It is dangerous, you see. Someone was telling me that by 2040 you will have to work more to provide sustenance to people who grow old. How will we provide sustenance? Our whole mental makeup is not for youth. We are structured in such a way that we don't have confidence in them. That is a very Indian way of looking at things. It has not changed, unfortunately, in my opinion. I might be wrong.

Q. If you had two–three words or a phrase that you would like to be remembered by once you retire, what would they be?

If I ever had a grave, I hope it would say that I believed in the Indian Constitution. Because I feel that is the best document for India, for Indians, for Muslims, for Dalits. That is the best document to attain social justice. I honestly feel that. Those principles or those dreams which were envisioned, if we are able to implement them, that would be the greatest thing that we can do for India. So I hope somebody would write that I'm a Constitutionalist. Apart from just hate speeches and controversies, those will definitely be there (laughs).

Devendra Fadnavis

When Devendra Fadnavis was appointed chief minister of Maharashtra in 2014, most political observers were quick to write him off. Fadnavis was then just 44, making him the second-youngest chief minister in the state's history, behind none other than Sharad Pawar. In addition, while he had held important positions in the Bharatiya Janata Party's (BJP's) state unit and was a three-term MLA, he had no previous ministerial experience and was hardly considered a strong leader in the state.

Besides, Maharashtra is a challenging state to govern. The political environment in the state is captured by competing interest groups—from big business houses to labour unions, from right to information (RTI) activists to the media. The bureaucracy is known to be particularly cumbersome, with many senior bureaucrats having deeply entrenched political loyalties. It is no surprise, then, that in the 40 years preceding Fadnavis, not a single Maharashtra chief minister had managed to complete their five-year term. Only one ever had in the state's history.

In addition to all these challenges, Devendra Fadnavis had to deal with a hostile, disgruntled ally in the form of the Shiv Sena, which spent most of his term as chief minister berating the BJP and its central leadership. He also had to tackle the most severe drought crisis the state had seen in over two decades, on top of the widespread rural distress and farmer suicides. Despite the deck being stacked against him, he was able to not only complete his five-year term but managed to do so with quite a few successes. On the administrative side, he ran a relatively clean government without any significant hiccups, even managing to peacefully tackle mass agitations (though not without criticism) and resist what he indicates were politically motivated attempts to unseat him. On the political side, the BJP won 23 of the 25 seats it contested in the 2019 Lok Sabha elections and emerged as the single largest party by some distance in the 2019 state elections.

During his five years as chief minister, Fadnavis's popularity increased tremendously, making him one of the most popular BJP leaders nationally. He also seems to have built excellent relations across the spectrum, such that even opposition leaders in the state rarely say a negative word about him. In a political space that has only become more antagonistic in recent years, that is quite a feat; a consequence, at least in part, of his accommodating approach and friendly personality.

We have the opportunity to interact with Fadnavis a couple of times, including a late-night sit-down conversation at Varsha, the chief minister's residence in Mumbai. After spending time with him, it is easy to see why he has very few enemies. He is remarkably soft-spoken, amiable, and goes out of his way to offer help. In our discussion with Fadnavis, we speak at length about the trials and tribulations of being a chief minister, the influence of the RSS on his politics and worldview, the role of his personality in managing dissent, and his outlook on policies like farm loan waivers. Our conversation is peppered with amusing anecdotes, like the story of a four-year-old Fadnavis insisting that his mother switch his school, Indira Convent, because it was named after the woman (Indira Gandhi) who put his father in jail during the Emergency. He comes across as forthcoming and thoughtful.

Fadnavis believes he was able to survive the full tenure as chief minister, despite all odds, because of his 'positive attitude' and his willingness to take everyone along. 'As a CM, every day is a challenge,' he says, conceding that he would initially get disconcerted by the litany of problems, but soon realized they were simply part of the job description. Beyond his personality and cooperative approach, he also credits the strict discipline and 'no-nonsense mentality' of the Modi–Shah-led BJP for helping him manage factionalism and dissent.

A large part of our conversation revolves around the philosophy and ideology of the RSS and how that has influenced Fadnavis. As his father was a devoted RSS *pracharak*, Fadnavis was born into the RSS and its creed. Unlike some other BJP leaders with similar strong roots in the RSS, however, he has always struck a moderate tone on issues surrounding religion. You are unlikely to find him making any controversial or provocative statements on such matters. He instead goes out of his way to deliver messages of inclusiveness. Fadnavis insists that he is moderate because of the RSS influence on his outlook, not despite it. The RSS ideology, he says, taught him never to discriminate and always to be inclusive. And according to him, those who discriminate based on faith are not subscribers to the RSS ideology.

Devendra Fadnavis has built a reputation of being an honest, able administrator who carries everyone along, somewhat reminiscent of former BJP prime minister Atal Bihari Vajpayee. That, coupled with his close ties with the RSS in his hometown of Nagpur, makes him one of the brightest stars among the next-generation BJP leaders.

Interview

Q. You joined politics while you were still in college. What made you join politics? Your father was a BJP Member of the Legislative Council (MLC) and your aunt was a cabinet minister. Did that play a role in you joining politics so young?

You know, I hadn't planned to join politics. I wanted to become a lawyer and was studying law. In my college days, I was active in student body politics with the Akhil Bharatiya Vidyarthi Parishad (ABVP). While I was in the final year of my degree, I got a chance to contest elections for the Municipal Corporation. I was not eligible before that because I hadn't turned 21. But fortunately for me, that was a time of reforms like the 74th amendment and other issues, due to which the elections were postponed. By the time they were scheduled again, I was eligible to contest. And as a result, I became the youngest corporator in Nagpur.

Q. You are the second-youngest Mayor in India's history, as well as the second-youngest chief minister of Maharashtra in history. Has it been challenging for you to take on these demanding roles at such a young age?

It is challenging at any age. When I got elected for the second time, out of the elected members, there were only eight people who had some experience, the rest of them were new. And I was the best performer amongst them for five years which is why I was selected as the mayor. When it was time for the legislative assembly election in 1999, I was offered a seat from West Nagpur. People had a lot of appreciation for my stint as the mayor and they elected me as a legislator. So, at the age of 29, I became a Member of the Legislative Assembly.

Q. *I am sure your father's arrest during the Emergency had a big impact on you. I read that you may have even left your school because it was called Indira Convent School. Is that true?*

That is true. I have no hard feelings for Mrs Indira Gandhi now. I was just four years old when my father was arrested and he was in jail for almost two years. I could only understand that Mrs Indira Gandhi had put him in jail. I was very angry with her and coincidentally my school's name was Indira Convent. So I told my mother that I wasn't going to study in this school anymore and I got admitted to a different school.

Q. *You were the longest-serving chief minister of Maharashtra in four decades. You were also the only one to complete the full term in four decades. What has been the secret to your success in a place like this which is clearly not easy for chief ministers to govern and stay around?*

I think it is only my positive attitude that has kept me going. There have been several protest rallies and agitations against me. Although some were genuine, there were some that were aimed at removing me from office. I think my positive approach to all these situations helped me successfully turn the crisis into opportunity. Hence, I could and have been delivering and that is why I have been able to survive for such a long time.

Q. *Could you think of any such situation which was crucial for your survival?*

There was a farmers' agitation during which there were a lot of people on the ground. The media covering the agitation were very hostile and blew the incident out of proportion. Such a portrayal was creating a lot of ill will. I started talking to them and found out that most of their demands had not been met in the last 20 years. Some of them were directly affected and were protesting, and there were many that were supporting them. With my positive approach towards the situation, I could enter into an agreement with them. I waived off their loans and introduced some other reforms. This helped the apparently violent agitation settle down. There was absolutely no violence. There have also been a number of agitations of reservations on the basis of caste. I have tried to handle them positively and took the decisions that were possible under the realm of our constitution.

Q. *Do you think this reservation policy is actually good for both social peace and economic development in the future? When people within your own party, like Mr Gadkari,have said clearly there are no government jobs, what is the purpose of reservation then?*

The people are at liberty to debate whether it is good or bad, but I think it is necessary. As of now, there is no other policy through which one can achieve affirmative action. It is only through reservation by way of which you can at least mete out justice to those who have been socially marginalized. If you look at the current scenario, reservation exists in the government sector. There is a huge private sector which is open to everybody. One cannot say that people are losing out due to the reservation policy because the entire private sector, which is developing at a fast pace, also exists. So I think reservation policy will always be debated because people who are benefitting from reservation will always want it and those who are not will always feel that they are missing out. I feel that presently, it is the only tool which is available to attain some sort of social equity.

Q. *You gave Marathas reservation. You gave farmers loan waivers. But even the farm loan waiver is not considered, by most people, as a long-term sustainable solution. The BJP has itself opposed it in many states. So what is the long-term solution for this, in terms of social equity?*

I totally agree that the farm loan waiver is not a solution that can change the fate of farmer. It is just one of the steps. But in a state like Maharashtra, if eventually due to drought or some agricultural crisis 40 per cent of your people are out of the institutional credit system, then their only fate at that point is to die. For a normal farmer the initial loan that he gets for sowing is what actually helps him. If he goes into default and is out of the institutional credit system, he is forced to go to the private moneylender, which results in all type of social problems. So my only reason to give them a waiver was to bring them back into the institutional credit system. Once they are back, we have a larger problem that needs to be addressed which is the need for sustainability in agriculture. Without sustainability, they will be pushed out of the system, yet again, and the government cannot continue to waive farm loans because it is a bad fiscal move.

We took up the challenge of water conservation. We created a lot of water conservation structures in 16,000 villages so that those villages can become water neutral. What is the result? Even though this year we were hit by extreme drought, our agricultural productivity went down by just 10 per cent as compared to last year. These measures have been very successful. Whatever measures you take there has to be a farm distress response mechanism.

Q. *Maharashtra is a very large and diverse state. You came in very young and relatively inexperienced compared to all your predecessors. You had so many different interest groups here and you had a hostile ally in the form of Shiv Sena. As you said you have a hostile media, you have bureaucracy, you have corporates. So how did you navigate all these different interest groups to achieve your goals in the last few years?*

My only advantage was that I had been working as a member of the assembly for 15 years. In these 15 years, I have been very vocal, I have been very active, and I have deliberated on practically every subject. So when I became chief minister, although I had never been a minister in the past, I had domain knowledge of every single sector and that helped me a lot.

Q. Are there factions within the BJP? And how do you manage the factional tension within the party?

Frankly speaking, I have not experienced factionalism in the last four-five years. Initially, people thought that the fact that I was far younger than my colleagues who were aspiring to be the chief minister, it would give rise to a lot of factionalism. But I think with my approach I could accommodate all of them, and I have not faced any problem within the party in the last four-five years.

Q. How much of your success in managing factionalism is contributed by the fact that in the BJP, you have this strong hand of the centre, that the party leadership doesn't allow much infighting and dissent within the state unit?

I think you are absolutely right because everybody knows that we have a no-nonsense mentality. No factionalism will be tolerated. We have a very strong central leadership and that has acted in my favour.

Q. What about the bureaucracy? We know that especially in Maharashtra, in Mumbai, the bureaucracy is hard to handle. There are a lot of loyalties to people from different political parties, as well as some deep-rooted relationships. So how did you as a first time minister and chief minister get the strength to deal with that? How did you navigate those challenges?

Bureaucracy was not new to me. For the 15 years that I was an MLA, I had been grilling the entire bureaucracy and the government as leader of the opposition. So the bureaucracy already knew that I had total domain knowledge. I think that the bureaucracy tends to cooperate with people who have domain knowledge. If I were to evaluate the bureaucracy, I feel that 50 per cent of them are very good and 50 per cent of them are average. One has to use them effectively and as it is rightly said that the 'bureaucracy is a horse on which you have to ride.' I tried to do that through some innovative ideas—I initiated the Key Responsibility Area (KRA) system for the bureaucracy. I gave them KRAs and have also started evaluating them. I started managing the projects through the War Room. All of this instilled a sense of accountability into them. They could see that there was a new work culture and to a large extent, they have cooperated.

Q. *You had so many successes in your five years. Are there any things that you look upon as a failure or a regret?*

There are many things that I would have liked to do. Five years are not sufficient to change a state. There are many infrastructural projects which I would have loved to see through.

Q. *For a long time, the BJP and especially you have proclaimed that Hindutva is an ideology which is not linked to any religion or dharma or who you pray to, but it is an all-inclusive idea of being Indian. While it is easy to say that, if you are a Muslim living in Mumbai and somebody says Hindutva is an idea which includes everybody, how do you convince them? Because some people will argue that even in Islam, Islamiat is a concept which includes everybody. So why not use the word Islamiat and why use the word Hindutva?*

It's because I don't know Islam. It is because I have been raised as a Hindu and I have always been taught tolerance. I have always been taught that being a Hindu is to be tolerant and have respect

60

for all faiths. History tells me that when people were persecuted around the world, they came to this land and this land has accepted them. It made them part of its culture. That is Hindutva. So I think Hindutva has always been all-inclusive. It is because of the politics of appeasement that society has been divided. Although I think it will take a little more time, eventually even the Muslims in this country will realize that Hindutva, which is preached by BJP or RSS, is a wider concept. It includes Muslims. I think that this realization has begun.

Q. *Regardless of your definition, Muslims hesitate to join your organization or come onboard with this ideology. Why don't Muslims see Hindutva and the RSS the same way?*

If you look at the birth of RSS—Dr Hedgewar was an active Congressman. He was chief of the *Vidarbha* Congress. Appeasement began in the Congress when they resolved that they will not sing the entire *Vande Mataram* because it hurts religious sentiments. However, our Muslim freedom fighters also used to sing *Vande Matram*. When the Congress started listening to voices of people like Jinnah who always said that there are two nations in India, that was the time when Dr Hedgewar said that unless we ground our identities as a nation of Hindus, this country would disintegrate. That is why he started RSS. He said that for 700 years invaders could invade our country because we did not have an identity. Hence, now we must take pride in being one country which is a Hindu country. And with that ideology, RSS was born. Since our country was divided on the basis of religion, it will take time for people to realize that Hindutva is a very larger term. It is not like any religion. I am very respectful even about the Semitic religions. They have their own ideologies and I have no problem with them. But Hindutva is not Semitic. My religion doesn't prevent me to go to a *dargah*. I go and I pray there because I feel my God is there. This inclusivity is the culture of India! If you look at the sects in Hinduism—those who believe in God are Hindus, those who don't believe in gods are Hindus, those who believe that God has sent a messenger are also Hindus, those who believe that nature is God are also Hindus. So in Hinduism, all type of faiths have always existed for more than 5,000 years.

Q. *Currently in India, there is a rise of mega gurus who have political clout. As a political party, what do you think of all these religious leaders becoming mega leaders in their own right, which is very unusual?*

I think it is not unusual for India. If you look at the history of India, religious leaders have always stood behind political leaders and have guided them because we have always believed that *dharma satta* (here dharma does not mean religion, it means righteousness) should be always above *raj satta*. Thus, in history we have seen that *dharma dand* has always been above *raj dand*. This has always been our culture. Chandragupta Maurya was a king but Chanakya created him. Sri Sri Ravi Shankar's ideology and teachings are inclusive and more about our culture. It's not about any faith or how you worship. I am not drawing any parallels but on the one hand, you have Shahi Imaam of, say, Jama Masjid who issues a *fatwa* saying that vote for this party. For years, Congress has been using him, and for years he has been issuing *fatwas* saying that vote for Congress. But nobody has criticized this. Today when religious leaders, social leaders, or non-political leaders are becoming active, they are being criticized. There are a lot of double standards.

Q. *You are looked as a leader with close ties to the RSS but still a moderate voice within the BJP. But on both sides, there are fringe elements who are polarizing the public with extreme, fanatical voices. How do you think we can get to a point where political parties are not incentivizing this kind of anti-religious rhetoric?*

First, let me clarify, I am moderate because I have been born and brought up in the RSS. I don't know what the perception is, but the reality is in RSS I have always been told to be a patriot, to be socially active and not to discriminate. That is why I am moderate. At the time of elections, there are some extreme reactions. I don't support that but electoral politics is a little different. So when a party appeases this community, a candidate from another party tries to woo the other community, which is not good. Our politics and our democratic sector has matured a lot, but it requires more maturity, which will come with time.

Q. *Can you talk about the impact that being a member of RSS has had on your politics and your outlook?*

The one thing they have taught me is to work selflessly. RSS has many organizations and its actual motto is to create good people. It is a man-making factory. They believe that people who believe in this country, who believe in a social cause, should lead. Their motto is 'Vyakti Nirmaan ka Kendra'. People may have different opinions about our ideology, but I don't think it is extreme. RSS has made me more inclusive and it is because of this that I am able to establish a dialogue with everybody.

Q. *So you think some people are misinterpreting the RSS philosophy when they put it in religious undertones to influence ideologies?*

Congress always knew that it is only RSS's ideology that can over-throw it, which is why they have always branded RSS as negative. When Mahatma Gandhi was assassinated, the blame was put on RSS. However, the judgement of the court exonerated RSS and made it clear that RSS had no role. Congress has tried to ban the RSS at least four times and the Supreme Court has come down heavily on them. So, all these perceptions are created for the purpose of vote bank politics.

Q. *Do you think RSS has had an impact on the values of politicians? What is the main difference between the members of the RSS and other politicians or public persons?*

I do not claim that a person who is not from the RSS cannot be a good person. There are good people in other organizations as well. I am aware of the possibility that somebody who is not from the RSS can be a better person than me. But when I evaluate myself, I feel that the RSS has contributed immensely in shaping my thoughts and it has made me more inclusive than normal people.

Q. *When we met Omar Abdullah we had a discussion on dynasty politics. He mentioned that although the BJP accuses the Congress and National Conference of dynasty politics, the BJP itself is run by the Sangh family. So what is the relationship between the RSS and the BJP?*

The *Sangh* doesn't run the BJP, the BJP is independent. The *Sangh* is like a father from where you derive inspiration and blessings. This is not the best example, but let's say you are running your own business independently, your father will always be your father. He will advise you and you will seek his blessings. That is the only relationship between BJP and RSS. Contrary to what Omar Abdullah said, RSS is not a single-family. A person with no identity becomes RSS chief. Till now all RSS chiefs have been unmarried, but even if we have a chief who is married and has a son, their sons will not become the RSS chief ever. Omar Abdullah is a good leader and I would not deny that, but in most of the cases, the only qualification these leaders have is that they are from the same family as the head.

Q. *Although the BJP and the Sangh are independent, has the BJP or have you had to take decisions that have actually gone against the interests or predisposition of the Sangh ?*

I don't think so, because if you look at the way the *Sangh* works, it is unaffected by political decisions. There are only a few larger decisions which may affect them, for example, they want us to have a very tough ideological position vis-à-vis Pakistan. So if we falter on that, the RSS will get affected. I have been in office for four and a half years and there has not been a single occasion when the RSS has intervened or dictated me. Organizations like Bhartiya Majdoor Sangh or the Industries Association of the RSS, have occasionally come to me and protested against some decisions that I have taken. But the RSS as an organization would never come.

Q. *Regarding your infrastructure work—you set up the War Room, you took on some of the biggest and most ambitious infrastructure projects in the state. However, you faced a lot of environmental protests and you had to deal with the different interest groups. How do you find the balance between infrastructural development and environmental sustainability, and make sure that you strike that balance in the best way possible?*

I acknowledged the issues raised by the environmentalists because it is high time that we think of sustainability. Having said that, looking at sustainability in a piecemeal manner won't help. For instance, to create a metro network in Mumbai I might have to cut down 500–700 trees. To cope with this, I am replanting 2,000 trees which are fully grown and have a survival rate of 95 per cent. After creating this metro network, I will be mitigating carbon footprint in Mumbai for which I would, otherwise, require 2 crore full-grown trees to be planted in Mumbai, which is impossible. So one has to look at the situation holistically. Recently, people have been opposed to the coastal road and they went to the Supreme Court. They feel that reclamation should not be done. However, in the rest of the world, all the countries that have invested in sustainable infrastructure development have built coastal roads by reclaiming land. Hence, it is how you reclaim and where you use it, that is important! After this reclamation we decided, and central government while giving us permission, said that this reclamation will not change the Coastal Regulation Zone (CRZ) line, so no new real estate will be constructed. Moreover, due to this reclamation, a huge green patch, something that Mumbai has never seen, is naturally being created. We are also creating a dedicated public transport corridor for green transport. These are all the benefits of this coastal road and reclamation. When the Prime Minister of Netherlands came to Mumbai, he was very bullish on the topic of the coastal road. He said that 300 years ago, the Dutch reclaimed lot of land in Mumbai and they were very keen to do such projects. He said that it is because of this reclamation that if in the future a tsunami arises, the deadly waves would be cut by that road and Mumbai would be saved. This is the kind of holistic approach that we need. When I initiated the work for the underground metro, there was a petition in a court which said that no construction activities should happen in the day time because it disrupts traffic. Parallelly, there was another petition filed by a different group, which said that no construction activities should happen at night because people are asleep and noise pollution happens. Now, how does one resolve the situation? I lost seven months due to these contradictory petitions and my cost escalated by 500 crores. I could have used all that money for more sustainability measures. I just want that we acknowledge the need for sustainability and we feel the need save the environment. I also feel that people who are raising their voice have no ill will. They also want to protect the environment. My only request to them is that they should look at the whole situation holistically.

Q. *You have done a great job being a politician, but do you sometimes at night wake up and think that maybe you should have been doing something else. If so, what is that something else?*

By education, I am a lawyer. I wanted to practise in the High Court and Supreme Court which I could not do. So given a chance even today I would love to become a lawyer.

Q. When you retire, what would you want to be remembered for?

I think that the only thing people should remember about me is that I tried to make a positive difference.

Jignesh Mevani

Over the last couple of decades, the Bharatiya Janata Party (BJP) has managed to turn the state of Gujarat into an impregnable electoral fortress. The 2017 assembly elections in the state became a battle of ego for both the ruling party and the Congress. As Gujarat is the home turf of both Prime Minister Modi and then BJP president Amit Shah, a loss for the BJP would greatly embarrass the two leaders. For the Congress, a surprise victory in Modi's home state would not only weaken him but also help lay the foundation for a much-needed pan-India revival. The BJP eventually emerged victorious but its tally was reduced to double digits for the first time since 1990, winning just 99 seats. The Congress, on the other hand, got its highest tally in the state since 1985, primarily because it managed to successfully piggyback on an energetic, high- decibel campaign against the BJP led by a troika of young activists—Jignesh Mevani, Hardik Patel, and Alpesh Thakor—that caught the imagination of the masses in Gujarat.

Jignesh Mevani, a former journalist, was using his recently earned law degree to help landless Dalits in his home state of Gujarat when he came across a viral video of a mob of cow vigilantes tying up and flogging the bodies of young Dalit men in the state's Una district, allegedly for picking up a cow carcass. Incensed at the crime, he decided to start a movement protesting atrocities against Dalits in the state. His movement received widespread support and by the time of the assembly elections the following year, Jignesh had become immensely popular across Gujarat. He decided to use the 2017 elections as a platform to campaign against what he repeatedly terms as the 'fascist' BJP government. Enthused by the support and media attention he was receiving, he decided, just 12 days before voting, to contest from Vadnag. Running as an independent candidate with some support from the Congress and Aam Aadmi Party (AAP), Jignesh managed to defeat the BJP candidate.

Two years after the Gujarat elections, we sit down with Jignesh in his apartment in Gandhinagar's MLA quarters. The modest apartment is a far cry from the typically large and sprawling homes of other politicians, many of whom are scions of well-known political families. The living room is filled with workers, supporters, and constituents, some seated on couches and others on the floor. There is little space to move and a lot of noise, so we are taken to a small adjoining room where Jignesh graciously offers us chairs while he sits uncomfortably on a bed. Over sandwiches and *chai*, we discuss a wide range of topics including his tryst with electoral politics, the advancement of the Dalits in India, and his personal failures and shortcomings.

Our conversation with Jignesh is unlike any other have had. Most of the prominent next-generation politicians in India are dynasts who have been groomed from a young age. They know when and what to speak, and when to remain silent. Jignesh on the other hand, not just because he sits on the far left of the ideological spectrum, is very open and at times even provocative. It's unsurprising that he consistently lands in trouble for making controversial remarks; he doesn't even try to be politically correct. You're unlikely to hear many other politicians calling the political system that they've chosen to be a part of 'an ocean of filth' that is 'corrupt to the core'. That, in a big way, also explains his mass appeal. He is perceived as an angry outsider who has entered the political system determined to transform it; a leader who has resisted the temptation—unlike Hardik and Alpesh—of joining a party to remain free from the shackles and compulsions of party politics. And he fully intends to keep it that way, insisting that his 'soul will not permit' him to join a party because he would then have to turn a blind eye to things that he fundamentally disagrees with.

Jignesh is refreshingly candid and remarkably self-aware. He might be the only MLA or MP who openly acknowledges, completely unprompted, that he is only doing an 'OK' job in his constituency. Spontaneously, he even discloses (albeit to make a political point), that he can be 'terribly patriarchal' and possessive in dealing with his girlfriends. He talks openly about his failures and weaknesses, including his lack of policy-related experience, but expresses a desire to adapt and learn.

Over the last couple of years, he has become popular in many parts of the country. During the 2019 campaign, he was seen addressing large rallies outside Gujarat, including in Bihar and UP, and was repeatedly invited by candidates to campaign for them. He is slowly emerging as a pan-India voice of the downtrodden, particularly the Dalits and minorities. To be able to arrive at this stage in the span of just a few years, with no family in politics and no party organization behind him, is a rare and significant accomplishment.

But unfortunately for Jignesh, in a political system like India's, one can only do so much staying outside the party system. He is well aware that his decision to stay as an independent might not allow him to affect the kind of far-reaching social and political changes which he hopes to achieve. That's why, for his long-term success in Indian politics, it is almost imperative that he fulfils his dream of creating a unique and impactful political platform in the years to come.

Interview

Q. Do you consider yourself more of a social activist or a politician?

It is a combination now. But the activist inside me does not let me, as they say in Hindi—'*mujhe chain se woh jeene nahi de raha hai*' (not letting me live in peace), so that part is still very intense inside me. Electorally it has just been a year and two-three months, so I am also sort of learning to navigate, learning to strategize. So the activist is still more dominating than the electoral politics person.

Q. With so much support for your movements and agitations, you are already looked upon as an important voice of the Dalit communities. What made you join the muddy world of electoral politics when you already have the support of the people?

As I have always claimed, the masses have a mindset that the ones who are electorally successful are the leaders, not the activists. So the mobilization that we see around us brings stagnancy at times, and that has happened with many social activists. But I am using this bourgeois glamour of an MP or an MLA to give a push to what I am already doing on the ground here.

Q. Are you finding a difference in the level of support?

Yes! My mass appeal has increased, my space in media has increased—I have a say in the government, I make bureaucrats accountable, and they have to respond to my files. The response I was getting as an activist was different from what I am getting now. They are afraid also because I am not just an MLA, I am an influential MLA because of my persona. So that has helped.

Q. You are still navigating electoral politics, so has the adjustment been difficult? What are some of the challenges that you've faced?

It has been difficult, and in the coming days, it is going to be even more difficult. The good thing is that I am conscious of the difficulties that I am going to face because working as an independent MLA and not having a full-fledged political party, not having their huge cadres, not having those resources, not having that experience is always a block and a limitation. But one good thing is that the kind of energy that I have and the efforts that I can put in endlessly—through days and nights I can work like a dog—compensates for many things that I am otherwise lacking. My never-ending efforts, my passion, and my commitment compensate for the things that I lack. But still, it is going to be very difficult.

Q. What are the kinds of obstacles and challenges that you envision?

I am a completely non-corrupt person. I don't have the resources which a person of mainstream electoral politics would need and require. In the absence of resources, it is extremely difficult to survive personally, to take care of your office—as in your office as an MLA and your office as an organization—and also to take care of the components of your organization. Otherwise, how would those people survive? I am getting a salary but they are not. So it is an endless struggle.

Q. Why have you chosen to remain independent? There would be so many things that you can do with the support of a party platform.

Yes, but there will be so many things that I will be saying yes to, things that are obnoxious and filthy. My soul will not permit that. I can't let myself into corrupt practices. I can't do a certain kind of politics, which most of the mainstream political parties are engaged in. So when I am independent, I don't have a boss. I don't have to take instructions. I take instructions from the poor people, follow my heart, and that is it.

Q. To have a large-scale impact, given that this is a representative democracy, by being independent are you not preventing your ideas from having a wider reach?

Yes, I am doing that. But if I survive the way I have been able to survive so far for the next two terms, then in the next decade maybe other progressive positive forces will emerge. And till that happens, I want to keep myself away from most of the nonsense that we witness and have to engage with when we are into mainstream politics.

Q. Can you provide some examples of the 'nonsense'? Most of the other politicians, because they belong to political parties, only speak of the virtues of electoral politics.

See, when you are in electoral politics, in this kind of capitalist system which is corrupt to the core, it is extremely difficult. Most people around you are just greedy for power and money. So if I become part of that culture, I can ensure that I will remain what I am, but then it will block many things for the others.

Q. What are the core principles that you would not be ready to compromise on?

No corrupt practices, no communal politics, no undue favours to anybody: these are the three main components that I would adhere to. And there are so many things that I would come to know and I would be in a position to explain to you maybe after a couple of years. I am also just learning. I have just begun to encounter the ocean of filth into which I have jumped. I am beginning to see many things. Many political parties have a setting with big leaders. If I join a party and massive deals are happening in the upper levels, if I remain silent or I am not in a position to take a stance, I will feel very spineless. I don't want to live like that. I will raise my voice, take my stance, and even if there are no results, my soul knows that I took up the cause with honesty.

Q. Arvind Kejriwal started out with agitations and then he created his own party, his own platform. Now he is leading a government in Delhi. Why not start your own party where you can create an organization built on the principles you have and what you stand for without any compromise?

That may happen in the coming years. Even if I have to do it, it will take a while. I am not claiming that I will do it. If all Kanhaiya Kumars, all Shehla Rashids, all Chandrashekhar Azads, all Hardik Patels, and Jignesh Mevanis come together, then a party is very much possible. But then that is not happening, or maybe all these components are waiting for the right opportunity. It is not going to happen so soon. But if we survive, if we are all able to electorally create some space and survive for a decade, then a huge platform is coming up. That is my gut feeling.

Q. What has stopped all of you from coming together?

We have miserably failed on one account; despite so much glamour, so much mass appeal, and mainstream media's attention, all of us could not launch a rock-solid youth platform. We can still do it and we will do it. But by now it should have been done. Maybe people haven't thought like that, or they haven't felt the need. But I am certainly feeling the need to act on it now.

Q. You are looked at as an icon of street and agitation politics, you have led many movements. How successful do you find this tactic of agitation and movements in effecting social change?

We are all subjected to neoliberalism, which has led to massive nationwide corporate loot, which in turn has led to severe kinds

74

of ecological, environmental, and economical disasters. And during the last two decades, people with a 'left' background and people from the stream of Gandhian thought have fought like anything. So many activists have fought brilliantly. We have seen great struggles when it comes to land in particular. But still, people have not been able to do much. There are projects they were not able to stop. But there are also projects in which Adani and Ambani were involved, Tata and Birla were involved, Vedanta and Posco were involved, which they were able to stop. So people have been able to do something. It is both ways. I had raised a slogan from a stage in Pune: '*Gaai ki poonch aap rakhlo, humei humaari zameen do*' (You keep the cow's tail, but give us our land). From that moment till now, we have been able to ensure the possession of nothing less than three to four thousand acres of land to the landless people of Gujarat. The land was allotted to landless Dalits two or three decades ago but was never given. It was given only on paper. The actual physical possession was never given. So we have successfully gained possession of three to four thousand acres of such land.

Q. *What do you say to people who say that you are compromising in some ways because even though you are an independent, you have the support of Congress and AAP?*

What we are facing as a nation, as I keep saying even at the risk of sounding terribly repetitive, is an unprecedented crisis. What is looming large over our heads is absolute complete fascism. We have to defeat these medieval, feudal, casteist, communal, fascist forces. The destruction of democracy is at work. The way intellectuals and rationalists have been attacked is unprecedented and has never happened before. Apex court judges came out and held a press conference saying that they (government) are tampering with our democracy, '*humaari* judiciary *ke saath khilwaad ho raha hai.*' During this unprecedented crisis, when I go abuse the BJP in

Kerala, I don't care if the CPM is winning. When I go to Bihar, I don't care that the Rashtriya Janata Dal (RJD) is winning. I don't care that when I speak against BJP in Rajasthan, Madhya Pradesh, or Gujarat, that the Congress benefits. I don't care if All India Trinamool Congress (TMC) wins in Bengal. If anyone benefits from my anti-RSS, anti-BJP stance, I don't care. I am primarily concerned with damaging the image of the BJP.

Q. *So you see them as the biggest evil right now and you are willing to accept any lesser evil …*

With the clarity that they (the other parties) are also evil. To put it in simple terms—all these people may not implement the Atrocity Act or the Indian Constitution in its true spirit, but BJP undoubtedly will put an end to this Atrocity Act, they will kill the Indian Constitution. This is the difference that we need to understand, in my view. This is what I have realized. And my standing together with all these so-called components of *mahagatbandhan* is a compromise, which I admit, because when it comes to navigating in electoral politics, it does lead to some compromise.

Q. *You decided to campaign and run for MLA just 12 days before the Gujarat elections. How was that first experience of electoral politics?*

It was like a dream. At the very last moment, I decided that if I have taken the movement so far, standing in the electoral space will itself be a slap in the face of BJP. They will be terribly disturbed. And it happened exactly that way. In fact, when I was contesting, Vijay Rupani who is the CM of a state, Yogi Adiyanath who is the CM of Uttar Pradesh, Amit Shah, Modi, all these people came to campaign against me. Against one independent MLA who has no clue about electoral politics, who didn't understand the grammar of electoral politics. Even after winning,

I said that electoral politics doesn't go well with people like me. The system is such that it can throw anyone out at any point. Still, so many people had to come and campaign against me. And the atmosphere was so charged, when I went from one village to another to campaign, it seemed like a movement was going on. The response was incredible, stunning and sublime. The reaction on people's faces was tremendous. One thousand Muslim women fasted for me as if it was Ramzaan. The support from the masses was just incredible.

Q. How are you building on that platform, that movement?

My constituency is just not Vadgam. I actually have three constituencies: the working-class, the caste issues of the Dalit community, and the youth. At this moment I am doing an 'OK' kind of job in Vadgam, not bad, not great, but an 'OK' kind of job. I travel all over the country like Kanshi Ram Ji because that part is also expected from me. If I confine myself to just Vadgam, my constituency, that would mean that I just want to ensure my electoral success next time. That is a very *swaarthi* (selfish) agenda. Secondly, when I keep telling the people that what we are facing as a nation is an unprecedented crisis and that we are subjected to fascism, I have to go states where the election is happening. So when the elections were happening in Rajasthan, Chattisgarh, MP, I was there campaigning madly.

Q. Have you been able to explain this to your constituency? And are they supporting you?

Yes. Obviously, some grievances will always be there, but then this is the level of consciousness of our people. They are not able to see the larger goal. In fact, it is my complaint to the activist fraternity of this country, and I am making a big statement, all the people who say that fascism has arrived—these people should have plunged into the elections in Rajasthan, MP, and Karnataka. They didn't do anything. I was the only person working madly in these states. Ashok Gehlot and Sachin Pilot started their campaign for Rajasthan Assembly elections in August (2018), I was getting detained and I was receiving prohibitory orders for entering into certain pockets of Rajasthan in May. This phrase 'Chowkidaar hi Chor hai' (the guard is a thief) is mine, I was the first person to use it way back in April. On 12th April, the Karnataka elections got over, on the morning of 14th April I got detained in Jaipur airport. I started my campaigning much before Congress could even imagine. So this kind of rigour on part of the mainstream electoral political parties and the civil societies of India was required but that hasn't happened.

Q. *You have said in other interviews that people look at you as only a Dalit leader even though you are much more than that. Do you feel a sense of responsibility now that you have been branded as a Dalit leader?*

Yes but I am not surprised that I'm branded as a Dalit leader, because even Ambedkar with all his greatness is always referred to just as a Dalit leader or the leader of the untouchables. This is what caste is. It doesn't spare even the progressives, it doesn't spare even the Dalits.

Q. *After the Una agitation, you decided to address the issues of Dalits and take their cause to a larger scale. What made you do that?*

I always knew that I have tremendous capacity and that I have a lot of progressive content compared to many Ambedkarites. The way my upbringing has been, the arts, theatre, cinema, and literature that I was exposed to during my college years, which were my formative years, has given me such openness. Many Ambedkarites and Dalit groups or activists reject or discard you only because you are a Brahmin or a Bania. This is also a form of Brahminism for me. My problem is with Brahminism, with the design of exploitation which exploits me on the basis of caste and class both. It is a twin-exploitation. I told myself, 'you are a person with potential and are deserving, so you take the lead. You float, you start sailing and leading from the front. Otherwise only people with old and outdated ideas will come forward.'

Q. *You have spoken against the atrocities Dalits face under the current government. But in spite of long periods of Congress rule (that is now your ally), the Dalits still find themselves in the position they do. Why do you think that after all these years the situation is still so bad?*

Because as a nation we have failed to realize that caste is not just a problem of the Dalit community but it is a problem of India. As a nation we have failed to realize, as Babasaheb Ambedkar puts it, that what is anti-national is caste. As a nation, we have nurtured the filth of caste and kept it alive, and we are not ashamed of that. One human being has to pick up the shit of another and we are pretty fine with that.

Q. *In Gandhi and Ambedkar's debate, Ambedkar was asking for a separate electorate. Would that have helped at this point?*

Yes, comparatively, it would have been better.

Q. *It is said that if the market runs properly, casteism will cease to exist …*

No. When neoliberalism was being introduced to us, this logic was given, but it has been so many years since 1991–2. Casteism is very much there. There are scholars who claim that we have become more casteist. So it hasn't worked. The flow of capital, the opening of the market has not been able to kill this monster of caste.

Q. *If economic growth, opening up of the economy has not helped the situation, then what is the solution?*

First, as a nation, we need to realize that caste has to bloody go. I am a man, and I am saying this on record, that I must have imbibed 'n' number of patriarchal notions. Whenever I am in a relationship, third-rate possessiveness comes out of me. If I look at myself objectively, I become terribly patriarchal in dealing with my partners and my girlfriends. I admit this. The same way as a nation we should first admit, that we are very casteist people. Until you acknowledge that something is rotten, you won't be able to deal with it, you don't think of it as filth. Secondly, the Dalit movement, progressive movement, all movements have to acknowledge that these are the five things that we have to do and then caste will get annihilated. We don't have any such blueprint, we have to make it together. If we study the practices of the Dalit movement so far, if we read Phule, Periyar, Ambedkar, and Marx there are indicators that will help in achieving the annihilation of caste-like inter-caste marriages, cultural programmes, etc. Why is a professor who teaches in a university, or why me, Jignesh Mevani, why are we not communal? Why am I not communal? I cannot be communal because of the exposure, orientation, and education that I have gotten. We need this type of education, cultural movement, massive campaign for social reforms, and land reforms. Caste is a multidimensional phenomenon so we have to hit back at all its dimensions. Inter-caste marriages are needed. The caste-based clusters that are evidently visible, they have to be destroyed. How? We have Sardar Awas Yojna, Indira and Ambedkar Awas Yojna—all the people from various castes who do not have a roof above their head, they should be allotted houses to live together in such colonies. These colonies should have space and swimming pools so that children from all castes and religions can swim together, play together, read together in a library. Only then there will be brotherhood between them, only then they will exchange their cultures, fall in love, and then inter-caste marriages will happen. And then who will say no? Most people would say yes. How will it happen? For that, we need a conducive environment. But for that we also have to decide that we do not want this phenomenon of caste, as a society, as a political party, as a movement, as a state.

Q. Why do you say there has been no impact of liberalization on caste?

Liberalization has resulted in land passing from the tiller to the tycoons. A project that will take us closer to the annihilation of caste is land reforms. Caste is a structural issue. So in India, who will become land owner and who will remain landless is designed by caste. To put it in the words of D.D. Kosambi (sounds very intellectual, as if I have read Kosambi a lot! But it is a brilliant statement which is engraved in my memory), 'In India classes arose in the form of caste.' Had Marx been in India for years and decades, he would have come up with this line in his manifesto, it is that sublime a statement. My class position being a Dalit in India is decided and determined by caste. Caste has decided who will ring the temple bell and who will clean the gutters. In fact, you would love to know this. Bhagat Singh who was just nineteen and a half and who didn't study the caste system in its totality or greatly, wrote an essay on untouchability, 'Achooton ka Sawaal'. When I read it, I was happily shattered. In the essay, he wrote that in Punjab province there was a special law called Land Alleviation Act just to ensure that even if you have wealth and money and you belong to Dalit community, you can't purchase land. Why? Because you have to remain out of that structure. So land reforms, cultural reforms, common schooling to the extent that a president's child and peon's child sit on the same bench, these are some of the things we need to do. I proposed five, you go to ten scholars, twenty-five such points of action will emerge and whatever is thought suitable from there should be worked upon. The Dalit and progressive movement is so fragmented and on top of it there is the issue with electoral politics that we are all struggling and failing for the most part.

Q. *But from the economic standpoint, a lot of people would argue that now if you go to big cities people don't know who is what caste and don't care …*

They do care. In studios in Chennai, in Bangalore, in Pune, in Mumbai, in Delhi, I am still introduced as a Dalit leader. Why not as a youth leader? Forget Dalit, forget privilege, why don't they simply call me an MLA from Gujarat? Why is Anil Teltumbde called a Dalit intellectual? He is a brilliant Marxist intellectual, one of the biggest public intellectuals that we have in the country today. His columns in *Economic and Political Weekly* (EPW) are really popular, he is brilliant. He talks about GST, demonetisation, fascism, neoliberalism, public health, and education. So why is he dubbed just as a Dalit leader? Of course, urbanization brings in cosmopolitan culture, it does help but it has not helped greatly. One should look at the long equation. At the same time, I am not cynical like many other Dalit activists who are against urbanization, I think it does help.

Q. *You say that you are the voice of the voiceless, you contest on issues of youth unemployment, issues of minorities, and the poor. What kind of policies do you think you are going to do differently?*

On that I do not claim that I have great clarity, I am also learning. My complaint is not that Modi did not create two crore jobs, my complaint is that none of the mainstream political parties are even saying how they will create employment. If I am asked, I can immediately propose two things. Fill up the 24 lakh government jobs that are already sanctioned. National Rural Employment Guarantee Act (NREGA) that is for 100 days, increase it to 250, 300 days. And where will the money for that come from? The 1 per cent people of this country who are sitting on 73 per cent property, put a wealth or some other tax on them. The capitalist system cannot resolve these issues. I am not advocating for a communist system but a socialist one.

Q. *India did follow a socialist system for a while. Do you think that we produced better results under that system considering that our growth rate is so much higher now?*

Its job is growth. It hasn't helped us at all. We have become more communal, more casteist. Farmer suicides are just not stopping, everyday we have farmers committing suicide. What have we gained from the market being up? Earlier you used to drink lemon juice, coconut water, and orange juice. Now you drink Coca Cola, Thums Up, and Pepsi. Earlier you used to eat *bajre ka rotla* with *gud*, now you eat pizza and are ruining your stomach.

Q. *So if at any point you and like-minded leaders come together and create a political organization, and if at any point you are in government, you will push for more socialist policies?*

Obviously. Because that is something which is in tune and in harmony with the idea of India, as is advised in the Preamble of the Indian constitution. We have to become a secular, socialist republic, not a fascist, capitalist, Hindutva regime. And as far as my constituency is concerned, since we are all struggling with the argument between socialism and capitalism, there is enough technology, innovation, and creativity in the world that no human being should be hungry, no human being should not have clothes on their body. Don't get trapped in the 'isms', let us first get the basics, let us get healthcare and education, we will talk about the rest later. We are still fighting for the basics. I think that if we had thoroughgoing land reforms in India, if we had weakened the caste system through land reforms and progressive movement, and on that land then set up a good agrarian infrastructure, and we had an agenda of nationalization, it would have been much better than neoliberalism.

Q. How would you describe your vision for India?

My vision for India has to be in harmony with the Preamble of the Indian Constitution. That is all that I would say.

Q. Could you talk about a couple of people who have inspired you and your approach to politics and activisim?

I am greatly inspired by Van Gogh—his life, his intensity, his passion for doing whatever he was engaged with, what a life and what a man! I am also inspired by leaders like Babasaheb Ambedkar and Bhagat Singh.

Q. How do you want to be remembered as a leader?

A. As a very innovative, creative, frank, open-minded, honest, anti-caste, and youth leader.

Jyotiraditya Scindia

In September 2001, thirty-year-old Jyotiraditya Scindia had just returned to India after completing his MBA at Stanford and had put together a team to start his first business venture, when his father, Madhavrao Scindia, the titular Maharaja of Gwalior and nine-term Lok Sabha Member of Parliament (MP), died in a tragic plane crash in Uttar Pradesh. Subsequently, the people of Guna—where his father had been the sitting MP—and Congress workers implored Jyotiraditya to fill the vacuum created by his father's death. Distraught, overwhelmed, and unprepared, he decided to jump headfirst into the world of politics. Jyotiraditya joined the Congress party and successfully contested the by-election from Guna, marking the beginning of what he calls a 'rollercoaster ride'.

The term seems appropriate for Scindia's political journey sincet—his meteoric rise within the Congress party and rather shocking switch to the BJP in March 2020. Scindia is considered to be a charismatic and astute politician. We, too, find him to be articulate and politically-savvy. He is careful and guarded with his words. This is not least surprising—with so many of his family members and ancestors in politics, Scindia was practically schooled in politics from an early age.

In about 15 odd years, Scindia won four elections to the Lok Sabha from his family bastion Guna. He was the youngest member of the Congress Working Committee. He held three different portfolios in Manmohan Singh's government, including the power portfolio, soon after India faced the most massive power outage ever seen across the world. He was appointed chief whip of the party in the Lok Sabha in 2014.

Five years later, however, the 2019 elections were not as kind to Scindia. Just before polling, he was appointed the Congress party's general secretary for the all-important western Uttar Pradesh. Despite the party's best efforts, its decision to stay out of the SP-BSP *gathbandhan* and the sweeping Bharatiya Janata Party (BJP) wave meant that 21 out of its 22 candidates in western UP lost their security deposits. Scindia also lost his family bastion, Guna, by over 1.2 lakh votes. It was the first time since 1984 and only the fourth time in history that a member of the Scindia royal family did not win the seat. Even worse, Scindia did not lose to a BJP strongman but rather to his former assistant—Dr Krishna Pal Singh Yadav.

Krishna Pal was Scindia's MP representative until 2018 when he switched over to the BJP because the Congress denied him a ticket for the assembly elections. His father, Raghuveer Singh, was also a longtime aide of Madhavrao Scindia. When Krishna Pal was nominated, a picture of him trying to take a selfie with Scindia circulated the internet, reportedly with the caption: 'Those who earlier lined up to click selfies with the "Maharaj" are now BJP candidates.' Elections in India can be great equalizers.

A few months before the 2019 elections, Scindia played a key role in helping the Congress wrest the crucial state of Madhya Pradesh from the BJP, which had ruled the state for 15 years. Once again, he got unlucky. His supporters pushed for him to become the chief minister but he fell victim to the generational tug of war within the Congress party. The then-party president Rahul Gandhi chose the more senior leader and a rumored Scindia detractor, Kamal Nath, for the post instead.

Rahul Gandhi promptly tweeted a picture of himself holding the hands of both leaders, captioned 'the two most powerful warriors are patience and time—Leo Tolstoy.' Those words proved to be both ironic and fateful. Only 15 months later, the seemingly impatient Scindia shocked the Congress party toppling the Kamal Nath government in Madhya Pradesh and joining the BJP along with 22 sitting MLAs. In his first interview after making the switch, he tells us that he was left with no choice but to switch after the Kamal Nath government shattered his dreams for the state by indulging in corruption, while harassing and persecuting those MLAs who were loyal to him. He also subtly criticizes the Congress leadership for refusing to adapt to India's changing realities, even while acknowledging that he still aligns with some of the party's ideology.

By parting ways with the floundering Congress, Scindia has made a big political calculation. The data shows that historically, Indian politics has not looked very favourably upon those who switch parties. It remains to be seen whether Scindia can buck this trend.

Interview

Q. You had gotten an MBA, you had studied at Doon, at Harvard, and at Stanford. You didn't have to go into politics. Was it a natural choice for you? There are other ways you can serve society—you can be in business, you can do social service. So why did you choose to join politics?

For me personally, there is a great difference between politics and public service. And my goal and aspiration is the latter and not the former. I see politics as a means to serve that goal. Now those means could be varied—from business to NGOs, there are many forms of doing that. I have grown up seeing politics at a very proximate distance, and the ability to be able to impact people's lives directly, not only through the legislative process of the Parliament but by really being the block builder of development in the area that one represents. I have seen that happen very closely with my father, and therefore, for me it was certainly a calling. Of course this was not a calling that I thought that I would have had to step up to so early in my life, because as you mentioned, I had just finished my MBA at the Stanford Graduate School of Business (GSB). I had graduated, and was actually looking at setting up a business. We had put a team together, got the first round of funding. But then sometimes in life fate doesn't deal you the right cards. My father passed away in a very tragic accident, and people looked to me to fill that vacuum and I felt responsible to fill that vacuum of public service. I stepped in, knowing that it is something that I genuinely felt motivated about from within but also knowing that it was something that I completely and totally was unprepared for. And it has been a rollercoaster ride for the last 20 years. It has been one in which I think I've had the privilege of interacting with great stalwarts, learning from a lot of people, and I think that in itself is an unbelievably eye-opening process. And then, to be able to imbibe what you have learnt from the experiences and to be able to affect those into action, is some-thing that I have been very passionate about and enjoy to this day. Again, the distinction I am making for you is between politics and public service.

Q. *You mentioned that it has been a rollercoaster ride. What have been some of those challenges for you, some of the frustrations for you? Of course, we know about your successes—you've had a lot of great things going for you. But I am sure beneath the surface it must not have been as easy, so could you talk a little bit about that?*

The learning curve was, at least for the first six–seven years, extremely steep, because you come in as a greenhorn into an ocean of great white sharks, great whites, and you have to learn to swim or be swallowed. So I think first, just bare survival, and I think it's the rough and tumble of grassroots politics—heat, dust, sweat, rain, hail—everything that you can imagine, that you need to weather. I think through it all, as I said, for me, the developmental paradigm is the most important. What I learned from my work experiences as a banker is to be able to seek projects and see them through to execution. I applied that very paradigm to my developmental projects. Whether you're building roads, irrigation projects, drinking water projects, or electrical projects, I made sure they follow timelines, spur charts, and I applied all of my skill sets to meet those challenges. The frustrating part is that bureaucratic processes sometimes take way too long. It has a sense of rigour embedded in it, but at the same time, there is a lot of red-tapeism. I encountered that and that was really frustrat-ing for someone who comes from a very professional background, having worked as a banker. But, one then learns to persevere, and when you persevere, you see your projects through to the end. I have also had very challenging assignments as a minister to bring about change, whether it was the Ministry of Power, Ministry of Communications IT and Posts, or the Ministry of Commerce and

Industry. I brought around a full business process restructuring (BPR) exercise for the Department of Posts in the form of Project Arrow, and eventually, the project won the prime minister's award for the most amount of monumental change that any department has brought about in the Government of India. As Commerce and Industry minister, my initiatives on transaction cost-cutting to be able to make sure that you ease the path for businesses in India, and then as Power minister, which I took over after the largest power outage. This covered putting in place processes of six–six months, make sure that you have levels of redundancy in place so that something like this never happens again, connecting the southern grid to the rest of India making it 'one nation one grid', bringing in huge amounts of thermal capacity. And then the last five years as the Chief Whip of the Congress party. Now as the member of the BJP, it is my resolve to work constructively towards the cause of nation-building, and then so it has been an exciting, trying, and at the same time a very fulfilling tenure.

Q. *You come from a royal family with a very rich history and legacy. Has that shaped your outlook on life and your politics in any way?*

Yes, in the most fundamental manner! My family's core tenet through multiple generations has always been to serve, whether it was through the earlier system, which was a monarchy, or whether it is the current system, which is a democratic system to be able to better people's lives. And my ancestors always strove to do that as well. So that thread runs very strong within me. And I take great amount of inspiration from the developmental work that my ancestors did for my region, which people still look up. Therefore, for me, it is even more important for me on two tracks—in essence, one, is obviously the developmental paradigm. More important than that is my own personal connect with each and everyone in my region because that to me is my biggest treasure: personal relationships with people. It doesn't matter if you're not there with them in their times of joy, but I always try and be with them when in times of tragedy or hardships.

Q. *You faced this unexpected election loss in your family bastion Guna. What were the key takeaways for you after that, and what kind of impact did the loss have on you personally, given your strong family and personal ties to the constituency?*

I think every election is a battle of ideology, vision, and commitment. That being said, you win some and you lose some. It's an election that I believe I fought with all my energy and for me, an election is not a mere voting exercise but rather a tenure of five years. The results unfortunately were not what one would have expected. The reasons behind the results could be many. I lost an election for the first time, I've won four, and a setback must only strengthen your resolve to work more earnestly to earn the trust of people back, something I deeply treasure in my life. For me, it's not politics but public service and therefore that passion must only be reinforced.

Q. *As you embark upon a new path with the BJP, is there any signature policy or project that you intend to focus on and adopt over the next few years?*

Well, my calling is very clear in life. I have had two inflection points in my life. One was 30th of September 2001, when I tragically lost my father. At that point, I decided to take the route of public service. The 10th of March 2020 constitutes the second most important inflection point in my life, and it was also coincidentally my father's 75th birthday. After spending 18 years with the Congress party, my goal is pretty much the same—public service. My calling is really to bring about development and progress in my state—and whatever role that I can play on a national front, whether it was through successive governments in the last 18 years where I was a minister in the central government or the five years I spent in opposition as the chief whip of the Congress party. Now, as a member of BJP going forward, I intend to pursue the very same calling. When you look at the vision, values, and mission for any organization, it's as important to look at them from an individual's perspective—and that steadfastly remains the same for me, which is public service and development.

Q. *You've been associated with the Congress since your teenage years, and over the last two decades, you've built so many relationships and a deep bond with the party. Can you talk a little bit about your personal emotions as you went through this decision-making process? Was it difficult for you emotionally to leave an organization that you have been associated with your entire adult life?*

Suffice it to say, it was obviously not an easy decision. It was a decision that I went through with great trial and tribulation before I eventually made up my mind.

Q. *In your press conference at the BJP headquarters where you took membership in the presence of BJP President, Mr J P Nadda, you indicated that the Congress was in denial of the reality and was not acknowledging new thought and leadership. The last time we spoke to you, you mentioned that you wouldn't leave the Congress despite possible grievances. What values of the Congress do you think changed that allowed you to become comfortable with switching out?*

With regard to my decision, I was impacted mainly by the situation in my home state, Madhya Pradesh (MP). I, along with party workers, had laboured for the last 15 years to establish a government that would bring about a paradigm shift in the way things were done in MP for the welfare of the people. My dream for MP had not just been shattered due to the Congress state government's leadership's lack of intent, but also because of the fact that politics and corruption had prevailed over public service. Additionally, representatives of the people and members of the cabinet who happened to be aligned with me were constantly harassed and persecuted. People's aspirations were put on the back burner. So the natural question the MLAs and ministers asked me was, 'what are you doing in this Congress government's environment of corruption and governance?' It was after constant pushbacks, and no recourse, even at the Congress' central leadership level, that I felt I was left with no choice.

Besides, India has changed, and for any organization or institution, be it a political one or a business organization, or even a university, adaptation is key to survival. If any organization doesn't constantly adapt to changing realities, then it faces an existential threat. And you have two options: either you face that reality and devise strategies to change, or you will have another reality that stares you in the face. And when you're faced with a situation where your organization just refuses the reality or refuses to change, then you know that your time is up.

Q. There are a lot of people who said that Mr Scindia shifted to the BJP because he had some personal ambitions. How do you respond to that?

See, I only have one ambition, which is public service and development. Politics is not my calling. I probably abhor it as much as you do. My calling is really for public service and making a real difference in people's lives. And if you look at my twenty-year-old record in public service, it's about development; it's about changing not only my constituency but my region.

Q. Do you think there are some ideological differences between the BJP and the Congress, which pushed you more towards one party

93

than the other or is it mostly about the ability of delivering on your goal of public service?

I think, as an individual, it is most important for you to be able to stand up for the truth. There are also a lot of things that the BJP has done, which I agree with. For example, the abolishment of Article 370. I was probably one of the few people who supported that (within the Congress). And I think it's important to be able to hear a viewpoint, even if it is one that is different from yours.

Q. *Some people would argue that within the BJP, there are some very conservative elements with a vastly differing ideology to yours and who are arguably opposed to the kind of progress you wish to see. Do you find that to be a challenge as you enter this new party?*

It's obvious that if you are going to a new work environment, you are going to face different challenges, than what you face right now. But that's fine. I do believe in that Prime Minister Modi is a person who has the best interests of the country at heart. I do believe that he is a very strong decision-maker, and I believe that he is a person who has the courage to take tough calls that are in the interest of the nation. And I think that is what the country needs today.

Q. *Can you say the same thing about the Congress party's leadership or not?*

No, you cannot. In fact, the kind of majority that the BJP garnered twice over comes from the bold leadership of Mr Narendra Modi, commitment, work ethic, and truly having the best interests of the country at heart, and, most importantly, taking the right decisions at the right time.

What's also very important is to be able to make the right calls; to be able to separate the wheat from the chaff. That's what leadership is all about—for you to be able to listen to different voices and then say, 'I have heard you all, and this is the way we should go.' Everything is not always about consensus and making sure that everyone is always on the same page. So it is firstly important for a leader to be able to hear all the views, but it's equally important for a leader to take a call, sometimes a difficult one. Now, if the country has changed, you've got to adapt. Not just that, it's important to be ahead of the curve. You've got to set the agenda for your people.

Q. So, in what ways do you think that India has changed?

India is an aspirational country. We are a people who look for new ideas, new thoughts, new leadership, and the ability to transform our existence. A lot of that comes from the belief in organizations and individuals who have the ability to do that. And I think India has moved a lot from being a socialist-modelled country to a sort of capitalist-modelled country to an entrepreneurial system where every individual is very aspirational. By the way, I think it's very important that the government and the country certainly provide the foundation and safety net for all our people to lead a healthy and secure life. So a social security net is vital to this proposition. I would like to make a distinction between social security network and a socialistic model—they are very distinct, and today we are in a hybrid model, which is needed for India to truly grow. You need to create that safety net environment (health, education, infrastructure), and then allow that aspirational India to poll-vault the country to new heights. And to be able to deliver on that is a great challenge for our political system. It's also a very healthy challenge, and I think that's extremely important for all of us, as it makes us accountable, which is good for any vibrant democracy.

Q. Do you not think that the Congress, under UPA 1 and UPA 2 (when you were also a minister), was successful in doing that? In a sense, some would argue that they were both providing a safety net in the form of MNREGA and other programmes, while also allowing individual entrepreneurship to flourish. So what do you think has changed? What do you think has happened in the thought process of the party that it is no longer able to do this?

The Congress was certainly more successful under UPA 1 than UPA 2. I think the bell curve was at its peak at the end of UPA 1 and the beginning of UPA 2. After that, the Congress had plummeted towards the negative slope of the bell curve, but I think in a society, in a company, or even in your family, it's very important to have differing viewpoints and voices. It is important to be able to actually grab on to a very different thought than what is normal. Being able to process that and take it forward is what will make the difference between those who are in a period of stasis and those who are ready for a period of constant change. I remember a person who had a very profound effect on me during my MBA at Stanford's Graduate School of Business. I had the good fortune of being taught by Andy Grove, one of the founders of Intel. In our last class, he wrote something on the board and said, 'I am just leaving two thoughts with you. Just keep these in mind no matter what you do in life. I wish you the best of luck.' And he left the classroom. When we scanned the board, the first line read 'the only constant in the world is change', and the second line read 'only the paranoid survive'. Those two sentences have had a great impact on me and I truly believe that the minute you stop being paranoid, your time is up.

Q. Once you retire a few decades from now, is there a phrase or a few words that you would like to be remembered by?

My life has always been about standing up for what I believe in and standing up for what is right. For me, the single-minded purpose has been to make a difference in people's lives—in my area, in my state, and whatever little I can contribute at the national level as well. So if I were to pass away tomorrow, I would like to be remembered as someone who did right, who believed in what was right, and someone who was caring—I think that's the most important thing. Those are the three qualities I admire most in a leader—being empathetic and caring, standing up for what one believes in and doing right by people. If you want me to put it in one phrase, it will simply be 'a good human being!'

Kalikesh Singh Deo

While the chorus against the dominance of dynasty politics is growing louder, it seems to have little sway in the eastern state of Odisha. During the 2019 elections, where the state had its assembly elections simultaneously with the Lok Sabha elections, it was quite common to see father–son, husband–wife, or sibling duos being offered Lok Sabha and Vidhan Sabha tickets from the same constituency across party lines. Bolangir, where the sitting two-term MP Kalikesh Narayan Singh Deo narrowly lost in 2019, is a shining example of a constituency where politics is all in the (royal) family. While Kalikesh fought the Lok Sabha elections, his younger brother, Arkesh, fought the assembly elections from the same constituency. The Bharatiya Janata Party (BJP) fielded Kalikesh's sister-in-law and former MP, Sangeeta Kumari Singh Deo, against Kalikesh. Narasingha Mishra, a veteran Congress leader, stood against Arkesh; Narasingha's son faced Kalikesh.

Despite his election loss in 2019, Kalikesh remains popular in Bolangir and across the state of Odisha. This is in large part due to his family's deep roots in the state. Kalikesh's grandfather, Rajendra Narayan Singh Deo, was the last ruler of the princely state of Patna and went on to become chief minister of Odisha.

In 1951, he was elected to the first Lok Sabha from Bolangir and over the course of his political career, represented the constituency many times as an MLA. Kalikesh's father, too, represented the same constituency in the Odisha assembly and was a founding member of the Biju Janata Dal (BJD). Kalikesh is embedded in this political tapestry, and his party, the constituency of Bolangir and politics itself are largely family inheritances, as is the case with most of the prominent young politicians in the country today. But unlike many of them, Kalikesh didn't directly jump into the political arena. Instead, he spent years working in the private sector, first in investment banking and then at the energy conglomerate Enron, gaining skills that he believes have made him a better politician.

Speaking with us at his home in Delhi, his golden Labrador by his side, Kalikesh ruminates about the family legacy. He contends that while he didn't have much of a say in these choices, the ideology of his party and its leader, Naveen Patnaik, deeply resonate with him. He points out that while the party is left-of-centre on welfare, it is still business-friendly and pro-market. Given his finance and business background, this is naturally appealing to him.

A big part of our discussion with Kalikesh revolves around the evolution of Indian politics over the 15-odd years that he has spent in it. He talks at length about the 'systematic decline' of institutions like the Parliament and state assemblies, and the failures of the judicial system. He offers his own ideas for parliamentary and judicial reform, such as removing the anti-defection law to allow MPs to freely express their thoughts and take positions contrary to those of their parties, without the fear of retribution. Otherwise, you may as well have 'loudspeakers and robots sitting and pressing a button,' he remarks, revealing his frustration.

He is vexed further by his struggle to implement some of his ideas for reform, primarily at the Parliament level, while he was an MP, despite his best efforts. This is symptomatic of the limited impact that regional parties have in driving macro-level reforms at the central level. The process involves building consensus among many other parties, which is often a time-consuming and somewhat futile exercise. Nonetheless, Kalikesh derives great satisfaction from bringing to fruition his personal projects. Many of these are based in Bolangir, which he hopes will have a big impact on the constituency over time. They include: skill development missions, employment drives, hospitals, and a school for training pilots. He also takes pride in the role and reputation that he had earned in Parliament, as a 'constructive' opposition leader who freely supported and opposed issues even if it sometimes meant going against the party-line.

Notwithstanding his easy entry into politics and other dynastic privileges, Kalikesh demonstrates a deep, careful understanding of issues concerning India's democracy and an earnest desire to drive change. As he continues to grow as a strong national voice from Odisha, it is likely that he will, over time, also be empowered with the resources needed to implement the reforms that he wishes to see.

Interview

Q. Over the fifteen years since you joined politics, how do you think you have evolved as a politician and as a person?

Over time one evolves, becomes more mature, one understands the intricacies of governance and is able to drive a lot more in governance. In 15 years as an elected member, five as an MLA and 10 as an MP, I have been able to get a sense of the delivery mechanism in the state because being an MLA allows you to be much closer to the ground. As an MP one gets to understand the broader policy and macro perspective of governance from the centre. I have realized that apart from doing whatever you can with the daily basic infrastructure, amenities for people, helping them as much as you can, you've got to also drive a few pet projects, things you are passionate about. So I have been pushing an employment drive, to help people in skill development and opportunities for higher education. We have managed to build a 350 crore government-run medical college and I say 'government-run' because the doctors need to be posted there for it to function. Otherwise, private-run hospitals won't work in a place like Bolangir. We are getting a pilot school opened because in the next five years 5,000 pilots will be hired since a lot of planes are being ordered by airlines. We've got a bunch of skill development initiatives going on. There has been a little more strategic thinking, a little more emphasis on trying to get good projects on the ground and pushing through these projects. It has not been easy but it is certainly satisfying.

Q. You are from the royal family, your grandfather was the Chief Minister of Orissa and your father was in politics. Has it been easy to kind of get out of their shadows? To what extent do you try and model yourself and your politics based on them? To what extent do you say 'I am going to try chart my own course here'?

I don't think you can ever get out of your parents' or your grand-parents' shadow because ultimately a large part of you is because of them and a large part of the initial goodwill is because of them. Of course, it depends upon how you perform after the first election. Why should I want to get out of anybody's shadow? I do what I think is best and what makes sense to me and what I believe is correct in any given situation and I hope that works for the people too. I don't think too much about trying to distinguish myself with the purpose. I think just my thoughts and my actions will ultimately speak for who I am.

Q. *How has politics evolved in this time? The role of technology and social media, different methods and mediums of communication in the last two elections was quite evident …*

Fifty per cent of the voters are under the age of 30. New technologies will always be used by the young, and they will adapt to it much easier. So politics and politicians have to evolve with that, you come across social media and other methods which are more techno-savvy and one will have to adapt to that and appeal to the younger voters. Another change is the strained relationship today between the opposition and the government, that's also new for me. In the old days, we invariably used to have good equations on a personal level. You would raise issues but not attack anyone personally. I think with this new government in the centre, we have crossed that boundary and now it's really an 'all is fair in love and war' sort of a situation. The atrocity of the attacks has become much more intense.

Q. *Does that hamper the ability of the ruling government to push through legislation or the parties to work together in a more constructive way?*

It does. When you have a personal equation and a personal relationship it really helps. Ultimately, you are dealing with people. It doesn't make sense to make enemies out of MPs. Slowly over the years the Parliament and the assembly itself is losing its importance in the entire structure. I think the executives, both in the state and in the assembly, have been trying to, for lack of a better word, usurp the space meant for legislation. The prime minister is also the leader of the majority party, and the three-line whip and the disqualification criteria don't allow MPs to speak their mind openly. One is also dependent on the leader of their party for the ticket ultimately. Nobody wants to irritate or work against the leadership in any political party. As a result, if the executive wants to decide something, it does not tolerate any dissent or differences. In such a scenario, the role of the Parliament itself has been diminished.

Q. Does the diminished role of the Parliament cause you concern? Is it a phenomenon that you attribute to the current government or has it been a systematic decline?

There is a systematic decline since the seventies and the eighties. It was in eighties that the no-confidence anti-defection bill came in, where if you wanted to defect you needed one-third support, and that was increased later to two-thirds. In effect, you won't have a defection in political parties. However, you need to be able to express an independent opinion, to not allow that is quite a shame. Secondly, any and every political party—when they come into the executive, they try and ride roughshod over the legislature, whether it's the Parliament or assembly. I think it's just the fault of the way our system has evolved. The courts don't interfere and that's unfortunate. Otherwise, there would be an appropriate forum to take this up. I think the jostling of space now is between the executive and the judiciary.

103

Q. *The judicial overreach of the Supreme Court has been under discussion. Do you think the Supreme Court is respecting and maintaining the* lakshman rekha *between the legislature and judiciary?*

No. I think there has been a judicial overreach in many cases. I think both the executive and the judiciary have failed in preserving the independence of the legislature.

Q. *What kind of parliamentary reforms would you like to bring in?*

The first thing I would do would be to have a primary system of tickets, so I don't have to be in my boss's good books to get the ticket. If my registered voters of the party in my constituency want me to stand from there then they will vote me in. Some sort of a primary system. The second reform that I would like to bring is to remove the anti-defection law. I think it is important that MPs are able to express their minds openly without fear of retribution or reprise because ultimately there is also an independent mind at work. Otherwise, why have individuals sitting there, just have loudspeakers and robots sitting and pressing a button. The standing committee that we have in various departments, they are basically advisory committees, so another thing I would like would be to give teeth to the standing committees. Why shouldn't the executive be held accountable by the legislature? That's the main function of the legislature. So what's wrong if departments report to committees? There is no harm.

Q. *Is it difficult to build consensus because BJD is one of the smaller parties in the Parliament?*

Well yes, it can get frustrating at times, it can be challenging at times. But I think if you can manage to do what you set out to do, the satisfaction of getting things done is far greater than the frustration.

Q. Why did you join national politics and become an MP instead of sticking around as an MLA and focusing more on state policies like your grandfather?

I was keen to become an MP. I wanted to get the experience of being an MP. In terms of the policy, you have a lot more impact as an MP than you would have as an MLA or a minister. Of course, if you run a department then that is a different ball game. So I have done five years as an MLA and 10 years as an MP and my party's nerve centre is in the state, so I am also very closely associated with the state government despite being an MP. I still work like an MLA on the ground, I am the district president of my party, I associate with the state government on policy issues, sometimes my opinion is sought and sometimes I give it without it being sought. And I now have friends in Delhi who can complement the development of the state and I think that's equally beneficial.

Q. BJD was a natural party choice for you. But at any point did you think that you should join one of the national parties to be able to have more of an impact? Today, for instance, if you were in the BJP, you could probably be a minister in the central government or at least be a part of a party that is capable of pushing a lot of legislation through. How do you think of such trade-offs?

Yes, I didn't have much of an option to begin with in terms of choosing parties because my father was one of the founding members along with the chief minister of this party. But more than that, I think what also subscribes to my line of thinking is the ethos and ideology of the party. It is left-of-centre in terms of welfare so it does a lot for the poor and deprived in Orissa, but it is right-of-centre on economic issues so it believes in a free market, it is business-friendly and industry-friendly, and it does not have an ideological perspective on that. What we are

105

also very clear about is that we do not want to be sucked into the environment of hate between religions and castes. We want a peaceful state; Orissa is a peaceful state and we want to keep it that way. Therefore, the ideology completely appeals to me, the leadership appeals to me. I have known Mr Naveen Patnaik for many years and I find that I relate much more to him than any of the leaders of other political parties as they stand today. So even if my father was not in BJD, I would still have made the choice to join BJD.

Q. *But you also have the Congress and other liberal parties that also focus a lot on economic welfare but to some extent are not anti-business or industry. So how do you think the BJD really differentiates itself from these other parties?*

Well, Congress is well-known to be left-of-centre. So it has not been very business-friendly. Let's not forget that the Congress was responsible for the so-called 'Indian growth rate' (Hindu growth rate) of less than 3 per cent for many years. So one doesn't always agree with Congress's economic policies. I think they are lopsided, unsustainable and bad for growth. Ultimately if it's bad for growth, it's not going to lead to sustainable development. It's going to be bad for the country.

Q. *How does the politics of the BJD and other similar parties compare with the two big national parties?*

I don't think India is a monolithic country. It is a very diverse country. Languages, problems, challenges, food, in every state and within every state, and district is different. It changes, it blends. Anybody who seeks to govern India from the comforts of Delhi will get it horribly wrong. You can't have a 'one shoe fits all' policy for development in India. So I have been a big votary of having different voices within the political system. At one time the Congress used to allow that, up until the sixties. The Congress itself used to have the far left within it and the right within it, the liberals and the conservatives, and different states were allowed to speak up. Now the Congress has become a monolith. BJP, unfortunately, is again becoming a monolith north-Indian party. So I think regional parties are here to stay. I think diversity will reflect the diversity of challenges that we really face and hopefully lead to better development.

Q. *Creating jobs is a huge challenge for India. No matter which government is in power there is a fear that we are creating far too little, compared to what we need. How do you think this can be addressed?*

I have been saying it since 2004 that if you don't address the youth which you view as an asset, it will be the biggest liability. And my fears are coming out to be true now because we just haven't created enough jobs, we just haven't created enough skill development platforms and our quality of education is far below what it should be. I think these are the three areas that we need to address. I think we need to have our concepts very clear. While we work on all kinds of job creation, our strengths are in engineering and in services, especially the IT-related services which are fast evolving, taking the impact of Artificial Intelligence (AI) on to it. So we need to be ready for that. We don't just need a centre for AI but we need to ensure that the skills of millions of people working in call centres are upgraded to adapt to the new AI technologies so that they can be useful even after the evolution takes place. Unfortunately, in the last four years we have had demonetization, we have had a faulty application of GST, and I think the final nail in the coffin has been the lack of liquidity amongst banks. The lending has completely stopped. You can't have growth without lending, you can't have jobs without investment.

Q. *These are problems that no government has been able to effectively address. What kinds of challenges do you think are preventing governments from doing all the things you just said?*

The real challenge, in my opinion, is the mindset of the political class and the executive. I feel that we are far too short-sighted and just think of our next six months or the ratings of the next one or two years. We don't take the trouble of explaining difficult choices to the electorate. I believe Indian people understand, no matter the level of literacy, no matter the level of awareness, if you explain to them as Mr Modi did during demonetization that there is difficulty in what you are doing but it is going to lead to a larger good. They will wait for it. But if like demonetization it has zero impact on all those goalposts he conceived at that time, then I believe they will take action against it. So you need to have a definitive plan, you need to work seriously towards it, you need to carry the entire political class on it.

Q. *As a young MP yourself, do you feel that the younger politicians face any specific challenges compared to the older peers, the more experienced lot?*

At the age of 44 I am still considered young. That is the biggest challenge itself. We should have a lot more younger people. If you go abroad, you have prime ministers who are 40–45. Obama, the Canadian prime minister, I mean anywhere, Norway, Sweden, just look at them. Our political system doesn't allow us to come up. It's like a club of few and you have to wait for your turn to enter it. Why can't people challenge their leadership in a transparent manner and gain control? You will find that nobody in the BJP can challenge their leadership right now, nobody in the Congress can challenge their leadership, for that matter any regional party either. I think there needs to be a system where younger people come out, make a bid for their positions with their ideas, not for the muscle and money that's being used ever more so in politics and for that I think what has to happen is that voters have to become a lot more aware and a lot more transparent.

Q. In spite of your influence on your party, are you able to effect the changes you want?

I think the issues of resistance for these ideas will be in every party because the leadership will always resist any shock to the system. If I am ever in a position to impact that change then I will.

Q. Odisha has stark diversity—it has well-developed areas, coastal areas, and other areas where there is abject poverty. While this might be true for every state in India, what are the challenges unique to the state?

The dichotomy of inequality exists everywhere in India, even in Delhi you have the super-rich and you have people who are starving at the same time. Odisha has been neglected by various governments in the centre for many years. The kind of investment that has gone into let's say northern states or western states to create irrigation for farmers to create infrastructure for business, it just hasn't come to Odisha. In the initial years, the kind of outreach Odisha should have had to industry probably didn't happen either. It has been a result of many factors. Within Odisha, there is a feeling that western Odisha and the the old districts of Kalahandi, Bolangir, and Koraput (KBK) region always get left out. But over the last 15 years, I find that this current government, the BJD government, has spent a lot of money on developing small village level infrastructure.

Q. How do you see the centre–state relationship in India and the relationships between one state and another? Have you seen it evolve in the last few years?

It certainly has changed, unfortunately not for the better. Despite the Finance Commission's recommendations and 10 per cent more money supposedly coming to states, what has happened instead is that all central government funding has been restricted to development programmes. Only a few programmes are being carried on by the centre. And the special grants that districts like Odisha used to get, in terms of Backward Regions Grant Fund (BRGF) or the Investor Awareness Programme (IAP) in Maoist areas have all stopped. In fact, Odisha is actually losing out in the new financial devolution, and other weaker states also do. They used to get a lot of supplemental grants. Jharkhand, Chhattisgarh, Bihar, Odisha, Telangana—all these states lose out under the new financial devolution bill. But notwithstanding that, I think even with the amount of money is that supposed to come, it comes more efficiently, more effectively and in a timely manner to the states which are being run by the BJP or the same party as the centre, than it does to other states. The ability of the central government to block and play politics around financial devolution or federalism shouldn't be there. It should be an automatic method of handing out money because ultimately there is a legitimate share, there's a legitimate, elected government and no government in the centre and state should be able to try and vitiate that.

K.T. Rama Rao

As we drive towards Begumpet in Hyderabad to meet with the Working president of the Telangana Rashtra Samithi (TRS), K.T. Rama Rao (or KTR, as he is commonly referred to), we pass by several roadside posters which highlight his achievements. Quite often, they are placed against the backdrop of construction activities that locals inform us are occurring at an alarming pace across the city. Adjacent to his office are a set of waiting rooms, where there is a constant stream of visitors, from party colleagues and officials to the general public. Our discussion, too, is conducted in the presence of a few bureaucrats, MLAs, and aides. As we speak for well over an hour, they simply sit and listen. It becomes immensely clear that in Telangana, KTR is both popular and powerful.

KTR is the product of a unique political environment. His father, K. Chandrashekar Rao (KCR), the current chief minister of Telangana, spearheaded a mass movement for the creation of a separate state of Telangana to be carved out of the erstwhile state of Andhra Pradesh. The creation of Telangana is historic because the administrative division of India into linguistic states started with the demand for a separate state for Telugu speakers—Andhra

Pradesh. With the creation of Telangana, India now has two states with Telugu as the official language. Understandably, KCR's image and the TRS are the dominant political force in Telangana.

The capital of Telangana, Hyderabad, is one of the fastest-growing cities in India. It is undergoing a robust transformation through its integration with the global economy and a construction boom that is giving many of its areas a major uplift. The TRS government is spearheading this development, with KTR playing a pivotal role. While his father, KCR has focused more on reviving the state's rural economy through ambitious welfare programmes, KTR, now controlling IT, commerce, and urban development in the cabinet, has taken it upon himself to personally drive these urban projects. He has surrounded himself with young men having one foot in the Silicon Valley and the other in Hyderabad as he tried to find technological solutions to the pain points of ordinary citizens. He also travelled around the world to build relations with technology leaders—from Satya Nadella of Microsoft to John Chambers of Cisco—and get them to commit to expanding their companies' presence in Hyderabad. This has earned him the image of a modernizer in the city.

KTR speaks openly about the personal and political challenges of governance in this day and age. Growing up in urban India, he reveals that he never paid any attention to the caste and community of the people around him. So, in the beginning, it would make him 'very uncomfortable' when party workers allocated tickets based on someone's caste and community. Over time, however, he has had to 'rethink and reorient' his outlook as he understood the historical reasons behind the prevalence of identity-based politics in India. He became conscious of social identities and their importance to people.

Another challenge he faced was having to reconcile his education and background with the demands of grassroots agitation politics. The many years he spent campaigning for Telangana statehood, he reveals, taught him that in India, there is no scientific and planned method of decision-making by the central government. In his words, you have to 'literally shout from the rooftops' to be heard because 'otherwise, nobody really cares'.

We discuss a host of issues with KTR including his personal challenges in politics, his views on devolution of power from the centre to the states and the impact of artificial intelligence on unemployment in India. From our conversation, it is quite clear that he has successfully transitioned from being an agitation leader to an accomplished administrator. He appears to be knowledge-able about different subjects and feels at home with different kinds of people, from senior bureaucrats to party colleagues to ordinary citizens who come to his office with different sets of demands. He is also very charismatic and easy in his dealings with these stakeholders. After the interview, we stay back to speak with a few of his aides. They all speak of him and his managerial style in glowing terms: KTR seems to have a certain aura among them.

From an agitation leader to a minister and now a party leader, KTR has witnessed a lot in a short period. His well-rounded political experience and the continued electoral success of his party make him well-positioned to become one of India's most powerful regional leaders in the future.

Interview

Q. How difficult is it to start with agitation and end up in administration, from a grassroots movement to a party in power in a state government?

You know, our government came into power in June 2014 and in end 2015, I had the good fortune of meeting the late Arun Jaitley, who was the then finance minister. He said something very interesting. He said that we don't see eye to eye on many things, in fact, there are very few things we agree on. But he said it is very rare to see in Indian politics the leader of an agitation, somebody who has made a huge hue and cry about statehood and rallied people around, created a ruckus in Parliament and shouted from rooftops to get his voice heard, for someone like KCR to transition into a very capable administrator, he said that it is a very rare transition because typically in India, one can either be a revolutionary or end up as a very good administrator just because you have the ability and skills, but rarely both. Our chief minister is extremely versatile and he is a man who comes from the grassroots. He is all for technology and modernization, but at the same time, he believes that India should not forget its roots and problems at the grass-root level. Today I am happy to share that Telangana is considered a role model for a number of things. In over 71 years of independence, every single prime minister and chief minister who has assumed office in different parts of the country have spoken about farmers and agrarian crisis, but not many could really come down right to it and say this what the issue is and this is how it should be resolved. All over the world, we have been seeing examples of various schemes being launched, but our chief minister launched a Direct Benefit Transfer (DBT) scheme—a Farm Input Assistance scheme—about two and a half years ago. It is called *Rythu Bandhu* which translates to 'farmer's friend'. That has now become a classic example of what to do.

It has both economics and politics; it is a fantastic combination of both. And see, I will not shy away from saying this—a lot of people talk about us launching populist schemes and ideas, and I would say the majority of India is poor, so if you carve out an economic policy which helps the poor of India and which helps you win an election, then why not do it? There was a time when people used to say that what Bengal thinks today India thinks tomorrow. Today that idiom can be applied to Telangana because our model has now been emulated by the prime minister himself, even though he perhaps will not acknowledge it publicly. He has literally copied our scheme, imitated it rather, and he has made it his own and is calling it *PM Kisaan*. We have no problems with it. Four other states have emulated us—Jharkhand, Bengal, Odisha, and Chattisgarh, and we are happy about it. So Telangana has become the role model on a number of accounts and I believe that with this chief minister who is so versatile, it is only going to go further and stronger. Since our leader is so versatile the transition from agitation to administration was fairly smooth and easy.

Q. *You have studied abroad, you have worked in the private sector and then you joined politics. You were on the streets with the Telangana agitation, then you became a cabinet minister and now you're leading the party. What have been your challenges and learnings?*

I was educated all along in urban pockets. I was educated for a bit in Karim Nagar then I came to Hyderabad then I went to Guntur, Hyderabad again, then Pune and then to the US. So I have worked my way through as a student in all urban pockets. When you are raised in urban India versus rural India, you have zero consciousness of caste, community, or religion because whoever sits next to you on your bench becomes your friend. You don't ask them their caste or community. But when you hit the ground in Indian politics, you are suddenly made aware of all these factors. Caste is discussed, community is discussed. And I had no clue. In the initial days, I refused to believe that caste would be an issue or community would be an issue when you are allocating a ticket or when you decide the candidatures etcetera. When people started discussing caste and community I would become very uncomfortable. I was like 'but this is not how it should be done.' When you start looking at how India has transitioned, when you look at how politics in India has been evolving, you realize that you cannot ignore or shy away from these factors because it is the reality—the downtrodden, the poor, socially marginalized, excluded communities in India have never had their voice in the policymaking and government. Today they are demanding a share, and there is nothing wrong in it. The Dalits, Muslims, and tribals want their voices to be heard and India has to strengthen itself, India has to survive. As a politician, you have to take cognizance of these voices, understand where they come from and you have to rethink and reorient yourself. That is one of the first things I had to do. Secondly, when you start making a case—for example, I came through an agitation. I was part of the Telangana Rashtra Samiti (TRS) from 2006 until 2014 for eight long years ... when you go through these various emotional phases, you also realize that we are the world's largest democracy in size, yet in a democratic setup like ours sometimes for your voice to be heard, you have to literally shout from the rooftops. Otherwise, nobody really cares. There has never been a scientific approach to any decision-making by the government in our country. There is something called a planning commission, there is something called a five-year plan. Now have we ever sat as a country, as a nation and said, 'Has this worked for us? Has this helped us?' Even though we call ourselves a federal republic, I have realized that people in Delhi don't care as much about what happens in Hyderabad or Chennai or for that matter Bhubaneshwar or Raipur. All they care about is their turf in Delhi and how they can maintain and protect it. When it really hits them that this could affect my political fortunes only then they sit up and take notice, otherwise they don't, it is as simple as that. So, fortunately or unfortunately, in India with a 1.3 billion population, if you want your voice to be heard, you need a voice in the Parliament, and sometimes you need to create a ruckus. Even the media doesn't seem to care unless you create a ruckus. So in the last 12 years, I have realized that there are ground realities, there are ground-level aspirations, there are grassroots-level aspirations that you cannot ignore. At the same time in a democracy, even if you are educated and qualified and even if you want a debate, you have to do a *dharna* and *hartal*. The police will grab you, drag you and throw you in a van like a piece of crap, but you just have to put up with it.

Q. *And what are the things that you have unlearnt in politics?*

Many! (laughs) Like I said, these sensibilities that you hold on to dearly. You shed that inhibition away and you do what you got to do. Like as much as I would like to see a casteless India which only rewards meritocracy, you have to understand that in India caste, community, and religious consciousness is a real thing. You also have to understand where it comes from. You have to understand their yearning and their aspiration, their demand to be heard. There is a ground for it, there is a basis, it is deeply rooted in something that has happened over generations. And, in a democracy as much as I would like to present that everything is good and everything I do is right, you also have to take some tough calls and you also have to sometimes—I wouldn't say lie through my teeth—but I would definitely say camouflage a bit, do a few things differently than how you would like to. So there are several things that you have got to learn, and similarly, there are things that you have got to unlearn simultaneously.

Q. *You hold onto the value of freedom of expression, but you had this debate with the writer, Kancha Ilaiah, where you indicated that you believe freedom of expression may not be absolute. Do you think there are limits to freedom of expression?*

117

Freedom of expression is a great thing and in a democracy nobody's voice should be suppressed, it is out of the question. But when you are expressing your views freely, in a democratic country everybody has got equal rights, if your voice or your opinion tends to create a disturbing situation or a law and order situation, when you are in government you have no choice but to control the situation that might escalate or control a situation that might go out of hands. To voice your opinion freely, yes I'll stand by it. I might not agree with you but I'll stand with you. For instance, I and Asaduddin Owaisi did not see eye to eye with respect to the formation of Telangana, he had a very different view before we became a separate state. But today we work together. Fact is, I respect him because he had a viewpoint. I'd rather have a viewpoint than waver and oscillate. Secondly, if somebody's opinion, if somebody's viewpoint can create trouble, can create a law and order situation which might escalate, I would definitely advise restraint, I would definitely say that you might want to say the same thing in a slightly more palatable fashion.

Q. *In the context of selection of* sarpanches *you recently said that 'If there is unanimity locally, I'll give you 50 lakhs from the MLA funds.' As a democrat, why do you think unanimity is so important in democracy at the local level?*

There are a lot of things that divide us and there a lot of things that unite us. In India, if you think about it, there are three things that unite Indians—religion, cricket, and war (possibly!). But the fact is that there are many more things that divide us, especially when it comes to an election. You could have run a great government, you could have done a great job as an administrator, but at the end of the day, there is caste, community, religion, money, and plenty of other things that will divide your voters. I am all for local governance, I have worked as Panchayat Raj Minister, I have gone through several successful models which have been implemented wonderfully by different states. Fact is, India still has to get over its ambivalence when it comes to decentralizing. If you are a federal republic there is no need for a concurrent list because it leads to a multiplicity of efforts. It doesn't make sense. India has now gone to a stage where we are a fast-growing nation of 1.3 billion with a very impressive Gross Domestic Product (GDP) growth rate over the last two decades. Now the time has come, when the government of India needs to say that stronger states will lead to a stronger country. And states are better administered when things are left alone to them. For instance, how would you decide between a state like Telangana which is growing fast at 17.7 per cent year on year for the last four to five years versus a state like (don't get me wrong on this) Jharkhand which was also created in the new millennium? How would you compare the two states in their growth rates and in their ability to administer and give the same dosage based on population, give the same devolution based on a loose fabric that you have created? The government of India should focus largely on defence, foreign policy, trade, and commerce, maybe external affairs, and maybe a few other subjects. Things like healthcare, education, agriculture should be left under the state's domain. Jharkhand has a large tribal population with 70 per cent tribals. Telangana has a completely different set of issues. We are harnessing our river waters, we are doing something truly astounding for our farmers. Our priorities are different, our agenda is different. For instance, when PM *Kisan* was launched, had honourable prime minister consulted us or talked to us and said that guys you are already doing *Rythu Bandhu*, would you like to dovetail this into your programme, we would have said yes. But now, in Telangana farmers get 16,000 per acre, whereas a farmer in Madhya Pradesh gets only 6,000 per acre. Because the state government here is more proactive so we are giving out much more. Likewise, we have a far more comprehensive health insurance programme in Telangana called *Arogyasri*. Now *Ayushman Bharat* is inferior to it without a question, I would not shy away

119

from saying that. But the Government of India wants to push it down our throat and say it is better. Why is there a multiplicity of efforts? Leave it to us. We have done the job for ten years, we know the game. We know what the loopholes are and what the gaps are. Why don't you give us that money so that we can dovetail it to an existing scheme? What happens here is in wanting political mileage, sometimes governments tend to duplicate efforts, the multiplicity of efforts is hurting the nation. The same logic holds between Hyderabad and villages, Hyderabad and the districts. We should also devolve.

Q. *You have played a role in bringing some of the world's biggest technology companies to Hyderabad. Across governments, we are facing a crisis in not being able to create jobs and opportunities for the youth. How do you see the role of technology in addressing that issue?*

We live in a knowledge economy. There are three things that make India stand apart in the knowledge economy. One, our collective ability today as Indians to possibly provide solutions for the entire world is truly an astounding opportunity. Unfortunately, governments and the private enterprises here as well have not tried to be innovative in coming out with new solutions. At best we have been copycats, at best we have just emulated what has been happening. What is so earth-shattering about Flipkart or Snapdeal? They are mere copies of Amazon. With all due respect to Bansals and the other guys. They are copycats. Where is that one unicorn enterprise from India which is completely innovative, and which has been a market leader? A small country like Finland, Israel, or Taiwan is able to come out with truly globally benchmark products. One dynamic I think we all need to get, is that our collective intellect should be harnessed. If we come to technology, people in government need not understand its programming or the coding aspect. All we need to understand is how that can be utilized for societal good. Take the pain points from your daily life, as the government, as the citizens of this country and try to address them through technology. When I became the Minister of Information Technology, we sat department by department to look at the common pain points for citizens and how can we address them through technology. One of the things we did was to give a challenge to the local startups to reduce the pains of commuters using their own vehicles. A local startup called Radical Tribe came up with a solution. They said that as long as a commuter has a smartphone (that is about 40 per cent of our phones) they need not worry if a cop stops them and asks them to show their license, registration cards or insurance. These can be digitally stored and the police only need to have a scanner so that anybody who gets stopped can merely show their phone and get their documents scanned. It's as simple as that. It has been downloaded more than 2.5 million times in Hyderabad! How do you leverage technology for societal good? We have provided 'phablets' to our agricultural extension offices. Now all the farmer has to do when he sees the pest in his crop—is take a picture and send it to the nearest agricultural extension officer. He will get back to you with an SMS that details out exactly what it could be. They have technology which can just quickly scan through millions and millions of images and can tell you exactly what it is and send back the response saying this is what you've got to be doing. You can be super proactive when it comes to leveraging technology. Therein you'll create a lot of jobs. People talk about AI and how it could lead to job loss. I would say that if you look at the overall economy, the manufacturing sector doesn't have the same sheen that it had about two and a half-three decades ago. Fact is, with the kind of population you have, with the kind of limited land you have, India has no choice but to focus on services. We've done very well when it comes to information technology services. But we need to do more in other aspects. For example, hospitality, tourism. Malaysia and Sri Lanka get more tourists than entire India combined. So why did we leave this huge opportunity which creates jobs for not so well-educated people as well? You need not be an engineer to be a part of the tourism industry. You need not be a professional student, professional degree guy to be a part of the hospitality industry. So services as a sector, unfortunately, has just been a by-product of other things that we have done. Whatever growth you see in the services sector today is actually a by-product and not a product of concerted efforts by the government. I think that needs to be the centre stage for the next decade at least because there are a lot of students who don't care about AI, lot of youngsters in India who don't feel threatened by AI. They are not technologists. They are looking for jobs outside of the tech space. So this is a bit over-hyped in my opinion, this whole debate about how AI is going to take over jobs—it is a part of evolution. Whenever there has been a breakthrough, people feared that it would change everything. I think we are in a fairly good space in India.

Q. *On the more personal side, can you tell us about your passions within politics, say two or three things you would hope to achieve in your political career, and a couple of passions outside of politics?*

India has a lot of ground to cover and you feel ashamed when you travel abroad and you go to different countries and you come back home—you feel ashamed because countries which have gone through a nuclear attack, which are constantly under threat from forces of nature, like earthquakes, tsunamis, cyclones. and typhoons, they seem to be doing alright. They seem to be evolving and they seem to be at least a 100 years ahead of you. India is such a well-endowed country. Yet we seem to be incapable of getting basics sorted. I would want to expedite that in my own limited capacity to make sure that we join that league as quickly as we can. I don't think India can afford to leap-frog, India has to pole-vault because we have lost precious time, 70 years, and things haven't changed. India moved up from the 153rd spot in 1990 on the Global Healthcare Quality and Access index to the 143rd spot now, 28 years later. So have we really moved? Ghana, Bangladesh, Sri Lanka, Pakistan are in the 70s and 50s on that list. And if you look at the country as a whole, what bothers you as a citizen, what bothers you as an Indian more than as a political leader, et cetera, is that we still have villages without roads, households without toilets, villages without electricity, we still have situations where despite the fact you have so much water there is no drinking water and not enough water for farmers. Unfortunately, it appears to me that the short-sighted, near-term desire to win the next elections seems to take precedence over everything else in terms of making a longer haul plan. I think that's what really holds us back. It has cost us dearly, whether we like it or not. Now I think India cannot afford to do it anymore. This generation is restless. Governments have to realize that the intolerance levels among people are growing in terms of the government and its ineptitude with respect to providing the basics. So as a politician I would like to ensure that my state, and by extension our country, gets the basics sorted. I mean I do have big dreams of Telangana owning its satellite in the air, doing a bunch of cool things for our farmers, for our students, training and skilling them, giving valuable inputs about the soil content and what needs to be done et cetera. All of that could also happen simultaneously, they are not mutually exclusive. But at the same we need to get the basics first addressed completely. Now on the personal front, I don't have much time and this whole myth about balancing your work life and family life is just a myth. Nobody, I think, actually has a balance. Like Shah Rukh Khan said in *Baazigar*, '*Kuch paane ke liye kuch khona padta hai.*' And '*Kuch kho ke paane waale ko Baazigar kehte hai.*' [To get something you have to lose something. The one who loses to win is the real gamber]. You have to balance it out and do whatever you can. On the personal front I'm preparing a bucket list because the other day my 10-year-old daughter asked me, 'Dad what is the craziest thing you have done in your life?' I really thought hard, long, dug deep and said what is it that I have done that I can tell her. I couldn't find an answer so I decided that together with my friends I am making a bucket list. *Kuch karna hai.* The biggest thing possibly that she has seen me doing is when I took a leap of faith and went on the rollercoaster at Atlantis at one point. I think that is the craziest thing I have done. I can't think of anything else. So I figured that I'll have to get some more things on my bucket list and hopefully someday I'll have an answer.

Q. *If you have two or three words or a phrase that you would like to be remembered by, what would it be?*

Well, I want to be remembered as a humanist. I don't care so much about political positions and whether or not you get a particular position, I don't really care about that. I want to be remembered as a guy who could do something for his fellow human beings and as a decent chap. A humanist who did not subscribe to a particular philosophy of his own, but somebody who stood up for his fellow human beings and did his bit for his country and his state. I think that is good enough.

Madhukeshwar Desai

Madhukeshwar Desai, the 32-year-old vice president of Bharatiya Janata Party's (BJP's) youth wing, the Bharatiya Janta Yuva Morcha (BJYM), hails from a distinguished political lineage. His great grandfather, Morarji Desai, was the fourth Prime Minister of India and a stalwart of Indian politics for over half a century. Despite the non-political vocations of the two generations before him which focussed on business instead, Madhukeshwar grew up interested in politics. He joined the BJP in 2011—at the young age of 23—garnering major media attention, given that Morarji Desai had spent many years in the Congress. In 2013, Madhukeshwar was made the National Vice president of the Yuva Morcha, making him the youngest person to hold the post in the history of the party's youth wing. Rewarded for his subsequent efforts, he was re-appointed for a second consecutive term in 2017.

Unlike most other contemporary politicians, Madhukeshwar hails from the intersection of the business and legal communities—he is an advocate by training. He pursues his professional career in law with as much fervour and dedication as his work for the BJP and BJYM. He is often seen at political events donning a crisp white shirt and black pants, the sartorial code of choice for South Mumbai lawyers. Madhukeshwar is currently the chief executive officer (CEO) of the Mumbai Centre for International Arbitration (MCIA), a joint effort between the Government of Maharashtra, the international and domestic arbitration community, and the business community. The Centre allows for business enterprises to arbitrate their disputes on Indian shores without getting ensnared in the country's infamously slow judicial system. With Madhukeshwar's outreach efforts, MCIA is well on its way to building a name for itself: in 2018, the Centre was referred a case directly by the Supreme Court.

For our meeting, we visit the upscale MCIA office, which overlooks Mumbai's picturesque Marine Drive stretch called the Queen's Necklace. Madhukeshwar is extremely conscious of his South Mumbai upbringing in a relatively wealthy and well-known family. He, however, wears his privilege lightly, making conscious and open efforts to step outside his comfort zone. Growing up, he confides, he could identify very little with his South Mumbai classmates, most of whom hailed from prominent business families and took many things for granted. It was only when he moved to Bangalore as a young adult that he found friends who were more grounded and motivated, and he, too, began to achieve better academic results.

Madhukeshwar joined the BJP primarily because he thinks it is the only party in India in which anyone can aspire to rise to the top. He also believes in some of the central tenets of the BJP's ideology, especially that all Indian citizens should be treated equally and that the country should move towards a uniform civil code. Soon after joining the party, Madhukeshwar helped organize L.K. Advani's *Jan Chetna Yatra* across the country. He made it a point to travel to every state of India, often by train so that he could connect with individuals from all walks of life. This journey was burdensome, often leaving him hospitalized or bed-ridden for weeks on end. Years later, in 2019, the party made good use of both his political and legal skills. He managed the BJP's campaign in the Mumbai North-Central constituency, where Poonam Mahajan was re-elected with a big margin. Even more pivotally, when a young BJP activist (Priyanka Sharma) was arrested in West Bengal during the campaign, allegedly for circulating a caricature of the state's chief minister (CM) Mamata Banerjee, the party relied on Madhukeshwar, among others, to take the battle for her release to the Supreme Court. The court ruled in their favour, lambasting the state government and handing BJP the key means to whip the All India Trinamool Congress (TMC) with during the campaign, earning the legal team much praise within the party. Madhukeshwar later told us that the victory in the Supreme Court felt even more satisfying because freedom of speech is an issue he cares about deeply.

Madhukeshwar Desai comes across as congenial and intelligent. He is the quintessential modern politician; having skillfully led the winning social media campaign for Mahajan, he is also deeply aware of the power of the internet and the visual media, which bodes well for him. While writing this book, we conducted three of our 20 interviews on camera. Madhukeshwar was the only interviewee who understood all aspects of a live image, the presentation before the camera, the profile of the interviewee, the lighting in the room, as well as the seating arrangement. For him, the delivery and form of a message are as important as the content.

Presently, Madhukeshwar is untested in electoral politics; it remains unclear whether his academic and legal acumen will be buttressed by the handiness needed to win elections in India. However, it is refreshing to meet politicians like Madhukeshwar who, despite their personal successes, have entered the system to offer institutional solutions to the nation's myriad problems.

Interview

*Q. You have had an upbringing in South Bombay, you have a lot of
different passions you have followed over the years, you have a
lot of different interests, your father and grandfather weren't in
politics, but of course, your great grandfather was. So what made
you join politics full-time?*

It is an interesting question that I get asked a lot and I have never
been able to give a fully satisfying answer. Since I was a child,
politics always interested me. When I actually started following
through with it, I realized that the amount of impact that you can
have with politics is far more than what you can have with say,
doing social work. While that is very important, for example, what
an non-governmental organization (NGO) does, the amount of
impact that you can have with politics is phenomenal. So that is
something that I found very interesting and that is something I
pursued. It is not the most obvious choice. Most people in my age
group, most people that I grew up with, some of them still think
I am quite silly for choosing what I choose to do. But it is something that I enjoy doing, and I would say that the day that I stop
enjoying doing it is the day that I will stop, but it still interests me
every single day.

*Q. There are many other ways where you can have a meaningful
impact in many people's lives. There are NGOs serving millions
of people, there are educational institutions training millions of
people. What is it about politics in India that gives it so much power
and play that you believe that once you are in politics you can
influence and introduce massive change?*

Two parts. For example, how I grew up, I grew up here in South
Mumbai. And over a period of time through my journey in politics, I have actually travelled and stayed in almost every single

state in the entire country. I have travelled on trains, travelled in buses, something that most people in South Mumbai have not done because they wouldn't need to do. It takes a lot for you to understand how privileged you are. If I can sort of break it down—I am male, I am rich, I am relatively good looking, I am straight and I speak English. A large majority of India is discriminated upon on a daily basis because they don't have one of these things. To understand and empathize why is it that they perceive their lives in a certain way is very important. That's a personal journey that I have had to go through and that is something that has made me better person. Coming to why government impacts everyone so much: just to take a dig at myself and South Bombay—if you have a bell in your room to call someone then I don't think the government really impacts you as much. But if you have a ration card instead, and you are dependent to some extent on either government subsidies through a ration, or you are dependent on low-cost government housing, or you are dependent on public healthcare and hospitals, then what the government does and says makes a huge difference to your life. So for you to understand and empathize with that whilst having grown up in this entire environment has been challenging for me but has been extremely rewarding—a duality that most people don't really get to play with.

Q. *What about politics has been most fulfilling for you? And what are some of the things that have been most frustrating or challenging for you?*

Nothing really compares to the joy and satisfaction that comes with the ability to help an individual out of a problem, however small that is. I don't see the same joy and satisfaction with my friends or colleagues who are not in politics with their respective jobs and what they do. Helping people gives me tremendous joy and it is the reason why I am in politics, so I can help people out. Having said that, my biggest issue or my biggest frustration is that the perception of power amongst people is such that they sometimes come to you with an issue that is not solvable and they presume that because you hold a position of power you can solve it or wave a magic wand. It becomes extremely frustrating because you can't explain to someone why you cannot resolve their issue and why a call from me will not change an entire system.

Q. *You have a reputation of being much more open-minded, some would say even liberal in your thinking on a lot of social conservative issues. How do you reconcile that? Have you found it difficult to articulate and advocate your position on those issues when your party's position has been more conservative?*

The most beautiful thing about my party is the fact that we have internal democracy. So if I disagree with something or I am not happy with something, I know I can take that up with my party leadership. There is a safe open space where I don't have to search for a camera to get two minutes of publicity to put my views forward and that has been accepted at multiple levels. That is between me and the party leadership of course. But that allows me to be intellectually honest with myself. And I do belong to the party because I do agree with 90 per cent or 95 per cent of what the party does and what the party stands for. With the remaining 5 per cent, we have a conversation about it and we see what we can do.

Q. *So what are the core principles that you follow that you think the party shares?*

I'll try and simplify as much as I can. If you want to be a politician in India, you have 13,000 political parties. This is the official statistic from the Election Commission of India. People's minds are blown when I tell them this. And every year there are new political parties that are coming up. So we have Rajnikant's party and

Kamal Hassan's party that have come up now, Aam Aadmi Party that started some time back, Rakhi Sawant's party also came up in between. So every single party, if you look at it, has either been created for an individual or for the family and for the purpose of the progress of that individual or family, whether that is an overtly stated mission or not. If you look at the BJP, for instance, that is not the case. We are founded in ideology. For me, what is the true test of this? The true test of this is succession, right? Tomorrow if Harsh creates an organization and says it is an institution and not a fiefdom, how would you really test it? You would only test it with succession. Has Harsh created for his children or has he created it for the public at large? If you look at Maharashtra, for instance. After Sharad Pawar ji, it will either be his daughter or his nephew who will take over as president of the party. After Balasaheb Thackrey, it was Uddhav ji and later it will be Aditya Thackrey who takes over the party. You go up north, after Farooq Abdullah ji it was Omar Abdullah ji. In south after former Prime Minister Deve Gowda his son Kumaraswamy who took over as president. Can either one of you tell me who will be the next president of the BJP? You can't. Because in my mind, I know for a fact that if I work hard on merit that I can aspire to one day hold the position of the president of the party. And as someone who works within the party, I can aspire to be the Prime Minister of India as well. But that is something that doesn't exist in other political parties because you know that there is a glass ceiling that exists and regardless of what your merit is, you may not ever actually achieve that. So as a young person, someone who can broadly, based on numbers, be defined as a millennial, I want to know that if I work hard and I do well that my party will support me and there is no artificial ceiling that I was not born to a specific family, or my family wasn't close enough to somebody else's family, which is why I am not a part of it. Today we are the largest political party in the entire world because people know that if they work right through, they can get there. And just to finish this point, if you look at all our presidents, let's take the last three presidents: Amit Shah ji was the treasurer of the *Yuva Morcha* about 15–20 years ago, Gadkari ji was the District president for the *Yuva Morcha* in Nagpur, Rajnath ji was again the Ward president (one step lower) of the *Yuva Morcha*. All of them have worked their way up and on merit have become the president of the party. So there isn't a fixed game that is being played where you know that someone's son or daughter is going to become party president.

Q. *A compelling reason for you to join the party is for your own personal career interests. The question is: what are the values that you share with the party? You said that 95 per cent of the time you agree with the party. So what are these values that you share with the party? Do you think those are your core values? Does the party share those values with you?*

So yes, why I would choose a party is a personal reason as well. What the party does and what the party demonstrates with its cadre also reflects with what the government does. And so if the party's reflection is on merit over say promoting one's progeny, then that is something that reflects in the government as well, and I'll give you an example. It is something that I have had a debate with people over and some have agreed with me and some haven't agreed with me and this is something that I think really differentiates us. If you look at the prime minister's mother, she is very old and she lives in a small one or two-bedroom house in Ahmedabad. When she falls sick she goes to the government hospital like millions of Indians. When the president of the Congress party were to fall sick, she goes on a private jet to another country and gets treatment and comes back. As a government, or as a party, when you say that my mother is going to go and get treatment in a facility where millions of other people get treatment, you push yourself to say that all government institutions must be at a certain level.

Q. *Your great grandfather, Mr Morarji Desai, was the prime minister of the country. He was part of the Congress, had disagreements with the Congress, and over time left the party. How much did that influence your choice of party? Or did it have no influence on your choice at all?*

I truly believe in Abraham Lincoln's quote that regardless of how tall your grandfather was, you have to do all your growing yourself. He did what was right for him at his time, and his legacy stands testament for it. It doesn't dictate beyond a point what I would do or what I would choose. And that is something that even in my family we are very clear about, that each generation would do what they have to do, what they think is right keeping in mind the values that have been passed on. Having said that, we would never do anything that would bring shame or disgrace to what he did.

Q. *On what kinds of issues do you feel like there is some form of dissonance? You agree with 95 per cent of the party's ideology and what it stands for. Where do you find that gap of 5 per cent?*

So that's something that we discuss internally in the party, and that is the reason that it gives us that safe space to discuss it, so we don't have to discuss it publicly.

Q. *What are your main passions? For instance, if you were to retire tomorrow. Or if there is a history book that is being written, about you what are the two or three things that you would want to be known for 50–60 years from now?*

I am passionate about a lot of things. I am passionate about cars and bikes and anything that has an engine, I really enjoy reading and I really enjoy music. Those are my passions that don't agree with this. But I do have a little bit of what you call Obsessive Compulsive Disorder (OCD). What that does is I am very, very curious about how things function and how things work, and identifying flaws in systems and making them better. If you come to an average politician's office, what do people come there to ask? They are effectively asking your help to navigate a complex system that exists and they sit at the top of that complex system by right of power. Instead of that, if you can break down the entire system and make it as simple as you possibly can, that is a pet peeve or a quirk that I have that I want to do. So I try and do that in every system. Even with the Arbitration Centre here. We have identified the problem, we have looked at what the issues were, we have found the quirks, and then we have tried to resolve it. That's something that I find very interesting, something I try to do. Romanticizing how you would be perceived by history, to my mind, leads you to write books like *Discovery of India* and take decisions based on how history would remember you as opposed to what would be right, or what is the need of the hour. So I will not fall into that. I would say in whatever situation I would be in and whatever decisions that I have to make, I pray and hope that I make the right decisions and history would remember me kindly for it.

Q. *Changing an entire system may require you to engage in a long bureaucratic fight, which may actually prevent you from helping people in the short run, because with helping people in the short run you may be sometimes bending rules or doing favours. If one gets pleasure out of helping people, which is a noble thing to do, how does one step back from that and find the time or the inclination to change an entire system? Because those may be very different processes. So how do you reconcile those two?*

I will sort of merge both of them together. I am a closet geek and I love reading about issues especially from an academic perspective. And I think that one thing that we should endeavour to do in India is really have more academics and government to come together and resolve issues, like you have in some of the

Nordic countries especially. What I mean by helping out people is not exercising my power to override someone else. When you interact with people and understand what their issues are, it is only then that you can come up with a framework. If you close yourself off and identify the problems only on an excel sheet, it gives you a very myopic perspective of what a problem is and how to solve it. It is only when you interact with people, and succeed or fail in solving their issues, that you get a holistic perspective of the reality. I think it is the way that we are in 2019. The way that time is structured now is that we end up reading a lot, but we end up reading a lot of nonsense as opposed to academic work, which I think is very important and which I tell all my friends and peers to do. In fact, somebody asked me recently that he wanted to join politics and I asked him what are the three books that he had read, and he didn't know. I told him to read *India After Gandhi* and Dominique Lapierre's book *Freedom at Midnight* to start off with. Thus, along with an academic perspective, if you don't interact with as many people, if you don't try and help them out and you don't try and resolve those issues, you'll never be able to confidently analyse a system and understand the tweaks a framework would need to make it easier for people to navigate.

Q. *But you know there is this common understanding that the BJP stands for a certain vision of Hindu nationalism. Development is not only its agenda but Hindu nationalism is a part of its agenda. So the question is—you do not seem to think that that's important and all, is that true? It doesn't matter to you personally, or ...?*

No no. Coming to let's say secularism, everyone likes to beat on that horse a lot. When did the word 'secularism' come into the preamble of the Constitution? It was Indira Gandhi that brought it in. After she got it in, Bapu Morarji Bhai became prime minister and he said that you cannot have something that is not defined. So we had an overwhelming majority in the Lok Sabha and it was decided that it should be defined as *Sarva Dharma Samabhav*—all religions be equal. That was then defeated in the Rajya Sabha that was governed by the Congress. It is often said and there is this perception that exists that we are unfair to minorities and that we are only doing things for Hindus, but tell me one thing that has been brought in that would justify that. To my mind, if I can draw an example again. I'll take you back to Rajiv Gandhi, and the reason I say Rajiv Gandhi is because he had a three-fourth majority in government. I won't compare any of the other governments because you had compulsions of coalitions et cetera. In the Shah Bano case when there were protests after the judgement came out, he actually brought in a law to make sure that the personal rights of Muslim men and Muslim women were 'safeguarded'. It was pandering to one specific religion. For Christians, at least for Roman Catholics, the Vatican is your holy city. For Hindus, depending on from which part of the country you are, you have different spots all across, Kashi Vishwanath being one of them. But there is only one subsidy that exists, now, of course, being phased out in India, as a by-product of the government of the day that brought it in which said that the government will sponsor a group of individuals to go to Hajj every year. It's the Supreme Court that read it down and said that it must be phased out. So when allegations are made to say that the party is overwhelmingly doing things only for Hindus, take a step back and look at the actions that the government has taken and everything that has been brought in has been brought in for everyone, right? Goods and Services Tax (GST) affects everyone equally, demonetization affected everyone equally, Real Estate Regulatory Authority (RERA) affects everyone equally, so that doesn't discriminate against you on the basis of your religion.

Q. *So we have talked about what we think the role of the government should be. Do you think the role of the courts—with Sabarimala,*

*section 377, issues of marital rape, should the courts, the bureau-
cracy, and the elected politicians be involved in telling us what the
appropriate religious beliefs and practices should be for individuals?*

We are a very religious country regardless of what we may show
otherwise, and you cannot divorce religion from anything. Even
if you have to sell a paper, while it is not really a religion, you
need to focus on politics, cricket, Bollywood, and astrology. If you
don't have a mix of those things, it will not go. And that's why
religion is deeply important to most people which is why it gets
highlighted so much whether it is in courts or in government or
in legislation.

Q. *What about community and marriage norms? Do you think the
same principle applies? Do you think the government should be
involved in these things?*

My perspective—and this is the perspective of my party and even
in the Directive Principles of State Policy in the Constitution—is
that we should move towards a uniform civil code. And I think
that would be important for society. In my personal opinion as
a lawyer and as someone who is politically active, I would say
that that is something that we should move towards. Whether its
Muslim personal laws, Christian personal laws, or Hindu personal
laws, I truly believe that we should move towards a place where
we move towards a uniform civil code.

Q. *But you do understand that within the Congress party for a very
long time and even within the BJP there are some people who
believe that introducing a uniform civil code is actually intruding
on the marriage norms of other communities, and even among the
Hindus there may be some people who resist that because there are
Hindu traditionalists who always said that it is not the role of the
state to tell me how I should run my life.*

If you look at the Constituent Assembly debates on the Hindu Marriage Act that had come up at that point in time and what the constituent assembly actually decided, it actually gives you an interesting perspective on what the role of the government is. Is it the role of the government to tell society where they should be? Is it the role of the government to say that this is reflective of society so, therefore, this is what we should do? Or is it a balance in between? I think the constituent assembly debates very clearly said that it is a balance in between. And from a religious perspective at least I don't think too much has changed from 1947 to today with the way that people feel, and therefore that is the answer.

Q. *You are managing to run the Mumbai Centre for International Arbitration (MCIA) and at the same time you are the vice president of the BJP Youth Wing. How do you strike this balance between your political career and professional career in law, and do you think this is sustainable, that you will be able to do it for the next 10–20 years as you continue to play an active role in politics?*

To be honest, I thought I was good at multitasking until I started this. I am not. But I think what is important is that I have a great support system, both at the MCIA as well as at home, so it allows me to do what is required to be done without it being too much of a stress. But I personally don't look at it as a challenge because both things really interest me, and as long as you do something that makes you get up and get out of bed every morning without it being taxing, I think it is rewarding in all ways.

Milind Deora

Milind Deora's political journey mirrors those of many other young dynasts from the Congress party. In 2004, Milind became one of the youngest members of the Lok Sabha at the age of 27, becoming part of a group of very young entrants—from Rahul Gandhi to Sachin Pilot—that year, dubbed by *India Today* magazine as 'The Class of 2004'. He was elected from South Mumbai. His father, Murli Deora, had previously represented the constituency four times, and was immensely popular within it. Milind won again in 2009 and was later inducted into the Manmohan Singh government. However, he faced consecutive electoral losses in 2014 and 2019 as a saffron surge ensured that the Congress drew a blank across Mumbai in both elections.

The story is all too familiar: there are many parallels with the journeys of Sachin Pilot, Jyotiraditya Scindia, Jitin Prasada, and others. There are, however, few things that Milind shares in common with the rest. His distinctive brand of politics makes him one of the most unique individuals across the political spectrum. With most politicians in India, there is significant dissonance between who they are in private and who they project themselves to be in the public sphere. One needs to peel off the veneers to understand their real selves. With Milind, in no small measure, what you see is what you get. He is comfortable in his skin and does not pretend to be anybody else, even when it may be politically disadvantageous.

We've met with Milind several times over the past few years, starting with an interaction at UC Berkeley in 2015. During the recent conversations that we have had with him in Mumbai, we spend a considerable amount of time trying to dissect his brand of politics and how he makes sense of it. In his trademark style of giving long-winded yet frank answers, often making comparisons with the American political system which he studies closely, Milind divulges a lot. We speak of several criticisms and issues of perception which he often faces, from his not being a full-time politician to his elite, urban background not allowing him to understand the problems of the poor to his close ties with the promoters of India's largest corporate houses.

'It doesn't affect me in any way,' he says about these perceptions people have of him. He insists that he can't play the game that many of his colleagues play where they move around Lutyens Delhi in shirts, jeans, and nice loafers, and just before reaching their constituency, switch to kurta-pajamas and get greeted with garlands. Milind prefers to be completely transparent—he almost always roams around in a shirt and pant whether it's for work or personal engagements, just like his father did. He narrates a story about how, once when on a round of a slum, he came across an individual who had been his server the previous night at a nice restaurant. Instead of being embarrassed, he mentioned his encounter with the individual in a speech to the entire audience.

'I don't understand rural issues at all,' he confesses, arguing that there are enough members of parliament (MPs) who understand and represent rural issues but not enough who understand issues of urban development. Understanding the challenges and aspirations of urban citizens is something that he prides himself on. And he sees the business community in South Mumbai as not only members of his constituency but also stakeholders in helping to meet these aspirations. 'I can't deny that I have the urban poor to Mukesh Ambani living here,' he says, defending the video he released during his 2019 campaign which had endorsements from different South Mumbaikars, most notably (and surprisingly) from business magnates, Mukesh Ambani and Uday Kotak.

The other distinctive feature about Milind's approach to his politics is that he is not afraid to speak his mind publicly, even if it means being at odds with his party. In many political systems, this may be a regular occurrence. In India, however, it is a rare phenomenon, primarily because the repercussions are often quick and severe. It requires a great deal of courage and self-confidence. Back when the UPA-II was in power, this earned him the reputation of being somewhat of a conscience keeper for the Congress party. It was only after Milind tweeted against the ordinance on convicted legislators passed by the Manmohan Singh government that Rahul Gandhi called a press conference and famously remarked that the ordinance should be torn up and thrown away, much to the embarrassment of Dr Manmohan Singh. A few months later, it was déjà vu as Rahul pulled up the Congress government in Maharashtra, once again on the heels of Milind's criticism. In 2019, Milind spoke out publicly against the working style of his colleague, Sanjay Nirupam, who was then the president of the Mumbai Congress. While he seems to regret venting out in public, it did force the party's central leadership into action—a month later, they replaced Nirupam with Milind, giving him the same prestigious post that his father held for 22 years.

At a time when political parties are getting increasingly centralized and the space for independent notions and dissent is fast shrinking, Milind's style of politics comes as a breath of fresh air. While he will probably never become a prominent mass leader, he has carved out a niche for himself as an important voice on urban issues across the country. That, coupled with the fact that he enjoys the friendship and trust of Rahul Gandhi, will ensure that he will continue to be of relevance within the Congress for a long time. Hopefully, he will also continue to play the role of the party's chief conscience keeper.

Interview

Q. You were born and raised in South Bombay, your family has business interests and you are passionate about so many other things, like music. What made you join politics at such a young age, and then over time, what is it that made you stick with it all these years?

The thing that made me take the plunge into politics and that keeps me motivated about it even now is the fact that apart from politics there is no other profession through which you can really make the kind of difference you can in society. By virtue of how I was raised, it was very clear to me that I would not get into politics, that I would study business and work in the family business. As a child, I was always exposed to public service more than I was exposed to politics. I was always part of my father's regular public service activities from providing free eye check-ups to the needy to his initiative of starting India's first digital literacy programme with Bill Gates in the mid-90s. In fact, after I worked in the private sector, I worked in an NGO and I took forward the initiative of providing digital literacy to some of the most needy and economically underprivileged schools in South Mumbai. Although one might think that the economic nerve centre of India only has fancy affluent schools, there are some government-aided schools which are some of the poorest schools in India. And when I got involved and started extending the programme that my father had started I began getting involved in politics through the back door. When I got into the Parliament and started interacting with my colleagues, I learnt that everyone had a different way of getting into politics. For some people, it was public service, for some people it was their identity, their caste, their community, and for me, it was very clear that social work and essentially social work around empowering the youth. When I actually became a full-time politician I realized that although you can do social work as an NGO or in the private sector with corporate social responsibility (CSR) funds, politics offers you the opportunity to take that work forward in a much more meaningful way.

Q. *Politics is obviously a full-time job. There is a perception of you that you are somewhat of a reluctant politician, that you are sometimes missing in action and you are not there on the ground fully. Why do you think that this perception exists?*

In India, I actually differ with the view that politics must be a full-time job. I personally believe that politics will move towards a place where you can have a full-time job and politics becomes a volunteering service for you, just like how it is in the United States. In the US if you go and talk to somebody who works in the Democratic National Committee (DNC) or people who are the administrative staff of the DNC, they may say that they are the Berkeley chapter head of the Democratic Party. They don't identify themselves as *karyakarta* who go around and wearing a certain old outfit that is meant to signify something that happened 70 years ago. Politics has evolved over time. Now every candidate, every campaign, and every election has a bunch of volunteers. People who have full-time jobs come in and volunteer. They move between the private sector, NGOs, and the government. I have been in politics for 15 years. I was an MP and I was a minister and had party duties as well. Any politician who is spending 24x7 in politics, I frankly do not know what they are doing with their time. I don't think it requires a full-time commitment unless you are an administrative person. If you have the ability to do something, it is up to you to do it for one hour a day, two hours a day, three hours a day. It depends on what you are doing and where you are in life. When I was a Lok Sabha MP and when I was a Union Minister, I had no time to do anything for those three years. From 2014–19 I had a lot of time to do things that I wanted to do. While I was involved with the party, I was travelling, was

144

engaged in business and did some consultancy work. I have been extremely busy recently with the general elections and the state elections in Maharashtra. But now the next election in Mumbai will be the Municipal Corporation election which will be in 2022, February. In the interim there will be time to do other things, I can't be doing this full-time. I don't blame the people who do this full-time. There are some people who just like shooting the breeze and it is just facetime for them. However, I think you can very well manage by doing things on your own. I think in India the time will come when you will find politicians who are actors in movies and shows and are very active in their constituency at the same time. For instance, I know that Kirron Kher manages her responsibilities as an MP from Chandigarh, as well as her position as a judge on India's Got Talent and other show business commitments. One can definitely do it.

Q. *You come from a more elite background than most politicians. Do you find it difficult to change this image?*

Most of the politicians in India live in large cities. For instance, if I were an MP from western Uttar Pradesh, my home would be a Lutyens bungalow in New Delhi. I would go to my constituency once every two or three weeks. In Delhi, I am moving around in a shirt and a pant or jeans and nice loafers, and the minute I have to board a train to my constituency, I wear a kurta-pyjama and I am greeted with a *haar* and I become a full-time *neta* for those three days. The rest of the time I am doing other things which may be in the realm of politics, or something with an NGO, maybe I am engaged in some business. So politicians *are* doing other things. It is a misconception that politicians are not doing something else in their life. If politicians aren't doing something else in their lives, what is their source of income? Because politics certainly does not allow you to support the kind of lifestyle most politicians have. I don't think my situation is anything unique. This perception may exist because I am from Mumbai and I represent a constituency like South Bombay. Although it is the richest constituency in India, people forget that South Mumbai is not just from Haji Ali to Marine Drive. The real South Mumbai has *chawls*, slums, congested and dilapidated buildings, vast tracts of Mumbai Port Trust land with slums and tenants on it. That is the heart of South Mumbai, and not the Marine Drive, Malabar Hill, and Peddar Road. Even my father, who was a much more grassroots politician than I am today, believed that he is not a full-time politician.

Q. *How do you deal with this perception of being an urban, elite South Mumbai politician? Do you find yourself, especially in election time, trying to change that perception?*

I don't think it matters to anyone on the ground. It is something that can be used against you, but it doesn't mean anything. It has not really affected me electorally. People in other parties may think that this is an elitist constituency and millions are spent on it, it doesn't really affect me in any way. I can't deny that I have one of the most urban constituencies and I can't deny that I am an urban guy. I can't deny that my constituency consists of people from urban poor all the way to Mukesh Ambani. I also can't deny that I represent all of them and they all come and support me in some way or the other. Mumbai is a mix of all kinds of people.

Q. *People had mixed views on the video that you released during the 2019 campaign, in which industrialists like Mukesh Ambani endorsed you. Some people suggested, how can we trust Milind to be neutral in policymaking if he has such close ties with industrialists.*

I cannot do the kind of politics wherein I am an urbane politician in Delhi and then I am a grassroots kurta pyjama wearing politician when I go to my constituency. I can't do that. It is very transparent here. For instance, it has happened with me that the person serving me an alcoholic drink during my dinner at a restaurant is somebody I met the next morning in my round of a slum. My outfit didn't change, I was still in my shirt and pant and I transparently acknowledged in my speeches that last night I was at the restaurant where he worked. That is how I do my politics. I prefer to know that it is transparent, unlike a lot of my colleagues and friends, who have to do the other kind of politics.

Now, there are important leaders in every constituency. In some areas the leader could be a don, in some areas the leader could be a religious priest. In South Mumbai, the important leaders are business leaders. They are the religious priests of South Mumbai. They not only have an impact on national policy but also on the economy and the politics of South Mumbai. In the video, I tried to authentically capture South Mumbai by including people who truly represent South Mumbai, from a *paanwala* to a simple shop-keeper to Uday Kotak or Mukesh Ambani. To me, that's all part of South Mumbai. If it was just one section, then that would have been wrong. I am not a socialist because I can't subscribe to the ideology of 'to hell with business'. Prithvi Jain, the president of one of the biggest trader groups called MASSMA, is also in that video. They represent small traders and are a very powerful body employ-ing lakhs of people. And I am not ashamed about it at all. It's not that I am living in and fighting from Borivali and I got Mukesh Ambani to use his celebrity status to get something. Then I might as well have got Salman Khan to make a video for me. However, the people in the video are important voices of South Mumbai who drive commerce and enterprise in South Mumbai.

Q. *Would your brand of politics differ if you had a rural constituency?*

Even if I had a rural constituency, let's say in rural Maharashtra, and I had to live in Mumbai and I regularly go to the constituency, I would still do the same thing. I would still be very transparent about who I am, what I wear, and what my lifestyle is. It is not a bad lifestyle, I am not doing something wrong. I am doing things everyone does. To me, Mumbai is about aspiration. I don't think that the man who served me in a restaurant and lives in a slum will judge his MP or his candidate for going to a nice restaurant or to a bad restaurant, or for taking time out. Mumbai is not ridden by caste or by that agitational kind of politics that you may find in other parts of India. It's driven by aspirations. Even the politics of Mumbai revolves around that, be it the *Shiv Sena* or the Maharashtra Navnirman Sena (MNS). Who has ownership of that aspiration? That's their politics.

Q. You seem to have reconciled with the fact that you will be considered an urban Mumbai politician. Do you want to have a more rural connect or become a leader for rural Maharashtra?

Not at all. I do not have any aspirations to go pan-Maharashtra. I have very little knowledge and understanding of rural issues. I know about agriculture, but I don't know much about what the problems of rural distress are. I think that although India is urbanizing very quickly, we are still a largely rural country and a country that is dependent on agriculture, and there are enough MPs to represent rural areas and rural aspirations. I think that urban India, urban aspirations, urban infrastructure and development, the services sector, the manufacturing sector, are areas which are very poorly represented in Parliament and in assemblies. It is very important for urban politics to come out if we want to grow and create jobs. Urban politics covers the services sector which is the biggest contributor to India's growth. It also covers the manufacturing sector, it covers jobs outside of agriculture, it covers urban infrastructure, it even covers the politics of urban migration. So, understanding urban politics and adequately representing it in Parliament and assemblies is something that has been ignored for many decades. In my experience from 2004 to now, I have seen that there are very few discussions on urban development. There is very little understanding amongst MPs on urban issues. There is far more understanding, even amongst urban MPs, about rural issues. So, there is enough representation of rural India, as it should be, because agriculture and food security are very important for our country. However, there certainly needs to be more representation for cities. As a country, we are failing to build tier-2, tier-3, tier-4 cities to absorb urbanization from rural areas to decongest large metros. The large five or six metros still remain the major economic growth drivers in the country. That's because of our lack of understanding and representation. I am proud of being an urban MP because I can then represent and voice some of these issues. I have colleagues who feel very proud, even if they studied in the United States, they know how to milk a cow. Like Sachin Pilot tells me that always. And that's good for him, and that's what a real rural MP should be like. To me, an urban politician must understand these urban issues.

Q. *The Congress party has leaders with aspirations. However, within the Congress party, there is a glass ceiling of sorts which is that only a Gandhi can run the show. Does that put a damper on the aspirations of the younger leaders to be a part of an organization where there is a glass ceiling? Because everyone would like to be the captain of the team.*

Congress is democratic in that if tomorrow the party were to overwhelmingly believe and express the view that a Gandhi should not be the leader, it could happen. There is a reason why the party believes a Gandhi is acceptable as a leader, that is an internal matter. From a public point of view to some people, the Congress might appear to not be a democratic organization whereas the Bharatiya Janata Party (BJP) does come across as a democratic organization. There may be an aspiring political activist who joins the Congress. There may also be a very ambitious young man who wants to be the prime minister one day and have an aversion to the Congress even if he agrees with the ideology. That might be an issue. However, we are democratic. To undercut the party's image as a rigid family-owned entity, the party has to communicate far more effectively that we are actually a democratic transparent party that is open to other suggestions.

Q. *The Congress performed terribly in the 2019 elections. You have always been known to express your views openly and candidly, and after the 2014 elections, you had publicly said that some of the people 'calling the shots' at the central level in the party were out of touch with the ground reality. What went wrong and what do you think the Congress needs to do?*

The Congress party has survived in India for a long time. The idea, the ethos, and the narrative of the Congress are still relevant to India. However, to take that narrative forward, to strengthen that narrative, and to communicate that narrative effectively, you need an effective organization. And that's something which we need to fix. An organization means many things, and all I'll say is that we need to figure out those pieces of the organization that should have been fixed in 2014 and during the last five years and fix them now. In my opinion, Congress may go from 50 seats to 100 seats, it may have a default figure of 120–130 seats in a non-polarized election. But for Congress to once again re-establish that its narrative and its ethos are the best for India, there will have to be major changes in the party, which I am not going to spell out. There are many people in this country who still believe in the Congress and what the Congress stands for. We need to know what is it that they want so that they come back and vote for Congress. That is what the party has to work on.

*Q. You said you want to know what the people want in order to go
back and vote for Congress. A lot of people point fingers at the
leadership of the party, at the Gandhi family and to the fact that it is
a family dynasty. This narrative has been exploited and pushed by
Mr Modi and Amit Shah and has gained considerable resonance…*

Dynastic politics is a global phenomenon and it is not unique to
Congress and India. There are enough dynasts in the BJP. Almost
all the BJP's regional allies are parties that are dynastic. I myself am
a dynast. I don't think dynastic politics is a problem. Regardless of
whether you are a dynast or not, presenting a strong effective narrative to the people of India is what's needed. For that, whether
it is Rahul Gandhi or Badal in Punjab, you need an organization
that can deliver this message, and you need to be aware and align
this narrative with what is happening on the ground and what
people are asking for. So for instance, take the *'chowkidar chor hai'*
slogan—is it effective or not effective that's what you have to measure. If there is a mood of nationalism after Balakot in the country,
how should you react to the surgical strikes—those are the things
you have to measure. You have to be smart and savvy about. If
you ask me, doing polling and all that is irrelevant. You just need
to have good instinct. To me, political instinct is very important.
Dynasty is a global phenomenon. It exists in many parties in India
and the world. It certainly exists in BJP, it certainly exists in the
allies, and it certainly exists in the Congress. I don't see dynasty
as a problem, I think that communicating a clear concise message
developing a narrative and communicating that narrative is of
utmost value. That is something we lacked in the last five years.
We were late in forming and disseminating a counter-narrative to
the BJP. I think another big issue was that what we were offering
was not clear enough. What we were offering socially was clear,
but economically, we were not clear. That was an area which we
could have focused on.

Q. In early 2019, you expressed your displeasure with the Mumbai Congress president at that time, Sanjay Nirupam. You came out publicly and exposed a bit of factionalism within the Mumbai Congress. At what stage does it make sense to come out publicly and express grievances versus dealing with it internally?

Ideally, one should never come out publicly. In politics sometimes, one feels a little claustrophobic, frustrated because of issues that have bottle up for too long, and then just lets it out in a public statement. It should not happen. Ideally, an organization should have a vent which allows hot air to come out. When there is an absence of such a vent, this happens. One can always look back and say I wish I was more patient. I am not a person who believes in being sensational and grabbing headlines. I don't really care about all that. Although there are some people who create a controversy every month to stay in the headlines, I don't have that insecurity or that need. I am not somebody who is proud of my outbursts that shouldn't have been made in public. And as you grow older you learn from that. Sometimes one feels suffocated and ends up doing what I did, but it shouldn't happen.

Q. How do you think about the 'love versus hate' that we heard about so much in the 2019 campaign? Even after losing Mr Rahul Gandhi has been saying he will fight the BJP's hate with love …

I think it is very hard to pinpoint what is love versus hate. In India when I look at it, I see the right-wing in India more violent that the left-wing. They are the ones who thrash Dalits and others, but if you look at America, you see the left as more violent, in some ways. I don't know if you'll agree with that. They are a little more intolerant even. So what is love versus hate, how do you describe what is illiberal politics anymore? It's becoming grey. Just like a Trump can stand up and say I am not a racist, show me a statement that clearly, unambiguously says I am racist. It might be hard to pin him down on that. You may have people in his party who are racist, he may say I am not racist, why would Kanye West support me? So a constituency will emerge who get tired of this left-and-right, I-am-here-I-am-there, I-don't-want-to-get-pigeonholed-into-this-is-what-you-stand-for. I think that societies are coming of age where no longer is there this notion of this is a leftist view socially and economically, this is a right view. Modi, for instance, has been economically very left-of-centre in many policies. In India, you can argue that right and left economics is measured on how many public sector undertakings (PSUs) you have privatized. And how much money you have made from selling PSU assets. And he has done zero on that. Why is Congress on the left? Manmohan Singh was a reformer in the truest sense. But he is still branded as a left politician. We opened the doors for the United States for foreign direct investment (FDI) in retail, for insurance bill, for GST, which we failed to pass. All the big reforms were Congress reforms. Extreme right you can argue. Economically. These things are very grey now. The lines are blurred. A constituency will emerge, which will say I am tired of these categorizations. It's like in music. I saw in music, people got tired of saying you are rock, you are alternative, now you are grunge, now you are this, and then a new art form emerged in the rock space which was indie. And indie today is the biggest rock genre. I really see that in politics.

Q. *Since you don't want to be that '24 hours politician' and you want to explore other interests, what are some of your passions outside of politics?*

One of my commonly known traits is that I am a very good observer of people and I am very good at foreseeing a trend well in advance. I have tested that foresight overtime in the private sector, in politics in India, and even internationally. I enjoy watching trends in the business. So if you ask me what is something I am passionate about, I would love, for instance, to host a show and where you engage in discussions about trends and break down what is happening around us. I feel that because politics globally is becoming so polarized and confrontational, almost every outlet of mainstream media is choosing sides. There is very little space to come in the middle. To develop such a space is a passion of mine. How can you, at least in India, create a property which brings all the different sides together and really looks at issues dispassionately? Although I will have the baggage of being on the left, I think that is an exciting space. I am also passionate about music. I am passionate about economics. I have survived so long in politics because of my economic developmental narrative, not because of my social identity or caste et cetera. My father was in a similar situation. He was a Marwari in Bombay, a non-Maharashtrian, and so it is a greater struggle for us because our politics has to be about other than who we are. So those are the areas that I am passionate about.

Q. *When you retire, how would you like to be remembered? Is there a line or phrase that you would like written on your grave?*

'Just know I chose my own fate. I drove by the fork in the road and went straight.'—Jay-Z (in the song called 'Renegade').

Omar Abdullah

Omar Abdullah hails from arguably Kashmir's most prominent political family. The Abdullahs have been at the forefront of Kashmir politics ever since Maharaja Hari Singh signed the accession of the princely state of Jammu and Kashmir to India in October 1947. Sheikh Abdullah (Omar's grandfather) became Prime Minister of Kashmir in 1948 and returned as chief minister in 1975. He then handed over the reins of power to Omar's father, Farooq Abdullah, who became the chief minister for the first time in 1982. In 2009, Omar Abdullah became the chief minister of Jammu and Kashmir at the young age of 38.

The rather storied careers of the Abdullah family belie the tension and turmoil that has been a constant feature of the politics in the valley. Since 1947, India and Pakistan have fought four open wars in the state, a separatist movement has been active in the area for decades, and since the 1990s, the state has been racked by violence and terrorism. It is estimated that there are 450,000 security personnel (including the army, paramilitary, and the local police) based in the state of Jammu and Kashmir, making it one of the most militarized regions in the entire world. The uncertain security and political environment have also meant that Jammu and Kashmir has been under president's Rule more often than any other state of India. Governing Jammu and Kashmir is a difficult feat, as is being a Kashmiri politician.

The Abdullah family's journey has been no less burdensome. Sheikh Abdullah spent over a decade in jail, and Farooq Abdullah was forced to move out of the country after being widely castigated for an accord with the Congress that led to the rise of militancy in Jammu and Kashmir. Omar himself entered politics despite his mother's objections and has faced multiple threats to his life, not to mention the recent eight-month long detention. Yet, for over two decades in politics, Omar has played multiple roles in Jammu and Kashmir and in central government. He has been a part of both the National Democratic Alliance (NDA) and United Progressive Alliance (UPA) alliances. He was elected to the Lok Sabha at the age of 29 and became the youngest minister in Vajpayee's government shortly after. He then became the president of his party, the J&K National Conference, and chief minister a few years later, this time in league with the Congress. During the Bharatiya Janata Party (BJP)-People's Democratic Party (PDP) rule in the then state (now union territory), as Leader of Opposition in the assembly, he was a vociferous critic of the BJP and its handling of the region.

As a Kashmiri politician from the valley, Omar has learned to walk multiple tightropes. In a state where the populace is often sharply divided between a separatist ideology and a nationalist one, there is barely any room in the middle. Omar Abdullah stands in that little sliver of space. He is Kashmiri and Indian, and like most Indians wears both identities proudly. For most Indians, the centre is also the safest place to be. For Omar, however, asserting this dual identity leaves him open to attacks from both sides—he is termed a collaborator by some and a separatist by others. 'I will never be Indian enough for that extreme right-wing nationalist politician. But then I'll also not be Kashmiri enough for those who don't see Kashmir's future as part of India,' Omar says to us. He has resigned himself to this reality and wishes the same were true of his father, who constantly feels the need to prove his patriotism. In troubled times, however, this is a peculiarly hard act to balance, even for Omar, especially when Kashmiri youth have been publicly targeted for just being Kashmiri in some parts of India, most blatantly after the Pulwama attacks, and of course, the events after the dilution of Article 370 in 2019.

At no point has the dilemma been sharper for Omar than immediately after the Modi government diluted Article 370 and abrogated Article 35A on August 5th, 2019, after which he was placed under detention in a government guest house for eight months, with almost no contact with the outside world. We have the chance to speak with Omar twice, the first conversation perhaps his last interview before his detention and the second conversation, his first interview after being released. Omar speaks at length about the detention experience and his emotional state throughout those difficult eight months. He reveals that he has come out of detention feeling resentful and bitter, and will take a long time to come to terms with what had happened. He is experiencing a wide range of emotions from anger (at the ruling government for its treatment of the residents of Jammu & Kashmir) to bewilderment (as to why autonomy and statehood were taken from the residents), and sadness (for the future of Jammu & Kashmir and its people).

Despite this welter of emotions, Omar retains an element of pragmatism as he mulls over his available options and possible next steps. He remains grounded, adhering to his beliefs, and being frank, even if it means expressing polarizing and unpopular opinions. He prides himself on being authentic and using the same tone, both in and out of the office; he does not varnish issues depending on the audience to make them palatable. This is apparent in our interview as well, where he comes across as very upfront, approachable, and forthcoming, even when visibly upset.

It remains to be seen whether this characteristic will serve him well politically in the long run, especially given the fate of the valley, which now hangs in an uneasy balance. Omar was a firm believer in Jammu and Kashmir's autonomy and special status. Yet, he still believes that its future lies as an integral part of India. The politics of the region has undergone a structural transformation with the transformation of Jammu and Kashmir to a union territory, the removal of its special status, and the bifurcation of the state. Cornered and isolated, Omar's political future rest almost entirely on how the new political realities play out in the valley.

Interview

*Q. You were born abroad, you have lived abroad, and before joining
politics you have worked in the private sector. Your mother didn't
want you to join politics. And of course, it is one thing to join
politics in India and a whole different ballgame to join politics in
Kashmir. So what really made you do it? Was it an easy decision?*

It was a relatively easy decision. I grew up not expecting to join
politics. But obviously, the family that I grew up in, it was part and
parcel of everyday life, first with my grandfather and then with
my father. Post-1990 with the outbreak of militancy in Jammu
and Kashmir and the complete cessation of any political activity,
it wasn't something that was at the forefront of my plans. I finished college, started working in the private sector for a few years,
but subsequently, things started to ease out in J&K and in 1996
we had Assembly elections and that is when the first seed was
planted and I started interacting with party colleagues. By then, I
had spent enough years in the private sector to know that it really
wasn't what I was looking for. I had tried two jobs but neither of
them gave me any sort of satisfaction that I was really making any
sort of impact. The work that I was doing wasn't really benefitting
anybody other than the organization that I was a part of. After
seeing electoral politics up close after the 1996 elections, I felt
that if I put in that kind of effort in work where I interact with
people, try to solve problems, and try to address issues, then perhaps there will be more satisfaction at the end of the day. That is
where the idea stemmed from. And the 1998 Parliament elections
came about, and colleagues from the party came to meet me and
said that it would be an opportune time to take the plunge. My
father warned me about it. It was more of a token warning so that
he could later tell my mother that 'Look, I told him not to but he
didn't listen.' So he ticked that box. So now whenever my mum
says anything, he says, 'Well I told him not to!' Ultimately he was

the one who signed off on my mandate. If he had said 'no' and he had meant it then, it wouldn't have happened. But yes, that is how it started.

Q. You have always lived with a lot of security. You have spoken about the threats to you and your family across the generations. Has being in politics come with immense personal costs?

As far as the security aspect is concerned, it came a little later in life. I was already towards the end of my teens when the trouble started in J&K. I am one of those generations that still have very warm memories of what a peaceful Jammu and Kashmir is like, which is something my children and the generations after that don't have. I know what it is like to cycle around Srinagar with absolute freedom, what it is like to drive around the valley with no worry about security and stuff like that. Obviously, all that changed in 1989–90 and that security has been a constant part of life after that. That said, politics has given me so many opportunities and I am here by choice. Therefore, it would be wrong on my part to complain about the problem that security poses. A certain amount of security I would still have even if I wasn't a politician because of the family I belong to. My mum always says that if you can't take the heat then stay out of the kitchen. I am here by choice, and I have no business complaining about the lifestyle changes that this forces me to make.

Q. A lot has been written about the alienation of the youth in Kashmir. How can we prevent the Kashmiri youth from aligning with extremist forces and remaining engaged with the democratic processes and mainstream politics?

The answer is in your question itself. The word you have used is 'engaged'. The problem is that over the last few years no one has engaged with them. Definitely, after 2014 there has been no engagement whatsoever. What little engagement has been there, has been for very limited political gains as opposed to looking for long-term solutions. And that is one of my pet peeves with the Modi government. There has been no effort made to engage the state of Jammu and Kashmir at all, particularly with the youth of Jammu and Kashmir. Some of them hold some political beliefs that are difficult to reconcile with, but they are not all like that. A large number of them actually took part in the 2014 Assembly and Parliament elections as voters, as political workers. So what changed after that which has pushed them to the margins? That's what we need to understand, and which we haven't done enough of. Only if the government in the centre goes about a process of engagement can we start undoing some of the damage that has been done. Because otherwise, you find youngsters who are well educated with the prospect of a decent life ahead of them setting all that aside to become militants. And once they join militancy, their life span is measured in days, not even in weeks or months. We have had instances, and I can quote more than one—for example, this associate professor from Kashmir University was teaching children in class on Thursday, he disappeared on Friday, he became a militant by Sunday, and he was dead on Monday. That was it. That was his lifespan the moment he decided to pick up the gun. And there are many more instances like that. Clearly, what is lacking at the moment is an effort to engage, and if we can build that into our process, we can start pulling back from the abyss that we are staring down.

Q. *Do you fear that we may lose an entire generation to militancy and violence?*

We have lost more than one generation. This violence that you are seeing now is 30 years old. Nobody at that time would have ever imagined. If you told me in 1989–90 that in 2019 I am going to be talking about Jammu and Kashmir still as a conflict-and-violence-ridden place where death is not an unusual phenomenon, I wouldn't have believed it to be possible. That is exactly where we are today. We have already lost a couple of generations to this violence and unless we stem it, it will just continue.

Q. *For a young Kashmiri man or woman growing up in a security environment, which is not easy to navigate, and then perhaps studying in a city like Hyderabad or Bangalore but having to be careful about revealing the Kashmiri identity out of fear, what do you think is the psychological impact?*

For me, this would be second or third-hand information because I have not had to live it. But I can understand for the average person on the street it is an extremely difficult environment within which to grow up, and it is an extremely difficult environment to live in. And it breeds a lot of resentment. A stray example—imagine a situation where you have to travel from North Kashmir to Srinagar or South Kashmir to Srinagar on a Wednesday or a Sunday, and you are told that you cannot visit because the security forces need the national highway for their own movement. So basically, you are a prisoner in your own home for two days of the week because vehicles of the security forces have to move. And even on the other days of the week, you are basically pushed off the road every time a CRPF or an army truck has to go past. Now can you imagine the sort of resentment that this would build up in people? This is our home, this is our land. On the one hand, we are told that Jammu and Kashmir is an integral part of India, and Jammu and Kashmir has to be treated the same way as other parts of the country have to. Yet when you see a dastardly sort of Naxalite attack in one part of the country, you see a completely muted reaction to that, and then you see what happens in Jammu and Kashmir and you see a completely different security reaction. It plays on the psyche of people. The identity of being somebody from Kashmir was less of a problem until recently when you came out to study in other parts of the country, whether you came to study in Pune or Mumbai or Chandigarh or anywhere else. But over the last three or four years, particularly with the Modi government in the centre, this attempt that has been made to paint all Kashmiris as stone pelting, *azadi* supporting anti-nationals has actually made this identity issue even more of one than it was earlier. You now find children being driven out of colleges or schools because they are Kashmiri. You find hoteliers putting signs on their guesthouses in Agra and other places saying that Kashmiris should not be given rooms here. There was one sign I saw that said 'Dogs are acceptable but Kashmiris are not.' Or then you have a constitutional authority like a governor of a state turning around and saying that Kashmir and Kashmiris should be boycotted economically, don't buy products from Kashmir, don't visit Kashmir, even if you want to go for the Amarnath Yatra, put it off for a few years so that we can crush Kashmiris economically as well. Obviously, all this plays into that mindset, whereas it is; you have people trying to pull you towards their side, you have the separatists, you have Pakistan, you have those that are using religion as a card in Jammu and Kashmir turning around and saying that there is no place for Muslims in India. You have these sorts of incidents. All it does is it heightens that sense of alienation, that sense of unease and it makes lives of people like us, who want Jammu and Kashmir to remain and thrive as a part of the union of India, much more difficult.

Q. *As a Kashmiri politician and chief minister if you say anything that expresses sentiments of regional autonomy strongly, you will be labelled a separatist who wants to break the country. On the other hand if you toe the line and you kind of make deals with the centre, you are accused at home for being a part of the central command. How do you walk that tight rope?*

I have reconciled myself to the fact that I will never be Indian enough for extreme right-wing nationalist politicians. But then I'll also not be Kashmiri enough for those who don't see Kashmir's future as part of India. And, therefore, it is best to be true to oneself.

Q. *You mentioned that 20–30 years ago if someone would have told you that 30 years from now Kashmir would still be a conflict zone, you would not have believed it. Considering your family is looked upon as guardians of Kashmiri politics, do you look upon that as a personal or a collective failure?*

To the extent that out of these 30 years I was in power for six years and my father was in office for six years, there is an element of personal failure in that. However, we work in a federal system, and therefore the failure is not just of the individual, the failure is of the collective. It's also a failure of the state. Sometimes we don't know what is good for us.

Q. *Do you have any personal regrets or anything else in your political life that you wish you had done differently?*

Well, there were two major incidents when I was in office that I wish had been handled differently. In 2009, there was an allegation of rape and murder of two women in South Kashmir in Shopian. I had just assumed office, and with the benefit of hindsight, that would not have been handled anywhere like it was handled at that time. So that's one. And of course, the 2010 summer agitation that we had to deal with which resulted in more than a hundred people dying. That continues to haunt me and always will. My failure was in not being able to convince the government of India that hanging Afzal Guru is not going to win them any votes in the general election and, in fact, would push Jammu and Kashmir back to the fringes. I wasn't able to convince them, and that is something I will always regret.

Q. What was your reaction on first hearing about the abrogation of Article 370? Can you tell us about your emotional state through the eight months during which you were in detention?

Well, I think the immediate reaction to the events of the August 5th 2019 was absolute shock. We were expecting something to happen because of all the rumours that had been floating around, and the orders that were being issued to forcibly vacate tourists and yatris (pilgrims) from the Valley. All of that had created a general sense of unease. The only thing we were not able to get a handle on was what was going to happen next. The National Conference Members of Parliament and I took some reassurance from our meeting with the Prime Minister. I think it was on the 2nd or 3rd of August. We were somewhat reassured that it wouldn't be as serious and as damaging as the rumours had led us to believe. But from midnight of the night of the 4th of August, when reports started coming in of people being detained, arrested, some removed from their homes and political leaders being placed under house arrest, we knew that we had to expect something pretty serious.

The fact that they would do all that they did—which is dilute Article 370, abrogate 35A, split the state into two and reduce the state into a union territory—I don't think any of us imagined that it would be such a drastic change. So, yes, the 5th of August pretty much passed in a haze because I was still locked up at home. The kids had these big padlocks on them. It was only in the evening when I had just finished walking (I was just trying to keep my exercise routine going) that somebody who works at my home came and told me that some government officers had come and they had orders to take me away. So I went and met this individual. He was one of the Srinagar District Magisterial staff, and he had a police officer with him, and they showed me the detention order. I was very matter of fact about it. I said, 'That's it, then. Give me a little bit of time, I'll shower, pack some clothes and I'll go with you.'

At that point in time, obviously, nobody had any idea how long it would last. I went and said bye to my dad and my sisters and everybody. They were sitting in the garden. And I told them that I was being taken to this government guest house and that I'd see them when I get out. I thought it would be a week or two, probably not more than that. And I packed accordingly. Those two weeks stretched to 232 days before I finally got out. Over those 232 days, there was no one single emotion or one single reaction. I went through the entire spectrum of emotions from anger to frustration to resentment to bitterness to sort of resigning myself to what had happened, and then going back to being angry about being detained and frustrated about it.

The one thing I was sure of was that I wasn't going to let them get me down. I wasn't going to let them mess with my head. There were a couple of times at the beginning where I felt a sense of anxiety creeping in. You know, just a few weeks before I was detained, I had had surgery on my hand for which I had to have an MRI. And I don't know if any of you have ever had one, but it's one of the worst experiences when you get sucked into that tube and it starts making noises. I think I'm borderline claustrophobic, so when I am taken into that machine, my heart starts racing, and it feels like the whole world is closing in on you. And I never thought I would feel that in an open room. But the first few days in detention, even in the large room that I was in, I still had this feeling of claustrophobia coming in on me. I just felt trapped. There was nobody to talk to. There was no contact with the outside world. It was three weeks before I saw my sister. It was five weeks before I saw a newspaper or a television news channel. Of course, we had no telephones, no internet or anything like that, so, I really was cut off from the world. But gradually, things improved, and I got through it.

Q. *How did you keep yourself occupied, and what did it feel like to be completely isolated for that long, especially for someone like you who*

is in public life and spends so much time in the company of others?
What did you do to make sure you're staying mentally sane?

I'm actually glad that I'm not one of those people who is uncomfortable in one's own company. I don't mind a little bit of time to
myself. Of course, 232 days to myself is a lot longer than I would
have liked. But I'm not one of those hard-core social animals that
have to be surrounded by people. I don't like being disconnected.
I don't like not knowing what's happening. Soon after the detention started, I took a leaf out of my boarding school days, and I
realized that if I had a routine that I followed, it would be a lot
easier to cope with.

So I immediately set myself a routine. I would wake up at a
particular time, eat breakfast, lunch, and dinner at very particular
times. As a person in detention, I had to have a medical check-up
with blood pressure and other tests taken every day. I set a fixed time
where the doctor would come and check my blood pressure, when
I would go out and exercise, when I would have my morning coffee
and read my newspaper, once they started allowing me to do so.
Everything was carved out, and having this routine really helped.
Otherwise, you get aimless and purposeless. I set aside time to read.
I had books brought to me and I finally caught up with reading a lot
of books that had piled up unread. I actually found that the single
biggest factor that helped me get through the detention was having
a routine that was pretty much carved in stone. Whether it was
sunny, snowing, or raining, my routine stayed the same.

Q. *Your time in detention, particularly with everything happening in*
Kashmir, must have been one of the most trying experiences that
you've gone through. Do you think it has shaped you in any way,
or had a more longer-term impact on you?

Well, I don't know what impact it will have in the long term. At
least at the moment, I know that I'm definitely more resentful

and more bitter. I'm angry because I don't know what I did to justify being detained the way I was. I can understand that in the initial aftermath of August 5th, the central government and the authorities in Srinagar were worried about how people would react to their move. But when there was no immediate law and order problem, there were no protests and things were met with a rather calm reaction. There was no justification for keeping us in as long as they did. And there are people who are still under detention. There are senior political leaders who are yet to be released. Dozens of people are in prisons outside Jammu and Kashmir—in Haryana, in Uttar Pradesh, and places like that. I still struggle to understand why we were treated this way. At the end of the day, we were part of the national mainstream. We put our lives on the line to fight elections in Jammu and Kashmir. And ironically, that was cited as a reason to continue to detain us. One of the clauses in my detention order talks about how I was able to influence people to come out and vote in large numbers in spite of a boycott call and a militant threat. I never realized that this was something that could be used against me. Tomorrow, how am I my going to convince people to come out and vote? What am I going to tell them? So, I mean, the overwhelming feeling that I have come out of detention with is a whole lot of bitterness and anger, which I'm trying to come to terms with. But I think it will be a while until I do.

Q. *You're implying that the news was met with calm in Jammu & Kashmir. Do you think that is the sentiment on the ground and that after what must have been an initial shock, the general population has taken it in their stride?*

No. The general population is angry about what happened. They're not going to come to terms with it easily. But they didn't react the way most people expected them to. If you saw the street protests of 2008, 2010, and 2016, you didn't see a repeat of that.

Partly, that may have been down to the fact that there was a far larger presence of security forces this time because they had time to plan for what would happen, as opposed to these three previous events that I sighted where they were caught by surprise.

I think people also found a different way of expressing their anger. They kept shops closed for months on end, kept children away from school for months on end. They stayed in their homes for months on end. They had a different way of expressing that anger and street protests weren't one of them. Justifying our detention by saying that we would have provoked street protests when they was no inclination towards street protests, is unjustifiable. People just found a completely different way of registering their anger, and they continue to do it today. It's not as if they've resigned themselves. None of us have resigned ourselves to what has happened. We're just not going to give the government an excuse to arrest us.

Q. *Have you spoken to anyone to try and get a sense of why you were detained for that long, and what was the justification?*

Truth be told, I haven't reached out to anyone. I'm not going to do it. If any of them feel the need to offer me an explanation, I would be happy to listen, but I don't think I'll buy it. And I'm not going to beg for one. Also, the day I came out from detention, the national lockdown was announced, and everyone has been really busy with the COVID-19 battle. I think it would be rather self-centered on my part to try to hijack the battle against COVID-19 and try instead to find out why we went through what we went through.

Q. *When we spoke to you last year, and really throughout your life, you've always maintained that you see Kashmir as an integral part of India, and that you're always going to fight for that. But you had also said to us that Article 370, in the form that it was, was a necessary precondition for Kashmir to be a part of India. Given the dilution of Article 370, has your stand on this most crucial matter evolved or changed in any way?*

Jammu & Kashmir is an integral part of India. As much as I would like to say that my detention and the circumstances of the 5th of August have caused me to shift my thinking on that, it hasn't. Because the position I've taken takes into account all sorts of factors, and I do not believe that Jammu & Kashmir has a future for itself outside of its relationship with India. However, that doesn't justify what India did to Jammu & Kashmir on the 5th of August, 2019.

My politics on this issue is still evolving. I still believe that we have to, constitutionally, try and fight to retrieve what we have lost on the 5th of August. And I'm not just talking about converting a union territory back into a state, because that's a minor part of it. One of the first things we did after the 5th of August was to approach the Supreme Court of India, and our petition is currently under the scrutiny of the Supreme Court. We hope that we will get justice from the Supreme Court.

A lot of people have asked me, 'why don't you ask the Government of India to reverse what they did on the 5th of August?' But, why would I ask Mr. Modi to reverse what Mr. Modi has done? It's stupid. It's pointless. It's just tokenism. It's the worst form of politics because all I'd be doing is trying to appease the voters, knowing full well that nothing will come out of it. And I don't want to do that. I think the politics of appeasement is the worst thing I can do to people here. So I don't know, I think things will evolve. I also haven't had a chance to sit down and talk to my colleagues and understand from them how they are thinking, what they feel about what happened. So as a party, we haven't been able to take a position it. Once we're done with COVID-19 and the rest of my colleagues in detention are released, then we will be able to sit and evolve a more thorough position on every-thing that happened on the 5th of August.

But the crux of it is that, yes, I still believe that Jammu & Kashmir is a part of India. But I also believe that Jammu & Kashmir has been treated very, very badly. Every single promise made to Jammu & Kashmir has been broken. And it's going to be very difficult for people like me to continue to justify why I believe Jammu & Kashmir must be a part of India. Delhi hasn't left us with much to talk about.

Q. Let's assume that normal electoral politics returns in Jammu & Kashmir. What do you think your and your party, the National Conference, would be advocating for?

That is the million-dollar question. What is the political slogan that the National Conference stands for today? I really wouldn't be able to answer that question for you. Other than, what sets us apart from this new entity, the Apni Party, which was set up a few months ago with the blessings of New Delhi and which has accepted the 5th of August as fait accompli and say that they will move on from that. We haven't and will not. We will continue to challenge what happened on the 5th of August. We will con-tinue to question why it was necessary. So while we will talk about the restoration of our statehood and the bifurcation of Jammu & Kashmir, we will also continue to challenge the Supreme Court for the reversal of what happened on the 5th of August. We believe that if the court were to take an objective view, what happened on that day does not stand legal scrutiny. And that's what we'll continue to fight for. But will there be any tweaking of this posi-tion, we will add or subtract anything to it? I honestly wouldn't be able to tell you until the party has had a chance to sit down and go forward from there. Personally, I see very little chance for myself to participate in any sort of electoral politics in the union territory of Jammu & Kashmir the way things stand, and I don't know how long that will last.

Q. *How do you this will now change the relationship between Kashmiris and the state of India, and the rest of the country, if at all?*

It was a relationship full of mistrust, which has been multiplied many, many times over. There is no reason why anyone, particularly in Kashmir, but also in large parts of Jammu, will trust what they hear from any government at the centre. We have been lied to by people sitting in the highest offices in the country. We were lied to by the governor sitting in Raj Bhavan, who represents the President of India, who represents the Union of India. He lied to our faces. He lied through the television channels. He lied through the newspapers. He told us that there was no threat to Jammu & Kashmir's special status and that we should go about our normal lives. It's very difficult to forget all this. It's difficult to imagine how we will go back to trusting what we are told. The wounds are very, very raw still. And it's not as if eight months in detention has lessened the intensity of all those wounds.

Q. *Do you worry about increased separatism and increased militancy once the security presence is reduced? What about the role of foreign actors in escalating the situation?*

Look, militancy is something that you can control. You can control it by force. The greater involvement of Pakistani-backed terrorists and militants is something that you can control as well, by stronger vigilance at the line of control. What you can't do is force people to feel more Indian than they feel. You can't force a sense of isolation, bitterness, anger, or a sense of separatism, out of people. And I dare say that in spite of the BJP and their voices in the media patting themselves on the back that the events of the 5th of August will end separatist sentiment in Jammu & Kashmir, I think it will have no such impact. If anything, those who are sitting on the fence are probably feeling more isolated and more separatist than they were before the 5th of August, 2019.

Q. In general, how long do you think a state can maintain physical control over a territory, largely through force?

Honestly, I think it can pretty much be indefinite. It depends on how many losses you're willing to take on the part of the security forces and on the part of the civilian population. If Israel-Palestine or numerous other examples are anything to go by, if you want to maintain a relationship with the region by force, you can do it indefinitely. But is that the relationship India wants with a part of its territory? You want to be known as an occupier of Jammu & Kashmir. That's not the relationship you claim to have with Jammu & Kashmir. You claim a relationship of equals. You claim a relationship where we should be no different than somebody from another part of the country. Then we must be afforded the same freedoms. We must be afforded the same opportunities, and we must be afforded the same right to dissent.

Well, I was taken away because the Government of India didn't want to hear a dissenting voice from us. How is that democracy? How do I go out tomorrow and tell people of Jammu & Kashmir to trust Indian democracy when that very democracy locked me up because they didn't want to hear a dissenting voice? My voice wasn't violent. I wasn't advocating people for freedom. I wasn't advocating for protest. There is not a single sound bite of mine that you can find where I have advocated the use of violence as a means to settle disputes. And I was locked away. So what do I tell people about the strength of Indian democracy? Unfortunately, today I have more questions than I have answers.

Q. For most of the decades after independence, your family, and to some extent, Mehbooba Mufti's family, have been the fulcrum of political leadership in Jammu & Kashmir. Given the recent events, do you think there's space for a new political class to emerge, or do you think that is going to be even more difficult?

It really depends on whether that new political class is sought to be created by New Delhi or if it evolves on its own. It's a question of credibility. If New Delhi wants to create an alternative leadership, it will not work. You will have people who will come forward, make statements, have the backing of the Government of India, but they won't have the backing of the people. I don't claim that the National Conference or I myself or my family has the backing of everybody in Kashmir. But we at least enjoy some degree of credibility, how much is open to debate. But parties that are foisted on the people by New Delhi enjoy none whatsoever. And we've seen this from 1953 onwards. As an alternative to my grandfather (Sheikh Abdullah), they tried to create Bakshi Sahab, Sadiq Sahab, Kasim Sahab and so many others, and they failed. With all the resources of the Government of India at their disposal, with all the money and with all the development, they still had to finally come back to my grandfather and say, 'look, we need to sit down with you and work something out.' New leadership that evolves because the people drive that leadership forward will take time, but it's not impossible. I'd like to believe that it will happen. But new leadership that New Delhi tries to foist on people will survive for an election or two and then disappear. They will enjoy no credibility whatsoever.

Q. A lot of your old allies, the Congress and many others, have supported the government's move on 370? Do you feel that the National Conference and, to some extent, the PDP, are politically isolated given these parties' positions? Do you feel a sense

174

of betrayal on behalf of these parties? And finally, do you see a potential alliance between you and the PDP going forward?

I think that we'll have to wait and see how local politics plays out within Jammu & Kashmir. At the moment, it appears as if the entire effort of New Delhi is focused on breaking up the PDP. Because this new formation they call Apni Party is largely made up of all the people of the PDP. This may explain why Mehbooba Mufti has been kept in detention longer than I have because they haven't met with the same success in breaking away people from the National Conference as they have in breaking away people from the PDP. We'll wait and see how that plays out. But obviously some amount of cooperation, some amount of working together with the PDP in the larger interest of general Kashmir cannot be ruled out.

Now, coming to your original question, do I feel betrayed by other parties in the rest of India? On the question of 370, not so much, because I understand that it was and remains a position or an issue on which it would have been very difficult for them to oppose the BJP. For these parties, it's realpolitik, it's survival. Why take up an issue that affects the maximum of five parliamentary seats, even if it is the right issue, at the cost of your popularity in the rest of the country? I would have liked to have seen at least a token resistance because, at the end of the day, Jammu & Kashmir's special status is the legacy of Pandit Jawaharlal Nehru. So maybe a little bit more. I understand that you don't want to oppose the revocation, but at least own it. Ask why it was felt necessary at that time for Jammu & Kashmir to be given special status. Because there was so much misinformation, there were so many lies that were propagated while I was locked up. And that was one of the most frustrating things—not being able to say what I wanted or not being able to come out with the facts that were counter to the propaganda that was being planted.

So that was a disappointment, but more than the revocation of 370, I think the thing that disappointed me more was the silence at Jammu and Kashmir being humiliated the way it was in being converted into a union territory. In all the years since independence, this is the first time a state has been downgraded. Otherwise, union territories have always been upgraded to states. Now, what did we do to deserve this treatment? If all this time, you have been telling the world that terrorism in Jammu & Kashmir is the product of Pakistan, that fundamentalism is the product of Pakistani involvement, that separatism exists because Pakistan has injected separatism into Jammu & Kashmir, then go and punish Pakistan. Why did you punish Jammu and Kashmir? Either you have been lying to the world and that what has happened in Jammu & Kashmir is not just down to Pakistan and there is a huge domestic constituency for it as well, in which case you punish us. Fine. But you can't tell the world that everything that has happened to Jammu & Kashmir, it has been Pakistan's doing and then choose to punish Jammu & Kashmir because you can't punish Pakistan.

How do you justify what you did in terms of reducing Jammu & Kashmir to a union territory and breaking it up? I understand that 370 and 35A were part of the BJP manifesto. They had to fulfill their promises, they did it, for better or worse. The consequences of this will be far-reaching. We will have to see how it plays out. But reducing Jammu & Kashmir to a union territory was never part of their manifesto. And all these other parties just went along with it and played dead when all this was going on in parliament. I'm so disappointed with leaders like Arvind Kejriwal, who perhaps can't oppose 370, which is fine, but should at least oppose reducing Jammu & Kashmir to a union territory. Every day, you are fighting for full statehood for Delhi. Every day, you are fighting because you are a chief minister with one and a half hands tied behind your back. And you are happy to watch Jammu & Kashmir being reduced to that status.

I'm so disappointed with parties like Telangana Rashtra Samithi (TRS) and others who fought for their own states to be carved out because they wanted that identity. They wanted the sense that they have their own place. And they happily went along while our identity was snatched away from us. So I'm not as disappointed in these parties about the 370 piece, but I'm really disappointed with them about this. We thought they were friends, political leaders. My father left his own election to go and campaign for Chandrababu Naidu, and he was one of the first people to jump straight off with the BJP and say, we support you on everything. These are betrayals that I will not forget easily.

Q. *The last time we met, you spoke about how difficult it is to manage Jammu & Kashmir because you have very different demographics, concerns and considerations in each of Jammu, Kashmir Valley and Ladakh. As far as Ladakh is concerned, given that it has got its own concerns and demographics, would it be better off, administratively, as a union territory?*

In the entire country, we're told that minority appeasement is a wrong thing. If that is the way it is, then so be it. Why does that not apply to Jammu & Kashmir as well? Jammu and Kashmir is an overwhelmingly Muslim majority state. Why is it that over here, minority appeasement is the order of the day. Nobody asked the people of Kargil if they wanted to be separated from Jammu & Kashmir. Why? Did they not have a right to a voice? If you think the Buddhists have no place in Jammu and Kashmir, fine. But then what did the people of Kargil do? Did they not deserve to be heard? So I do not understand how it is that what is sauce for the goose is not sauce for the gander. I mean, in the rest of the country, appeasement is bad, but in Jammu & Kashmir, appeasement is the order of the day. You can't have it both ways.

Because the BJP can't win elections here, they have to completely rewrite the rules. I mean, it's almost like what the world did with hockey - year after year, Olympics after Olympics, India went and won the gold medal or Pakistan won it, and the rest of the world couldn't deal with that. So they just dropped the entire rule book on hockey. They changed everything, and we barely managed to win anything after that. This is exactly what the BJP wants to do with Jammu & Kashmir. They can't win elections a fair way. They can't win elections an honest way. So they decide to break up the state and do a delimitation ahead of time. Everything about the 5th of August was about bringing Jammu and Kashmir at par with the rest of the country. If that is your stated aim, no argument. But then, why you have decided to cherry-pick? You keep the Public Safety Act in place because you want to misuse it. You detain me under Public Safety Act, which exists nowhere else in the country except Jammu and Kashmir. The whole purpose was to bring Jammu and Kashmir at par with the rest of the country. Then why have you got that Public Safety Act? Now, if you have to bring Jammu & Kashmir at the par with the rest of the country, then why don't we have delimitation with the rest of the country? Why don't we have assembly elections now and delimitation when it's due in 2026 or something like that? But no, you will single out Jammu & Kashmir with one or two of the small Northeast states, and you'll have delimitations here. Why? Because you can't win elections here on your own. And so you want to completely rejig the whole process and mess things up. You also have a completely different domicile law that applies in places that you want to protect like Himachal, Lakshadweep, Andaman, the Northeast and elsewhere. But in Jammu & Kashmir, you have domicile laws which will rewrite the demographic structure of the territory.

Q: *It seems that what has surprised you and upset you the most are that the things that are guaranteed under the Indian Constitution have been denied to you and to the people of Jammu & Kashmir, and that the Indian constitution wasn't protected.*

Absolutely. It is disappointing that the body that we look towards to protect the Indian constitution—the courts of India—took so long to wake up to what was happening. Even today, Mehbooba Mufti's case is not being heard in the Supreme Court at the moment, even though she has been detained for over 260 days. How do you justify this? On the one hand, you have the Vice President of India in the Rajya Sabha waxing eloquent about how dissent is the cornerstone of democracy and how without dissent, democracy doesn't exist. And then you lock up scores of people in Jammu and Kashmir simply because you don't want them dissent. My sister spent a night in Central Jail in Srinagar because she was involved in a silent protest in Srinagar, holding up a banner. That's all she did. There were 15 women. She was the youngest, and she's just a year younger than me. She was the youngest woman in that protest, so you can imagine the age profile of that protest, and all 15 of them were taken for a night to central jail because the right to dissent does not exist here the way it does everywhere. That's it. These are the things that will be very difficult for me to explain to people if I were to wish to continue in electoral politics. And that's why I still don't know which way it will go.

Q. *Do you worry that if you boycott electoral politics going forward, you will cede more ground to the same forces that you believe are imposing harm and injustice on the people of Jammu & Kashmir?*

My party won't boycott elections. I'm not saying the National Conference will leave electoral politics because then the National Conference ceases to exist as a mainstream political party. And we are clearly not a separatist party. We are not a party that's demanding azadi (freedom). We are a party that is part of the mainstream. So I'm not for a moment advocating that the National Conference leaves mainstream politics or electoral politics. I'm talking purely about myself. I don't see myself as a member of the Assembly of the Union Territory of Jammu & Kashmir. I've been chief minister of one of the most empowered assemblies of this country. I'm not going to be chief minister of a union territory, where perhaps I can't even decide which peon I want working in my office. That's not for me.

Q. So you are not sure whether you want to continue in electoral politics under the current framework?

I really am not sure.

Q. When you retire, what are the two or three words or phrases that you would want to be remembered for? Something that could be put on your grave.

I would like to be remembered as a peacemaker. If I can play even a small part in resolving a generations-old problem in Jammu and Kashmir, that's honestly more than one can ask for.

Poonam Mahajan

As we step into Poonam Mahajan's apartment in Mumbai, we are greeted by her young daughter and an excited cocker spaniel. Over some home-cooked *vada pav* and *bhel puri*, Poonam Mahajan, the president of the Bharatiya Janata Party's (BJP's) Youth Wing and MP from Mumbai North Central, speaks candidly. We talk about her family crises, the importance of the BJP in her life, juggling motherhood with the demands of 24×7 politics, and pursuing her passion for the preservation of wildlife. We find in her a politician who is deeply embedded inside the party, has a modern outlook towards the development of Mumbai, and yet is deeply aware of and beholden to the more informal exchanges that characterize Indian politics.

Poonam's father, Pramod Mahajan, was one of BJP's most prominent second-generation leaders when he passed away at the young age of 56, shot dead by his own brother. She reveals that it wasn't her father's passing but 'how he passed away and what happened after it' that made it an immensely traumatic time for her. As she entered politics under pressure from party workers, the mystery surrounding the tragedy was the subject of insensitive and unrelenting media coverage. Furthermore, while grieving her father's demise, her brother Rahul Mahajan, too, gained infamy over a drug overdose charge (that was later dismissed). This left the 26-year-old Poonam to deal with both her father and brother's legal cases. 'Such things should not happen to anybody,' she tells us.

Poonam's entry into politics was also not easy. Unlike a Sachin Pilot or Jyotiraditya Scindia who also joined politics following their fathers' untimely passing, Poonam didn't have a seat to contest from since Pramod Mahajan was not an MP at the time of his death. In fact, a few years later when Poonam was first given a ticket—for the Maharashtra assembly elections in 2009—she actually lost by a big margin. Yet, she continued to work for the party, particularly for the Youth Wing. She was rewarded with a ticket to contest the Lok Sabha elections in 2014, an opportunity she grabbed with both hands as she defeated Congress's Priya Dutt by almost 2 lakh votes. She has never looked back since, and was re-elected in 2019.

The active engagement of her father with the party's organization appears to have left a deep impression on Poonam. She sees the BJP as a party of cadres, a party in which maintaining personal relationships within the cadre is part and parcel of being a politician. She speaks fondly of the organization, how it looks after all of its party workers, the small pension her mother still gets because she is the widow of a party 'karyakarta', and the transformation of her 'uncles' (father's friends) into colleagues. While membership in a cadre-based party has distinct advantages, it is not without its challenges. Even though the BJP does not impose any gag orders on its members, it does expect some degree of adherence to its ideological positions. BJP politicians, like Poonam, working in a cadre-based ideological party, do not have the same degrees of freedom as dynasts who sit atop party organizations do.

The ideological and institutional constraints do not, however, influence the fact that Poonam Mahajan is a Mumbai politician. And as one, her main concerns are joblessness, infrastructural development (especially toilets), and ensuring that Mumbai remains an important global city, part of a global village where international influences and trends have a long-lasting impact. She balances the need for infrastructural development with environmental protection. Mumbai needs green spaces, and she speaks passionately of her efforts to replace '*jhopad-pattis*' (slums) with trees. In the corner of her living room, we notice a rather large sculpture of a pink elephant. When we ask her about it, her ardour for wildlife is perceptible; indeed, she even praises Indira Gandhi for passing the Wildlife Protection Act in 1972. She helps sell such sculptures for raising funds for elephant conservation through a charity that she is associated with.

When we had mentioned to Poonam's party colleague, Varun Gandhi, that we would be meeting her, he was effusive with praise for her, revealing that she is very caring and goes out of her way to help and support others. We see this in action ourselves—Poonam repeatedly offers to help us with this book and other endeavours. She is warm, friendly, and very comfortable in her own skin, often making jokes at her own expense. She is also unpretentious and straightforward, refusing to give us the typical political double talk and preferring to tell it like it is.

While Poonam says her entry into politics was 'accidental,' her rise in politics is certainly not. At just 39, she now has both the platform and the resources to build a lasting political legacy.

Interview

Q. *You can impact millions of lives by being a social worker or being a businesswoman. Politics comes with its fair share of challenges. So, why did you choose to join politics?*

I will give you my father's example. When any MLA, MC, MP, or if any party worker passes away, the first thing my father used to do (especially if that person was a public representative) was he would give his wife or son or daughter that one opportunity. It is not always about winning the seat. Sometimes you lose too. It is not always the emotional game that you have to pick. But that's the only source of survival for the family because that party worker has not done anything else his entire life. In most cases, he has only done party work. My father also started a pension scheme in the party. My mother also gets it. It is not much but it is given since a senior level of the party has passed away suddenly so that is how the party takes care of you. So, that's a matter of survival at that time. About why I got into politics—I will be very honest. I had no idea I will be in politics. I will not say that the first step was that I wanted to change the world or make a difference. It was something which I felt was right. But I was still unsure when I entered. After my father's death the political gurus and bosses with whom I work now, my uncle, friend, someone was coming to me every day asking me to join the party. And getting into that foray suddenly is actually very difficult for a person who does not have any backing. And I didn't have any backing. I will not say my entry into politics, at least at first, was with an agenda. I can't lie. Everybody asks me why you got into politics. I never say to make a difference. I say it was an accidental entry for me. Family wise, everybody expected my brother to lead because it is very typical of an Indian family or Italian family or any other family that the son will take over from the father. And he is older than me too. But the situation changed a lot. I had my father's legal case. We had a very different situation with my brother's legal cases. I learnt a lot from my father's case and my brother's. That time I didn't have any backing. And thankfully, I pulled through that transition and now I have now been in politics for 12 years. I am 39; I started at 26. My defeat in Vidhan Sabha elections and my victory in the two Lok Sabha elections, my work as an MP, and as a Youth Wing president all have taught me a lot. I believe that it is a blessing, and I need to make an impact or it's a disservice to humanity, and to myself.

Q. What are the things that you would love to be remembered for? Secondly, what are the challenges you face right now in trying to do to the things you want to do, both as a politician and, as a female politician?

I don't know if I will be remembered or not. I haven't even thought about it. I have a plan for the next five years and one for 20 years from now. That's how I work. I don't jump straight from now to 20 years later. I just want to go step by step, because I have seen enough defeats and victories. My father used to say 'Sammaan milne ke like panso apmaan sehen karne padte hai' (To gain respect one has to bear five hundred insults). I have learnt my lesson and that's how I have even wired myself. My political heroes are very different. It's a cliché, but my father is my hero! Why? It has been 12 years since he has passed away. I entered Parliament in 2014, and in more than five years since then, there hasn't been a single day when somebody—a peon, minister or MP from any party—has not told me a different story about my father. Earlier, they could not connect with the family to tell that Pramod ji did this for me or this is the experience I had. Now when they come to know about me, they share such beautiful experiences. That's what I want to be. If I was aware of these experiences when I was starting out in politics then I would have had more arrogance. But now, because of them, I have humility. This man has done so much and I didn't even know. I am not a feminist. But feminism is important to me. Russia is my favourite country, and Russia's best time was when Catherine, the Great, was the Tsarina. Of course, there is a suspicious story about her becoming a queen, but during her rule art, culture, politics—everything was at its peak, she created the golden age for Russia. The golden age of Britain was also under a queen! I believe that if a woman has the capacity, and she is ready to accept it then she should take charge.

Q. *But within the Indian political system, women get very little representation. The presumption about the BJP on the street is that it is a male-centred party …*

No, no. BJP is the only party that has enough women. We had two women together in the Security Council—the defence minister, Nirmala ji and the late external affairs minister, Sushma ji. Now Nirmala Ji is the Finance minister. And we have many other female leaders. I myself had the chance to open the IIM Bill in Parliament, against Shashi Tharoor. And now, I am the Youth Wing president. We have seven wings in BJP, the Kisan morcha, ST morchas, et cetera, and the Yuva morcha is the most important because most of the BJP leadership emerged from the youth wing leaders. Shivraj Singh Chauhan, my father, Rajnath Singh, J.P. Nadda, Dharmendra Pradhan—all were national Youth Wing presidents. One or two failed, others just took off. I was just told, 'Poonam, you are becoming the Youth Wing president.' They did not say that because you are a woman you should be the Women's Wing president. No! They said you become the Youth Wing president. I said, 'Thank you Amit Bhai! I'll start working.' It starts from the family. I said this on Barkha Dutt's show as well, I could see the blue sky since childhood. I didn't have any glass ceiling. I imbibed gender equality from my parents. My father never woke me up early. 'Let Poonam sleep. Wake Rahul up!' he would say. My brother can make better tea than me and I can give better speeches than him. My mother never had a problem with this. And luckily my mother-in-law is also such a chilled out person, I still don't enter the kitchen. I have always seen parity. I always tell the women in my team that sometimes women do not want women to succeed. When we help each other, we are still in competition. I know that people talk behind my back. One of my Youth Wing people said, 'Now womenfolk will lead the youth.' That poor guy is working under me now. I just gave him a lot of work to see how a woman can make you work! But this happens everywhere.

Q. *So you have not found it to be a challenge in any way?*

Yes, it is a challenge as a mother. I'll tell you about one incident and I'll quote the person. Kirron Kher and I were chatting. One male MP came to us and said, '*Hum logo ne ek discussion kiya tha, tum log aaye nahi.*' (You both didn't attend the meeting we just had.) Kirron Kher is a strong lady. She answered him, '*Kya karein bhai saab, humari biwiyaan nahi hai.*' (what to do, we don't have wives.) I loved her answer. I said, '*Sardaarni kaam par lag gayi.*' I was teasing her. I said, 'KK you spoke so well.' She said, '*Kyuki biwiyaan nahi hai, toh beta bimaar pade to humein hi karna padta hai yeh.*' (Because we don't have wives, if our son falls sick we only have to take care of him.) The answer really struck me and I use it everywhere. Because *theek hai* (alright) I am the mother to my constituency, I have to be a motherly person to my Youth Wing, lakhs and lakhs of people who are working under me, my team. When my daughter is unwell and I am not there, that's a challenge, it hurts me. But we as a family work together. I don't see challenges as a woman. No, I was not raised like that. If I am not raised like that, how will I see that challenge? So thankfully I am not raised like that.

Q. *What about the family crises that you have faced? You were only 26 when your father passed away. How did the incident impact you?*

My father passing away was not an issue. The issue was how he passed away and what happened after it. My family was completely used by the media. I am a very private person. I don't believe you need to do a lot of PR to stay connected. If you are a good person, people connect with you. If you are a useful person, people connect with you. So after my father's death, one Hindi news channel started this Diwali Bonanza Win a Gold Coin contest. There was a question on the ticker. Who killed Pramod Mahajan? The options were brother, uncle, et cetera, and one could win a gold prize. That struck me hard and actually put me in a shell. But in life, I think people's destinies are planned and one has to manoeuvre around it. You just have to work towards it. You don't know what's happening. And I face a lot of things. I have faced court cases. When my father's case was going on I had learnt the deposition by heart. I was not a lawyer. Every day from ten-thirty in the morning to five in the evening, I used to sit on a bench next to a very famous criminal who had his case in the next court. Life has been really, really difficult for me, such things should not happen to anybody.

Q. *What are the things you would not compromise on, in political life?*

I don't compromise on my promise. I am very clear as a Member of Parliament. If people come to me with an agenda and a problem to solve which is under my jurisdiction, I explain to them how it works. Because I am not the only party involved. There are five hundred things you have to do. But if I promise then I do it. Or I tell them I can't do it. Sometimes, being a woman helps me. You can't argue with women. You can argue with a man. So I use that quite well. And people have gotten used to it in my constituency. I have not had to compromise greatly. I am telling you about the brighter, positive wave in my party. When you are clear with your ideas, even your organization and people who are heading the organization know how to treat you. That's what I believe. And if there is something where I have to compromise, I turn things around when I work. If I can't do that why am I a politician? I find a way. I know how to do it. What kind of a politician are you that you don't know how to work on your way and your ethics and beliefs?

Q. *Why are you in the BJP? What is different about the BJP, from say Shiv Sena or the Congress?*

Let me give you a very clichéd answer again. I am in BJP because my father was in BJP and I have seen the atmosphere growing up. A lot of people have told me that I am different from BJP, I say what do you mean by that? Just because you have typecast a particular party and their leaders, you think that I am different. Why I am in BJP is because what I am is what the BJP is. I am quite comfortable in my thought process. I believe in the ideas that BJP has always put forward. Such as the ideology of reaching out to the last person. Congress is a party of voters, it plays games. BJP is a party of workers, *karyakarta*. And I believe in that; team-work, everyone getting together, even families. Now the party has grown too big but I have seen the party's meeting happening in my house, which was a two-and-a-half bedroom house, and this happened till 2004. Leaders in BJP have never told me not to say this or that. I have very strong views on some things, such as freedom of speech, and I assert them very strongly. They have never told me why did you say this or that.

Q. *Do you think there is a fundamental organizational difference between your party and the others?*

I am lucky. Because in other parties politicians have to follow a gag order. This has been told, this has to be done. We also get orders—it's not that we don't get our three lines, but typically we have ideological orders which the BJP always align to. We support it. It's always like that—99.9 per cent. My father always taught me that nobody is bigger than the organization. Organization is created by people, not by a person. So, that is how it works here. I pity people that they don't have this kind of organizational structure. It's very easy to credit one person for the success of a party, the party leaders. But when there is a defeat the party collectively has to work on it. And we do, all the time.

Q. *We have the youngest population in the world. Half the population is below the age of 25. Two-thirds is less than 35 years of age. As president of the BJP's Youth Wing, you have insight into the problems of the youth in India. Can you talk a little bit about your experiences and thoughts on this? How should leaders of the future be prepared for it?*

Any leadership in this country that wants to sustain itself has to think and work in a very different way. Young people, millennials like my son and others who will be voters in four or five years, are actually going to drive this nation forward. They have vague ideas about the nation. Their minds which are constantly surrounded by technology and everything, are more confused than us. My son has attention deficit hyperactivity disorder (ADHD). I had to change my son's school because he has ADHD and his school did not understand the concept. They said that he is brilliant but he doesn't sit in the class. I asked what I should do. They told me that it was my fault. I did not know much about it myself. It took a lot of time for me to understand. And ADHD is not an elite thing. When teachers in villages beat children for not paying attention in class—that could be ADHD. Leaders need a basic understanding of education in order to work on such things. We are working on a lot of other aspects like this. I always say the youth are the energy of this nation, if we harness it, it will give us electricity. Otherwise, there will be an explosion. With things like education. We as parents, we as younger leaders should understand what's changing and what are the disruptions that are likely to occur. In '96, we had this big *Rashtriya Adhiveshan*, when Atalji became the PM, which was organized by my father. The front page of every newspaper ran the headline 'The 5-star culture of BJP' because my father was holding his Motorola phone in the picture. He was really angry that day. After he cooled down he called a press conference, where he said, 'It's a wonderful photo to put on the front page. In ten years, even a herdsman will be using a cell phone to call his companion ahead of him to say "Wait for me, I am coming".' And that's exactly what happened by 2006. So it is about how as a leader you understand disruption, accept it, and work with it.

Priyanka Gandhi Vadra

Priyanka Gandhi Vadra has always been somewhat of an enigma for large sections of the Indian public. This is in part because she bears an uncanny resemblance to her grandmother, Indira Gandhi, in both her looks and mannerisms. It's also because many find her to be extremely charismatic and the natural inheritor of politics in the Nehru-Gandhi family. 'Will she, won't she?'—the question of whether she would formally enter politics remained a matter of intense speculation for the better part of the last two decades and has only added to her aura. Meanwhile, little was ever known about the self-admittedly reclusive Priyanka who stayed far away from the limelight.

In 1999, the 27-year-old Priyanka was struggling to choose whether or not to contest the Lok Sabha elections when her friend suggested she leave Delhi and go on a retreat to be able to make an independent decision. Somewhat accidentally, Priyanka landed up at a *Vipassana* centre where she spent 10 days doing their meditation course. In the process, she came to the realization that she did not want to join politics. She also discovered a few things about herself, most notably that she was still holding on to repressed anger and pain since her father's assassination, eight years prior. For most of the next two decades, she remained the ultimate insider on the outside, her political activity restricted to small roles she played during the election campaigns of her mother and her brother.

A few weeks before the 2019 elections, however, Priyanka surprised everybody by announcing her formal entry into politics. What was most surprising about the move was that she did not take up a large national role or contest from a seat. She chose, instead, to take on the party's most daunting challenge—to revive its organization and fortunes in the key state of Uttar Pradesh as the general secretary of All India Congress Committee (AICC)—a move that earned her much praise and media fanfare. Priyanka believes that the Congress has a strong vision and ideology but lacks the organizational structure to be able to effectively communicate that vision to the public. Acknowledging the pressure from her brother to join the party for a good while, she nonetheless insists that the decision was one she made herself, arrived at after a process of deep introspection.

It is difficult to truly appreciate Priyanka's choices without understanding her unique family history and its influence on her life. In her case, the personal and political have been inextricably linked to each other from an early age. It is for this reason that our interview with her is unlike any other: we spend a large part discussing her personal life. We speak of, among many things, the influence of her grandmother's and father's assassinations on her upbringing, the bond she shares with her brother Rahul Gandhi, and her approach to dealing with the allegations of impropriety levelled against her husband, Robert Vadra, which she reveals deeply impacted her children. Despite her reputation for being a very private person, we are pleasantly surprised to find that she is more than willing to open up on a wide range of topics for the very first time.

Sharing vivid memories and anecdotes, Priyanka gives us a deep and nuanced understanding of what it meant to grow up in the Nehru-Gandhi household, particularly in the 1970s and 1980s when the family was at the height of its power, prominence, and also, vulnerability. She reveals that her and Rahul's childhood and education were completely disrupted after Indira Gandhi's assassination—they were forced to leave schools abruptly, were not allowed to leave the house or meet their friends for months on end, and essentially spent many years homeschooled with little access to the public sphere outside.

Evidently, the assassinations also had a deep personal impact. After Indira died, Priyanka and Rahul lived in fear of their father meeting a similar fate. She wouldn't sleep until he got home every night and would 'think that every time he was going away, he was not coming back'. Being upset became a habit for both her and her brother; this was exacerbated by the 'long stretches of loneliness' when they were confined to their house while their parents were busy with official duties. After their father's assassination a few years later, Priyanka reveals it took her many years to process her feelings of pain and anger. It required a sustained personal effort, covering everything from meditation courses to even a visit to the Vellore jail to meet one of her father's assassins, Nalini, in a bid to receive closure.

On meeting Priyanka, it is easy to understand why a lot of people find her charismatic. She has a warm and natural presence about her. Unlike other politicians, Priyanka is open, straightforward, and very comfortable in revealing her personal contradictions, weaknesses, and true feelings. It is easy to tell that she is very self-aware and comfortable in her own skin.

Whether or not these personal qualities will translate into political success, with or without political ambition, remains an open question. Priyanka joined the Congress at a particularly perilous time—the party is being trounced on all parameters by the Modi–Shah juggernaut. Besides, it is yet to be seen if she will claim a bigger, more pan-India role; and even if she does, how she will tackle the risk of overshadowing her elder brother. For now, she is singularly focused on the task at hand—reviving the Congress in Uttar Pradesh. She is open about the party's shortcomings in the state and is acutely aware of the scale of the challenge ahead.

What is clear to us, however, is that she is in this for the long haul. And if she were given a larger role in the party, she would likely be a force to reckon with, even for the best in the business.

Interview

Q. People know very little about your interests and passions outside of politics. Could you talk about some of those? What is it that you like to do in your free time when you are away from all of this?

Well, I have been a housewife for many years, so my downtime is generally cleaning up the kitchen or cooking something. I love photography and I am also a master Scuba diver. I have done some courses on freediving with my brother. I love wildlife so I try to go to the jungle as much as I can with the kids. I read a lot and I also write a little bit.

Q. What do you write?

Well, I just generally would write for many years for myself for a record of what was going on in general. But I have never published anything like that. I have got a book deal recently, to write about my experiences about my meeting one of the ladies who was involved in the conspiracy to assassinate my father. It is a memoir-style sort of thing.

Q. Just after Mrs Indira Gandhi's assassination, your father, Rajiv Gandhi, said in an interview, 'what is very difficult is what the children have to go through. They can't go out and play. They can't be normal children …. And, if anybody had to really sacrifice, it's been the children.' He even said that your education had been 'messed up'. Would you say that your upbringing had been impacted severely? Did you have a sheltered and protected childhood?

Our upbringing and education was heavily impacted by the events in our family's life. I was 12 and my brother was 14 when my grandmother was shot. We lived in the same house as her.

Until about a few months before that, during Operation Blue Star, our lives were pretty normal. If we had bodyguards we were not aware of them. They would probably be people in plain clothes, employed in the school as servers et cetera, but we had no knowledge. Unlike what is projected about us, our family was not and is not very rich, opulent, or flamboyant. We grew up in a very frugal home considering my grandmother was the prime minister and my father was a pilot. We played on the streets with other kids and had a gang of about 30–40 kids who would cycle all over the place and create mischief. Just about a month and a half before my grandmother was shot, both of us were suddenly pulled out of boarding school. One day somebody came to pick us up and brought us home. Thereafter we were put into schools in Delhi. About a month and a half after we were enrolled in schools in Delhi, there was an incident when it was suspected that there was an attempt to kidnap us. Then my grandmother was shot and we were withdrawn from school. Thereafter, from the age of 12 to till when we went to college, we were homeschooled. So, certainly, our education and our socialization were greatly impacted. Since our interaction with kids in our age group became very limited to one or two kids, we were sheltered in that aspect. However, we were not sheltered otherwise because we were actually in a very adult world. We were hearing about the political problems, the problems that my father was facing, dealing with the attacks on my father by the media and the opposition, and also the dynamics between people around our parents changing drastically with the rise and fall of power. So we dealt with an adult world at a very young age. But, at the same time, we were sheltered from having a normal childhood. We were not allowed out anywhere, except for maybe one hour on a weekend, but we could not go to the same place again. There were all sorts of rules.

Q. *Do you think that is when you became a little bit reclusive and learnt to be comfortable in your own skin?*

197

I actually think I became reclusive later. I was an extremely extroverted and competitive child in school. I would participate in everything and partly also got thrown into everything because they thought that my grandmother would come and watch. So, one of the things about growing up in this kind of world is that your assessment of yourself is very hard to achieve. You don't know if you are in the gymnastics team because you are a good gymnast or because your grandmother is going to come and watch your gymnastics competition. So, as a child, that throws up certain issues. I think I became reclusive later when the tension from the media increased. In fact, we were used to having a very private life. And as children, especially because we were confined to the home my mother protected our privacy fiercely, as well as her own. She did not want my father to be in politics. She treasured her private life with him. We grew up away from the media glare. There were never really any pictures of us in the media, unless we were in an official function. I think as an adult I became more reclusive when I had my own children. The media world had changed completely and it had become much more intrusive. I think it was almost a protective measure to preserve my own privacy and my kids.

Q. *Could you talk more about the dynamics around the family chang-ing with political rise? In what ways did they change?*

One great privilege of being brought up in a family like mine is that you get to observe human behaviour around power very closely. It teaches you a lot about how to deal with those things and it teaches you a lot about life. There were dynamics around my father which experienced change. For example, by the time he became the prime minister, my father had his cousins and friends in politics. I think one of his best friends was his defence minister and his second cousin was the home minister. There were huge public falling outs between the three of them. So things like that. As a child, you understand and interpret these situations in your own way and as an adult, you look at them differently and you learn from them. So, definitely, there were changes. I think power, by its very nature, isolates. The access to those sources of power is valuable and is controlled, and that throws up certain dynamics.

Q. *How has your experience as a child with a disrupted upbringing and being part of an important political family informed your approach to raising your own children and family?*

So the first thing is that I wanted to prevent my children from experiencing the violence and the stress that we did. My grand-mother was shot when I was 12, my father was killed when I was 19. So the seven-year period between the two assassinations, we actually lived in fear of my father's assassination. I would not go to sleep until I heard him coming back home at night. And I would think that every time he was going away, he was not coming back. So, a lot of my effort towards my children has been to give them a very normal childhood. They have grown up quite differently than the way I did. Not in terms of the value systems, though. The value systems are probably almost identical for them. But, in just the fact that they have lived pretty freely. Of course, there have been times when they had bodyguards. But, I have attempted to give them a very normal life and to keep them out of the media glare completely. So, for example, they do not have public social media accounts in their own names, because I have encouraged them to keep their private life private as well. They have dif-ferent usernames and their friends know that they have private accounts. My daughter didn't know who the prime minister was until she was about in class five or six. It didn't register to them what their family is. For example, my son until he went to Doon school, which was a boarding school, where he suddenly discov-ered that everybody had a view of his family, everybody had an opinion. Somehow they remained fairly sheltered till they were 12–13. Because also, the schools they went to, all the kids grew up with them. So they used to just come in and out of the house like normal, and my house had nothing really fancy about it. It is just like anybody else's.

Q. *You have grown up in a house with very strong women around you. Do you think that there are any distinct challenges women face in politics? What has your experience been?*

I think women face more challenges than men do in all spheres of life. In politics, especially at the grassroots level, when I see a woman who is politically active, I really admire and respect her because I know the sort of social pressure she has to go through. For example, for her to come for a rally at five in the evening in a rural area by herself is already much more difficult for her than for a man. For her to gather 50 women, put them in the car somehow and bring them there is even more difficult, especially in rural and semi-urban settings. Women have to handle many things at a time, we are multitaskers. I finished my daughter's IB presentation at 2 am last night and woke up at 6 am to do some other files that the Income Tax and the Enforcement Directorate were asking for, and here I am at 9 am. And plus I have people coming home for dinner, so I had to arrange for that. So, women just by the nature of the things that we handle, we have to handle more. We, in India, and in the rest of the world as well, face a lot of social pressures that men don't. So I think it's really admirable when a woman puts herself forward and takes on something which is as public and as outward-facing as politics, especially if she comes from a non-affluent background.

Q. *You were really young when your grandmother and your father were assassinated. What are some lessons or values you feel you imbibed from them that had a lasting impact on you and influenced your approach to both politics and life in general?*

Both my grandmother and father impacted me greatly. They had a very similar value system. They have taught me the value of truth, honesty, and giving your best to whatever you are doing. When I was a housewife, I tried to be a good mother, gave my best to do that job well. And now that I am in politics, I try my best to do this well. There are so many things that one learns from their parents and grandparents, I don't think one can quantify it. I have learnt a lot from their lives and deaths, and even from the violence of their deaths. I learnt a lot about myself also. There was anger and a lot of feelings after that I had to deal with and process it, and I experienced how slowly you come to understand anger and pain differently through time.

Q. *Everybody has their own way of dealing with these kinds of things. How did you deal with the anger and the pain?*

I think when an event like that happens, the natural reaction is anger. As a child, you don't realize that you have anger, but as you start growing older, you realize that you are carrying some anger within you. I actually did a lot of *Vipassana* meditation courses, which I accidentally attended without knowing what they were all about. Back in 1999, there was a question of whether I should stand for an election, and I thought to myself, that I would not be able to make up my mind over here because everybody is going to tell me what they think I should do. So, I should go somewhere quieter and a friend of mine told me why don't you go to this retreat, it lasts 10 days. I had no idea that it was a Buddhist retreat. So, I went off to a *Vipassana* centre to make this decision and in the process, I discovered quite a lot about myself. I discovered that my concerns were not as grandiose as I thought they were. I had anger and hurt that I had not processed and I began dealing with those. It was about eight years after my father's death that I actually started processing these feelings.

Q. Not everyone gets rid of these feelings. Do you think that you are much less in anger and pain now compared to when you were younger?

I used to think that one does not get rid of these feelings. But I realized that one can get rid of those feelings and I don't feel anger like that anymore. I think when this sort of trauma happens, one tends to get used to being upset. It becomes a way of being. And I think for us because we were confined to home, there were long stretches of loneliness, where just two of us hanging around in an empty house, parents were touring quite a lot for work. So, we sort of got used to that thing, of being alone and having to deal with pain in some form or the other. Sometimes I think it tends to become a subconscious habit without realizing it and I think it is quite easy to break if you make up your mind, if you are able to see it in a correct perspective. I think a lot of it hinges on the idea of being a victim. If you get rid of that idea, then it is much easier to process pain.

Q. You have spent long stretches of time with your brother Rahul in your house. Given the upbringing, the tragedies, and the amount of time you spent together processing these kinds of emotions, you probably have a different bond with him compared to any other sibling relationship. How similar are you to him? And in what ways are you different people?

I think he is much calmer than I am. If I have any vestiges of anger, he has got even less. He is definitely wiser. He thinks more long term than I do. I am more in the moment. He will think 15 years ahead, if you ask me about 15 years ahead I will be too busy processing the next five days to be able to think that far. So those are some fundamental differences between us. In terms of our views about life and the world, we are very similar. We both believe in non-violence and we both try to be as honest as possible. Our value system is very similar and we are very close.

When we were kids we fought like crazy. It was probably because we had nothing else to do at home. We would have to be pulled apart at official ceremonies. I remember once when we were in Russia, my mother was holding one of us trying to keep us away from beating each other while my father was at some war memorial. So we used to fight a lot but at the same time, we were very close. Now, I would say that he is my best friend. He is able to say certain things which I don't like to hear often because he thinks much more deeply than I do about things, and he ends up being correct. So I realize that what he tells me is for my own good. And I am equally frank with him.

Q. *There has always been a huge clamour for you to join politics. Since you were young, many people have spoken about how you are a natural politician in your family. Obviously, people draw parallels with your grandmother. You are charismatic, you are comfortable with people, your oratory skills are great, you are comfortable with giving speeches in Hindi. In an interview with Barkha Dutt 10 years ago, you affirmed this in a small way where you said that, while you are reclusive, you are comfortable with people and this does come naturally to you. So, would you say that it is still true, 10 years later?*

I think that a lot of people who are actually good communicators and are able to be comfortable in public are actually reclusive in private. I think that has a lot to do with maybe the kind of social situations they find themselves in private. If you took me to a party, you would find me sitting in a corner not talking to anyone. If you take me to a village, I will be talking to everybody. I think it also a function of how curious you are about things in certain situations.

I think some things have become associated with me by default. I look like my grandmother so people assume I am like her in many ways. There are certain traits that I probably share with her like I would share with my mother or father or grandparents, like any child would. But, I think a lot of that got associated with me. I am as comfortable with people as they are with me. I think part of that comfort with me comes because what they are expecting is completely different. People come to us with a lot of preconceived notions about how we are and perhaps they think that we are going to be arrogant and nasty. They realize that we are normal people full of weaknesses, full of flaws in our character, just like them. It is also the function of when you sit and speak to people, they realize that you are just like them and they then open up to you and are comfortable with you. I think it is a mutual thing. I don't think I create excessive comfort in anyone. I think it is just the function of how they also react to me.

Q. *Back then you had also said that you are very clear that you don't want to be in politics and there are certain aspects of politics that you are not suited to. What aspects of political life do you feel you are not comfortable with?*

I think the thing that I was afraid of in 1999, and even today, was the public exposure. The fact that one would have to deal constantly with media, that part of it I find hard to … Everything else, I am absolutely fine. That part is something that if I could avoid, I would avoid.

Q. *Almost two decades back when you went to Vipassana, it helped you to decide not to contest elections and not to join politics. So, this time in 2019, what was the thought process you went through to arrive at a decision that now is the right time for you to join politics?*

I was very young when I first went for *Vipassana*, and young people sometimes go into the 'can I save the world' mode. So

Vipassana brought me down to the earth in three days. I realized my mind was full of trivial, small, and petty stuff and I realized that my preoccupations were much smaller and much more real than what I was imagining them to be. That made me feel that I was not ready to be in politics because the reasons why I thought I should have been in politics were actually flawed. So, I stayed out of it. Now, I have arrived at a very different place in my life now. Since I had created a so-called private life, I lived with my husband, I did my own things, brought up my own children, in my mind, I had created some sort of disconnect between me and the political world around me. So, I had assumed that because I took these decisions, I was somehow not connected, in the way that people thought I was, to that world. I completely stayed out of it. I did not participate in any political activity, any political decisions, contrary to what was believed. I saw myself as separate. I think over the last few years, as one grows older, you understand that you are not separated just because you are making certain personal decisions. I think you begin to understand that you are connected to the world in a way that you cannot disconnect yourself sometimes. A lot of the privileges I had, a lot of the life I was having—I am not talking about the tangible privileges I had, I am talking about, for example, the privilege to observe human beings so closely in extraordinary situations—were coming out of the fact that I was part of the universe of politics. As you grow older you realize these things more deeply. I think that process was happening in any case and that was a personal process. And as you realize that, you see your responsibilities as different. My ability to say 'No, I am not going to be involved in any of these and I am just going to look after my kids' that got diminished because I was on my own growing personally in a particular direction, and also because of what was happening in the country and around me. So, now I think more than ever what we are seeing is the destruction of everything that our freedom fighters fought for and built. All democratic institutions are under attack, whether it is the media or judiciary or Right to Information (RTI). Watching all this happening around you, and thinking that you are going to take care of your kids and pretend that you have nothing to do with it, became an impossibility. I just could not do it anymore. I just realized that there is so much that is going wrong. As I said, I have never been a crusader, it has never been about 'saving the world' and all that. But, certainly, there is something that you can do. Even if it is changing the minds of 10 people, you should be doing it, in such a situation as we are in today. That is the primary motivation. It was my own decision. I had always said that if I do join politics, it will be because I want to join it. Not because of anybody's pressure.

Q. *So it seems like the decision came naturally to you and that this is just something you arrived at your own, given the circumstances around you and the place that you felt you were at this stage of your life. So it wasn't your mother or brother convincing you to join?*

My brother had been telling me that for the last six or seven years that I should work with him. I have been disagreeing with him on many things related to that. He had been telling me for a long time. Yes, it was definitely my own decision. I had always said that anyway if I do join politics it will be because I want to join it. Not because of anybody's pressure.

Q. *So now you, your brother and your mother are all key influencing decision-makers in the party and you're also a very tight-knit family. How does that dynamic play out? I am sure that each one of you has different political instincts, different approaches, there may be a generation gap at some level. How do you strike that balance where you don't want to step on each other's toes but you do want to express your own instincts and let them play out?*

So far I have been looking after the Congress party in the eastern side of Uttar Pradesh. So, I really stuck to that and that is generally because it is a focused area. So, it is a separation in any case. I obviously give my views when we discuss politics, about certain events or decisions that have been taken. We are very open with each other about giving views. And whoever is the decision-maker, whether it is my mother or brother, it is their independent decision as well. All three of us have this personality where we hear everybody out and then do what we think is right. So far it has not been an issue.

Q. *In recent years your family has been in the limelight, with Prime Minister Modi and the BJP top brass all attacking your husband for impropriety in land dealings. How do you respond to this? How do you deal with this at the dining table with your children? How do you approach these topics and what kind of impact does it have on them?*

So when my son was around ten and my daughter was eight, I thought it was a good idea to let them know people said things about my family and they had to learn how to deal with this. We surfed the internet together and I found an article which said that my Italian grandmother was a KGB spy who used to smuggle antiques out of India, but my grandmother is such a typical Italian grandmother. She spends all her time in the kitchen cooking pasta sauce, cleaning the house, doing the ironing, and my kids knew that. So, when they saw the article they burst out laughing. We had a big laugh imagining her smuggling antiques, speaking Russian, and meeting KGB people on the sly somewhere. That was their first introduction to the fact that they should not believe everything they see or read about their family and they should assess it themselves, and also that they should not take it so seriously beyond a point. Having said that, over the last few years, with the BJP government at the centre, their father has been under tremendous attack and stress. He has been interrogated for hours by the Enforcement Directorate. Now that the kids are much older, they are exposed to television debates and all sorts of things almost on a daily basis. So, it has been hard for them. My son was in an all-boys boarding school, and he faced a lot of difficulties there because of these things. My daughter here has had to deal with things. Also, they worry about their father. But, on the whole, they are tough kids and they have learned to take it in their stride. There are moments where they are more stressed than others, but we deal with it together as a family. We discuss things and don't hide things. After all the allegations were made about my husband, my first reaction was to pay a visit to my 13-year-old son and to show him every single transaction. I talked to him about the allegations, and told him that this is what is being alleged, this is what the truth is, and that he has to assess it for himself. I explained this to my daughter as well. I don't hide things from my children, even the mistakes I make or the weaknesses I have. I am very open with them.

Q. Why not go through the same process for the public, in some way? Why not put out your version of the facts in the public domain?

It was very difficult. Initially, our party generally reacted with silence to these things. I think it has taken the Congress party a while to understand what the new media is like. Back in the 1980s, there would be an article in the newspaper from which you kept a dignified silence and kept working. That formula worked. Today, it doesn't work anymore. Today, unless you say, your word is not out there. Firstly, I think it took our party a while to get into that space. Secondly, frankly, neither the media nor anybody else was listening. There was very little space to put out your version of things. And I think by the time I got wiser to the fact that we should be speaking out and saying what our version of things are, the other versions were quite well entrenched.

You know, the other day somebody came to my house and said: 'This is your house!' I said 'Yeah'. He replied, 'This is shocking.' I replied, 'What do you mean?'. I was really not sure what that meant. 'You have cane furniture?' I replied, 'Yes well, this is my furniture.' So, I think they were expecting some Ambani style opulence, which they don't find. He had arrived earlier than I did. And he told me: '*Yaha toh main bula bula ke thak gaya, koyi aaya hi nahi. Maine toh sochcha tha ki itne saare* waiters *honge*, bearers *honge!*' (I came to your house and grew tired trying to call for someone. I had thought there must be so many waiters and bearers in the house). And then a few minutes the maid started coming out in her sloppy *salwar kameez* and he was looking at her thinking what is going on here. I think the BJP campaign's impression has been so strong and so well entrenched that even people who are close to us, who see our way of life, have probably questioned things. It was such a well-orchestrated campaign that went on for so long, that by the time we woke up to the fact that we ought to be telling our side, the damage had already been done. I think the impression was clearly formed. The government has been there for five years, it is on its sixth year now. Surely if there was something extremely incriminating, they would have found it by now. But it so happens that during election time they decide to call my husband to be cross-examined eight hours a day on a particular date that suits them, and then they go quiet. It is clearly a politically orchestrated campaign, and the propaganda machinery and media machinery has thrived on it. I think it would be partly our shortcoming that we did not get our act together and start saying our version early enough, and now perhaps people are not willing to hear it.

Q. *It sounds like you've given up on that. But do you worry that you and your kids will carry that baggage until it has been clarified and resolved in a sense?*

I don't think of it as baggage at all. To me, the truth matters. So, to me it doesn't matter. I mean, beyond a point, yes of course, as politician public figure, these things matter in your career in that sense. But, I really do believe that eventually, the truth matters more. For my kids, see I had to carry baggage of assassination, they would have to carry baggage of political propaganda against their family and another kid in a village carries a baggage of poverty, does not have food to eat, another one carries the baggage of having sick parents whom he can't take to hospital. I am certainly not one of those people who sit here and say what a painful life. I have experienced what I have experienced. I won't say anymore any less than anybody else has it; it is a different set of problems and different set of stresses.

Q. You have joined Congress at a very precarious time for the party. Your party is up against a different beast altogether. Why do you think that Congress is in the position that it finds itself today and how do you think the Congress can recover?

I can speak more for UP than the entire country because that is my immediate experience. I have actually asked these questions to all the party workers I have met there, including the 15 workers you may have seen sitting outside who are waiting to meet me. It is also a question I am trying to understand, why are we where we are? There are many, many factors, we are an old party that had been in power for 10 years at a stretch before the last election. That has created a certain inertia, there was a certain amount of arrogance, there was a certain disconnect with the public. We cannot ignore these facts. But, at the same time, there was a lot of good which was done. As a political party, unless you're connecting to the people you won't succeed. At the moment, as a party in UP, for instance, we are not connecting to the people. We are actually functioning within ourselves. So, for example, we have 440 member state committee. Just the fact it has 440 members means that it is probably non-functional. It is meant to be an executive committee. The process of selecting these people is also jaded now. Mostly it is based on patronage than on merit. I think the task really is to find young, good people who believe in the ideology of the Congress and who connected to the public. Currently, it is a mixture of people who have been there for years, say in a state like UP where Congress has not been in power for 30 years, they are a little tired and jaded, their elections come and go, and they are not sure whether we are going for an alliance or whether we'll fight on our own. What is the incentive for younger, more passionate people? If they don't think that at some point they will be able to fight an election or will be able to enter the power structure, then they lose the incentive. So that is part of it. Part of it is, as I said, is disconnect with people. I often ask the party workers what they do all day, and they tell me that they participate in party demonstrations, et cetera. However, if there is a problem in the village, are you the first guy there? Are you the guy to whom people come? Do you take them to the local police station to file a complaint with them? Do you fight for them against the local thug? That element of connecting with the public, at least in Uttar Pradesh, seems to have slipped. I imagine that at some level because we are such an old party and because a lot of our office bearers have been there for a long time that this has happened. I think that possibly that has happened in other areas as well. I would think of building those areas well. But it is a long haul.

Q. *There is a big ongoing debate over the role that your family should be playing within the party and in politics, some people say that Gandhis are the glue of the party and if they are no longer in charge, the party will split as it has in the past. On the other hand, there is a call for fresh leadership, there is a resonating sentiment that dynasts should not be automatically given higher posts in parties and that there should be an election, nurturing of younger talent, et cetera.*

211

How do you envision your family's role in the party going forward and how do you think about this debate and these tradeoffs?

As I see my brother's role and my role, if we could enable that process of actually empowering other young people to participate and become leaders, then we would have achieved something. I see that as my role. As my brother said very clearly in his resignation letter post the elections that he thinks that he should take responsibility for the last election. And perhaps not in the letter but elsewhere, he said that none of us should be the president of the party and I am in full agreement with him. I think that the party should find its own path also.

Q. There is also a sense that even if you have another president, the Gandhi family's looming presence in the party and there is a certain unique attachment and adulation among the party workers for your family, given the history and everything. They look up to you, your brother, and your mother as their true leaders. So, don't you think that being in politics while having someone else run the party will create a kind of awkward dynamic where people are still looking to you for inspiration and decisions? Wouldn't it undermine the sitting president of the party to have all of you still active in the party? What do you think of those tradeoffs?

I think it would only undermine somebody if that was the way we wanted to be. But if we wanted to step back and give other people the freedom to take decisions and do anything, I don't see why there should be an incumbrance. It depends very much on the way we look at it and I don't think that any of us look at it that way. I think if there were to be another party president, he would be my boss. If he tells me tomorrow that he doesn't want me in Uttar Pradesh but wants me to be in Andaman and Nicobar, then I would jolly well go to Andaman and Nicobar. It depends on me—I could say 'sorry I don't care, I'm going to do what I want.'

212

But, I don't think that any of us have that attitude. I think that we actually believe in the democratization of our party. My brother did a lot of work to that end. He conducted those elections in Youth Congress and National Students' Union of India (NSUI) because he wanted to enable new and young talent to come in. In fact, oddly enough, he was attacked from within his party for it.

Q. Some people say that one of the reasons why the Congress finds itself in trouble is that it has lost the independent ideological vision that distinguishes it from other regional parties. What do you think the Congress needs to do to present an alternative vision for India that is common, national, and that resonates with people? Do you imagine and contemplate such a vision? If so, what would compose that vision?

I think ideologically, the Congress party is very clear, but it has not been communicated with that clarity to the public in a long time. I think part of that issue is perhaps the internal shift of some of the leaders of the Congress party towards the end of the last government where the ideological stances were diluted to some extent. So there wasn't as much clarity as there might have been earlier. But that is also the way the Congress party works, there are different energies in the Congress party. There are leaders who are towards the right, those who are more towards the left, and there are those who are more towards the centre. It is not like the BJP where everything is uniform thought. There is space in the Congress party for different kinds of thinking, and it all comes together and everybody discusses and moves forward. I think where we might have failed is in the public articulation of that ideology. Perhaps one of the things the Congress party could do is actually have a brainstorming session where we come out with a very clear vision. One such thing was our manifesto this year. Our manifesto for this election, which was produced through consultation with different sections of the public and the

Congress leaders, is actually a good testament for what we stand for, in terms of policy and also ideologically. But again, we had a beautiful manifesto, but how much of that we were actually able to reach out to the public is where we fall short. I think that the ideology is there, and in some form or another the articulation is there. But it is not clear enough to the public. I think that is perhaps where we fail.

Q. *The prevailing sentiment among a large section of Congress sym-*
    pathizers, supporters, and workers is that the only person that can
    save the party, who can fight Modi and Amit Shah effectively is
    Priyanka Gandhi. And after the election, multiple people said that
    she should be the new president of the Congress. Could we ever see
    you as the leader and the driving force of this party?

If we look back at the last three or four years, I don't think any-body has fought Modi as hard as my brother has. I was not as vocal as him in the last election. He has been extremely vocal. He has taken the fight, whether it was to Gujarat during the assembly elections or afterwards in the general elections. Firstly, I would like to say that, to me, my brother is my leader and he will always be. Secondly, I see hundreds of people in UP and in different parts of the country who are very well equipped to fight the BJP. There are young and good enough leaders. I cannot tell the future, I do not know what is going to happen in the future. But, I think there are plenty of people who are capable to lead the party as well.

Q. *In this case where your brother has, after two elections, decided*
    that it is time to step down, do you see yourself taking on that kind
    of challenge at any point? Would you give it a shot?

I think I really have my work cut out for me in UP. It is an immense task, if we do manage to revive the party in UP, it will actually do a lot to the party in the rest of the country as well. It's a huge task.

I am at ground zero, and it is going to take a lot of time, a lot of focus, and frankly, I am quite happy doing it. I really do believe that if we do manage to build there it will be a huge contribution to the party. So, I feel that I would like to focus there and put my head down and work hard there.

Q. *How would you like to be remembered once you retire? Are there any phrases that you would hope to be associated with?*

Believe it or not, I am anti-legacy. I just do not believe in it. Even today, I am in politics not because I have a legacy to preserve, but because I believe that I better not ignore the privilege I have and do something, be it as small as possible if I am in a position to do it. I think kids should not have a legacy. We should not leave them with a legacy of good or legacy of bad. They should be free. And therefore, I frankly need not be remembered.

Rahul Gandhi

I t was autumn in 2017 and the campus of the University of
California, Berkeley was bustling with activity at the start of
the new academic year. Small groups of students had banded
together to commemorate the victims of the 9/11 terror attacks,
which had occurred 16 years ago to the day. A group of Special
Protection Guard (SPG) officers started inspecting the event
venue and surroundings. Two hours later, Rahul Gandhi would
be interacting with the students of the university and other
residents of the San Francisco Bay Area, in an event we had
painstakingly organized. The Special Protection Guard officers
had flown in overnight from New Delhi, without giving us any
prior notice. They had intercepted threats to Rahul Gandhi from
Sikh groups operating out of California. Indeed, we had received
letters from such groups asking for the event to be called off.
When we persisted, citing free speech, our event and livestream
links were hacked and redirected to YouTube videos of prominent
Sikh politicians berating Rahul Gandhi. As it started to rain, we
wondered if the event would see a low turnout. Much to our surprise, hundreds of students had already lined up outside Berkeley's
iconic International House, braving the heavy rain and wind.

Eventually, the main hall was packed and even the adjacent room started overflowing.

In the weeks leading up to this event, we were admittedly nervous about how it would pan out. Rahul Gandhi had never given a public interview in such a setting, and certainly not on the international stage. There were rumours that he was especially averse to interviews after a particularly harrowing experience on Indian television, at the hands of Arnab Goswami during the 2014 elections. Since then, he had mostly been in a shell, refusing to interact with the media. Hence, our impression of Rahul Gandhi was built out of hearsay and public perceptions, which were particularly unfavourable at the time. Vitriolic stereotypes about him were in heavy circulation: he was called lazy, unintelligent, and in politics out of compulsion rather than passion. His critics also claimed that he was often arrogant, aloof, and entitled.

When Rahul arrived a few minutes later, we got a chance to spend an hour or so with him. We were struck by his warm composure. He had no airs about himself, appeared calm and collected, and acted with the utmost decorum. As we sat in a room before the interview, Milind Deora, who was accompanying Rahul Gandhi, joked that Harsh was about to give him the same treatment as Arnab Goswami had tried to do in 2014. Rahul laughed, turned to Harsh, and said, 'Ask me anything you want and in any tone you want.' He kept to his word. The interview was no-holds-barred and extremely candid: we asked whatever we wanted, as did members of the audience, and he answered each and every question. At no point were we to refrain from broaching certain topics or questions. By the end, we realized that contrary to what the political rumour mill had propped Rahul up to be, he was forthcoming, generous, and frank.

A large section of the gathering came out of the event saying that their perceptions of Rahul Gandhi had been changed after seeing him in person. Back in India, too, the interview made headlines, dominating the prime-time debates across almost all television news channels and trending on social media platforms. Perhaps realizing the impact of the interview, the BJP fielded cabinet minister, Smriti Irani, to respond to Rahul's comments. In a press conference, she said, 'A failed dynast today chose to speak about his failed political journeys in the US.' It seems that Rahul Gandhi came across so well that many people, in fact, believed that the conversation was scripted. Over two years later, people still remember this event, often suggesting that it marked a turning point for Rahul as it gave him the confidence to put himself out there in a manner that he had never done before.

As we meet Rahul in 2019 for this book, it is once again a difficult time for him: only a few months back, he had been trounced in the 2019 elections. The massive loss, despite his best efforts, led him to give up the post of Congress president, leaving his party in a state of chaos and confusion. We inevitably spent a lot of time discussing his anointed dynastic privilege, the elections, and the next steps for the Congress, yet Rahul also speaks about his passions and motivations.

Many of our impressions from Berkeley are solidified when we interview him at his home in Delhi. Since this interview is more private, he opens up more and paints a picture of the emotional landscape of his mind: his thoughts and feelings, his response to the sharp vicissitudes of fortune, his interests, and his long-term vision. At one point, he offers to cook us omelettes, insisting that they would be the best we've ever eaten. From cooking to scuba diving to martial arts, Rahul is a man of multiple interests. He reads widely, and his taste is eclectic, ranging from Middle Eastern history to Chinese philosophy. He surprises us with a recitation of the lines of one of the poems of Mahmoud Darwish, a Palestinian poet. It also becomes apparent that in Delhi, Rahul values his privacy but gets very little of it. He is continuously in the presence of people, including his security detail. Even if he just wishes to exercise, his security tags along. Only occasionally they may let him run alone, instead choosing to follow at a respectful distance. Getting personal space, Rahul reveals, is often the main reason behind his multiple foreign trips.

One could easily assume that Rahul is quite sheltered since he is constantly surrounded by people and lives enclosed in a security bubble. As it happens, Rahul is quite aware of what is occurring in India. He has a good sense of the issues faced by the citizenry and is conscious of what is said about him by his opponents. He believes that his politics is his fight for the wellbeing of the common person and not for any personal gains. With a well-rounded character, Rahul comes across as self-assured, confident, and equanimous. His main task, he reveals, is to provide a better and more participatory politics not only for the country but also for the Congress Party. While we laud his commitment to reforming the party, we leave the interview wondering if he will be able to deal with the scale of the challenges and transformations needed in the Congress Party.

Rahul Gandhi is a respectful, personable, and discerning politician, yet can be a staunch critic of the state when required. He cares deeply about India and the Congress Party and plays his part with merit, without brandishing his privilege or pedigree. His general demeanour makes us wonder if he's ruthless enough for the cut-throat world of Indian politics, particularly when propped up against the Modi–Shah combine. Rahul's political future depends in large part on whether he can survive at a moment when politics appears to take no prisoners.

Interview

Q. You've had a very different life and upbringing as compared to anyone else, sometimes making it hard for a lot of people outside to relate to you. You've had a sheltered upbringing, you've been surrounded by security right through your life. You've had to move schools and colleges at different points because of security reasons, do you feel it's sometimes lonely being Rahul Gandhi?

My upbringing wasn't sheltered at all. My grandmother was assassinated in 1984 and my father in 1991. Mine has been a harsh and volatile upbringing, surrounded by security men.

I wouldn't say I've been lonely, because as a political leader you meet so many people every day! Over time I've evolved my own way of connecting with people by listening to what they're saying and being quite open to them. I enjoy those interactions. I learn from them. And it leaves me feeling quite fulfilled. Besides, like everyone else, I have my family and some very close friends that I enjoy spending time with away from work.

Q. People outside know very little about what you do outside of politics. We see you surrounded by cameras all day and doing your work, but what are some of the passions and interests you harbour or you have harboured in the past, outside of politics, in your personal life?

By nature, I'm a curious person. When I get interested in something I tend to deep dive into it, to understand its nature. That's just the way I operate. I will tend to go into detail and build a certain level of competence and understanding in that subject. Amongst the broad sweep of subjects I'm interested in are Indian philosophy, Buddhism, the history of the Mongols, WWI/WWII history, Middle Eastern history, Pakistani history, and Chinese philosophy. I tend to follow a shot-gun approach and focus on a single subject at a time, studying it in-depth.

As far as sports and hobbies go, I'm passionate about Aikido, a Japanese martial art in which I have a Black Belt. I'm a pilot. I love diving and I'm both a free diver and a scuba divemaster. I enjoy running and cooking. In fact, I can cook you the best omelettes you'll ever have!

Q. *You have all these passions and interests, so there's always been a sense from the outside, a lot of your critics have said that it seems like you're in politics out of compulsion and not passion. Is this your true calling? Going back in time, is this what you would do over again?*

I hate labels. Politics is a label. There's a tendency to put a label (politics for instance) on a person and then try to define him or her in the context of that label. Politics is very important to me, it takes up a lot of my time, but, I have other interests as well.

My political approach is built around listening to people and trying to help them achieve what they want to achieve. I go to people who I think need my help and I will raise their issues and try and fight for them. I spend a lot of time thinking about politics and discussing it. I love what I do. I'm passionate about it. I'm certainly not doing what I do out of any compulsion.

Q. *You've probably heard this question before, where people say you keep having to run away and leave for vacations. Is that a way for you to get outside of this craziness and harbour some of your passions?*

In India, I live my life surrounded by security men, 24×7. As a consequence, in India, I have very little privacy, other than when I'm in my own home. When I'm out of India, I have more space, more privacy. I enjoy learning from other cultures and I love inter-acting with people from different parts of the world. I don't see my trips abroad as vacations. For example, when I'm in the United States and if I visit Berkeley to interact with students over there, I learn from that experience. There are new ideas I'm exposed to; new ways of looking at things. These are extremely enriching experiences and that's what I enjoy most about travelling abroad. The truth is, I'm up against a formidable Rashtriya Swayamsevak Sangh (RSS)–Bharatiya Janata Party (BJP) political machine that attacks me 24×7, because it sees me as a threat, because it sees the ideas that I represent as a threat. So it has to paint me as someone who isn't interested, as someone with no understanding, as someone who only wants to go abroad on vacation. The fact that you are asking me this question, proves that their propaganda is somewhat successful.

Q. *We discussed this in Berkeley as well. How do you counter this machine that you're talking about? Clearly, it's working, it's reso-nating with people.*

It doesn't work with all people. It works and resonates with some people in an environment where all Indian institutions are captured. Where the press is completely under the control of the establishment. Where the Election Commission creates an election schedule that takes into account the RSS–BJP's political needs. There is a capture of the system aided by a tremendous amount of money and power. Of course, that's going to have an impact, but it also helps shape me. It forces me to adapt, to be more effective in my communication, more aggressive perhaps.

Q. *So you're not frustrated?*

Of course not! My duty as an opposition leader is to work for the weaker and marginalized sections of the society in this country that needs someone to stand by them, fight for them, so that their voices are heard. I'm constantly evolving. That has nothing to do with electoral victories or defeats and leaves me feeling anything but frustrated.

Q. The sense I'm getting is that you're in it for the long run, you're here for the people. Elections will come and go, but that's not going to have an impact on whether you remain in politics or not.

Absolutely! I'm here for the long haul. I don't run away from challenges.

Q. What keeps you ticking? What keeps you sticking with it?

I believe that the RSS–BJP ideology is dangerous for the country and that the imposition of that ideology on India and the capture of our key institutions, is going to have a very tragic outcome for the country. I love the people of my country, and in the twenty-first century dividing India along religious lines, along sectarian lines, ethnic lines, North–South lines, and East–West lines is going to irreparably damage us. I will do whatever I can to prevent this from happening. This is what keeps me ticking.

Q. You've always framed these elections as an ideological battle. Even after the elections, you said that this was a battle of ideologies and that this battle would continue. Why do you think Indian voters are resonating a lot more with Mr Modi and the BJP's ideology than the one you and your alliance partners are professing?.

The Indian economic model that worked in the 1990s and till about 2012 is not working anymore. The Indian people are unable to see a path out of massive unemployment, rural distress, and the bleak situation they find themselves in. They are worried, they are tense, and in that feeling of worry and tension they need something to hold on to and that something, unfortunately, is Mr Narendra Modi. Ironically, it is Mr Modi himself who has been largely responsible for the mess the country is in today, particularly our economy. One strategy Mr Modi has used effectively is to present India with an enemy, to focus their anger and frustration on, thus turning the spotlight away from his own incompetence and failures. It worked in the 2019 elections, but this approach has a limited shelf life and will eventually fail. I don't see this as a failure of the Congress ideology, I see this as a victory for the RSS–BJP propaganda machine backed by a subservient media, the capture of institutions, and tremendous amounts of money.

Q. I'm interested in this model you're talking about. You say that the economic model of India has failed.

Yes, it's run its course. Every model is designed or based on the peculiar circumstances of the time it was developed for. We don't live in 1990, we live in 2019. It's pretty clear that what produced wealth in the 1990s and till about 2010–12, is now accelerating inequality and has created a nation where people can't get a proper education, can't access healthcare, and where jobs are not being created. So one needs to rethink some of our basic economic ideas that we've taken for granted for almost three decades and try and figure out a new economic model that will help us break out of the shackles of extreme inequality that is generating tremendous anger and anxiety in our society. The tragedy is, that, that work is not being done. The tragedy is that we are having conversations about all sorts of things, but not about how unemployment can be reduced. We are not doing the thinking on how inequality can be done away with. If you looked at our 2019 election manifesto, you'll see that some of the thinking on how this process can be started, is in there. It's clear in the manifesto how inequality can be dealt with. We explained how you could develop a higher education system that is accessible to the people, how education can be made more relevant, and what can be done to solve India's agricultural problem. The blueprint of a new economic model is in our manifesto. But the RSS–BJP continue to live in denial.

The today Gross Domestic Product (GDP) growth has crashed to 5 per cent, the lowest in over six years. Manufacturing growth is down to just 0.6 per cent, which means manufacturing is dying in India and we're importing goods mostly from China. There is massive unemployment. But the BJP–RSS refuse to accept that India has an economic problem. So how will you begin fixing a problem whose existence you refuse to even acknowledge?

Q. *You spoke a little about how Chinese manufacturing is one of the reasons why we're in the mess we are in. Can you talk a little bit about that?*

China has completely dominated global manufacturing. They have built a modern manufacturing system that has out-competed everybody. That's one reason we are unable to create jobs here. I'm not blaming China, I'm just saying that they have done something effectively and we need to think about how we can compete with that. The Western world and India to an extent gave up on the manufacturing sector. They said that the Chinese are doing manufacturing, and we'll focus on services, marketing, and sales, and on building fancy logos and putting those on the back of products manufactured in China. That's not going to cut it. The Western world has realized that and India too must wake up to this reality. There's no solution on the table at present, but we need to make finding a solution to this massive problem a national priority. Manufacturing is going to change and it's going to be affected by modern technology, and I think there's an opportunity there for India, if India tries to grab it. But there is no sense of that right now.

Q. *We had a government under Dr Manmohan Singh who was the architect of the modern economic system in India between 2004 and 2014. We had the first majority government in 30 years under Mr Modi and we're still not seeing that new economic model develop?*

By about 2012, it became clear to us that the basic economic model we were following wasn't working as effectively as it had five to 10 years ago. It had some serious flaws in it. We began some initial work on rethinking that model, but we never got a chance to implement it as in 2014 the BJP came to power. Unfortunately, they continued with the same flawed economic model, without spending any time on fixing it. Consequently, we've dug ourselves into a deep economic mess. Other than rebranding our old Government programmes, created in Dr Manmohan Singh's time, very little fresh thinking has gone into how to fix our economic model so that we can deal with growing inequality and unemployment.

Q. *What you're saying is that if you had a government in power right now, you'd have to rethink this system as a whole. You're talking about a paradigm shift in how we view our policy preparation?*

Precisely! In the 1990s, when we first developed the economic model that India is following even today, we were a largely rural nation. Thirty years later, there is rapid urbanization taking place in India. That itself is cause for a massive rethink of our economic model as the basic assumptions that it's built on, have changed dramatically. People in urban India, in our cities and rapidly growing towns, behave very differently than people in villages. People from villages travel to towns and cities in search of employment. We had conceived of instruments and schemes like AADHAR and MNREGA to ease that transition, to allow seamless migration of large numbers of people between villages and cities. And to

226

allow them to go back to the villages when they felt the need to. The current government hasn't moved past those tools. It hasn't shown how they intend to solve India's urban issues. How they intend to provide a billion people access to a world-class education system. Or good quality and affordable healthcare to every Indian, not just the rich. There's so much that's broken that needs fixing.

Q. *As you said right now, you had the highest unemployment in 45 years, you had a weak economy across most macroeconomic indicators, socially, we had a polarized country. In a situation like this, you had a historic opportunity to uproot the BJP government. What went wrong?*

It's not what went wrong. It's what we had to fight! We didn't fight just the RSS–BJP. They were just the face or one component of what we fought. We fought all the institutions captured by the RSS–BJP. The entire Indian media captured and threatened by the RSS–BJP. Stacked against us were all the big businesses that were forced to support the BJP, financially allowing them to spend billions of dollars on their campaign. The entire system has been captured and redesigned to help one political party. Go and look at the funding, at the electoral bonds. See how much the BJP gets, how much the Congress gets, and how much the other parties get? We are no longer fighting a political party, but the entire institutional architecture of the country, which has now been firmly captured by the RSS–BJP.

Q. *That's a scary thought for the Congress as you think about future elections. You have state elections coming up, general elections in another five years. How do you approach it then, if you're saying you're not fighting a party but the whole system?*

When there is capture, there will also be resistance. That's the nature of the universe. What is capture? An attempt at taking away wealth from people. Who are you taking that wealth away from? From the poorest people in the country. But, they're not just going to sit there and say 'okay, take it', they're going to ask what's going on? How is what is happening fair? It's only a matter of time.

Q. *What impact did this election loss have on you personally? Were you expecting it? Were you surprised? Of course, you worked really hard. Did it hit hard?*

I didn't expect the BJP to get 300 seats. Frankly, nobody did! There are questions being asked about how it was possible for the BJP to get 300 seats when there was so much popular discontent against them and how they could predict the precise number of seats so accurately so many months in advance. But I'm not going to get into that. I'm working with the assumption that we held a free and fair election. As a politician, I respect the will of the people. They say we want to try Mr Narendra Modi again, okay, try him again. I laid down a clear vision for India, but the Indian people didn't agree with me. That's fine. That's the nature of a democracy.

Q. *The Congress finds itself in an extremely weak position right now ... is it in terminal decline?*

The Congress is not just an organization, it is also a set of ideas. Ideas like compassion, love, affection, respect, seeing yourself in the other, and seeing the other in yourself, religious tolerance, these are ideas that the Congress represents and these ideas have survived in India for thousands of years. The Congress may have lost an election and be weakened electorally, but the ideas we represent are as relevant today as they ever were, which makes me confident that we will bounce back.

Q. So what does worry you when you think about this loss?

What worries me is that you have a country of 1.3 billion people which is much more divided today than it was in 2014. You have South India which feels like the government is against them; you have the minorities—Muslims, Sikhs, Christians, Parsis, and others who are terrified. You have Tribal communities who are being exploited, threatened, and displaced so that the natural wealth of their lands can be extracted and stolen from them. This deliberate division of the country is not something that is sustainable and there will be far-reaching consequences for sure. That worries me. What also worries me is that we have some of the best talent in the world but at present, they see no future. Opportunities for our young people are drying up. Millions of talented, educated youth are unemployed. We have some of the hardest working farmers in the world, but we can't give them a life of dignity. These are the things that worry me. Electoral victories and defeats are a part of any politician's life in a democracy.

Q. You said that 2014 was a big learning experience for you, now you're saying that the Congress will reinvent itself. It hasn't done it after 2014, it's very clear that …

Let's get this in perspective. Nobody would argue against the fact that it was I and the Congress Party that fought most aggressively against the RSS–BJP between 2014–19. Nobody would argue that it was not the Congress Party which was countering the BJP and standing against it. Nobody can argue that we gave the BJP a bloody nose in the state elections in Gujarat, that we won Madhya Pradesh, Chhattisgarh, Rajasthan, and kept the BJP out in Karnataka. What India is soon going to realize is that the democratic process has been subverted, that now it is not one party against another, but the opposition parties against the power of the Indian state. This has not happened before. It has not happened in post-Independence India. That is the challenge we are facing and that we need to adapt to and prepare to fight.

Q. Given this situation, what is the Congress going to do? How will it be reinvented? And be made electorally more competitive against the BJP?

Congress has always stood for the aspirations of the people, and for their protection. That's the design. That's what we did during the freedom struggle and what it's done ever since. The Congress is a conversation and a set of ideas. The Congress believes in building a consensus to take India forward. That's not what the RSS–BJP do. They have a narrow, rigid, view of India that they want to impose on the Indian people. They're not bothered about how the Indian people feel about this. There is no dialogue. No debate. No consensus. Eventually, it is the rising anger against the imposition of their ideology on every Indian, that will lead to the electoral downfall of the BJP.

Q. So you're hoping not that Congress changes its trajectory, but that the public is …

I'm not hoping for anything. I'm absolutely certain that the capture of Indian institutions is not sustainable, and that the Indian people will realize that their most valuable asset, their voice, has been taken away from them. And that the Congress actually listens to and respects the voice of the people and is a much better alternative for India and the Indian people than the RSS–BJP.

Q. You are by far the most popular leader within the Congress. When the Congress workers are asked who they want to be led by, they point at you. After the elections, there was a clamour for you to stay on as president, but you stepped down. Could you tell us a little about why you did that?

The Congress Party lost the 2019 elections, under my command. The Congress has to develop a culture of accountability and that begins right at the top. I'm pretty clear in my mind that I am accountable for the 2019 loss and that I had to step down as a consequence.

Q. *Was that a decision supported by your family?*

We've obviously discussed this as a family and I've listened to and appreciated my mother and sister's perspectives. But I feel that the culture of accountability is missing at present in the Congress Party and the only way to inject that into the Congress system is by beginning at the top.

Q. *But would you be open in the future, if the party says they want you to come back as president, to lead the ship?*

I'm here, standing by the Congress Party and ready to fight for it because I believe in the Congress Party. I don't need to be the Congress president in order to fight for the Congress Party or to work on strengthening it.

Q. *For the Congress, the Gandhi family is its biggest asset, but it's also a liability because the BJP keeps bringing back this namdaar and kamdaar.*

That's just propaganda. I can give you a list of over a hundred senior RSS–BJP leaders all of whom come from political dynasties. As far as my mother, my sister, and I are concerned, we are driven by ideology. We fundamentally believe in the Congress ideology and will not compromise with our belief just to grab political power. The RSS–BJP that keeps changing like a chameleon in its blind pursuit of power, understands the power of the Gandhi family's commitment to the Congress ideology. In fact, they fear it, which is why we are the primary targets of their propaganda and systematic disinformation.

Q. *A lot of people who support your ideology, for whom this ideology really resonates and who are repulsed by the onslaught of the BJP ideology on the country, they are pinning their hopes on you, your family, and the Congress to come back electorally. What I'm trying to ask is do you have a strategy in play for yourself, family, and party, instead of depending on the public for …*

The Congress is an old party that has fought many, many national and state elections since Independence. The fundamental difference between the Congress and the BJP is that while the Congress is an instrument of the people of India, the BJP is an instrument of an organization—the RSS. We know how to fight the RSS–BJP organizationally and politically and have successfully done it in the past. In fact, leading up to the General Elections, we defeated the RSS–BJP in election after election across India. Obviously, in a democracy, it is the people who will finally decide the outcome of an election and any strategy we develop has to be effective in convincing a majority of the electorate that the Congress ideology and the Congress Party is a better alternative than the RSS–BJP.

Q. *Has it helped you to have your sister, who you call your best friend and confidante, join the party? What kind of role do you envision for her and yourself in the party?*

My sister is an extremely capable person, who has to chart her own political course. I'm happy that she's working in Uttar Pradesh because I think there's a huge opportunity for the Congress Party to make a strong comeback in the next state elections over there.

Q. Was it easy to convince her to join? To finally come into politics?

Priyanka and I had spoken about this before and her view was that while her children were growing up and still in school, she wouldn't be able to do justice to a full-time political career. Now that they're going to college, she can immerse herself fully and do justice to the role she has agreed to play as a general-secretary of the Congress Party.

Q. When you retire, what are the last two-or-three words or phrase you'd like to be remembered by? Something that would be on your grave, or something that would be etched in the memories of people?

I'm not too bothered about what people will say about me after I've gone. I'm more interested in the here and now and in what I do, what I stand for, who I stand with, and who I can help.

Jawaharlal Nehru said that he'd like his ashes to be scattered in the Himalayas. He didn't even want a memorial in his name. I don't think he was too bothered about what people were going to say after he was gone. Or whether they would remember him or not. I think he was much more bothered about his actions, while he was still alive! I think that's a good model to follow.

Rajyavardhan Singh Rathore

Hearing the name Rajyavardhan Singh Rathore, one immediately recalls images of a young man standing on the podium at the 2004 Athens Olympics, India's first individual Olympic silver medal in over a century around his neck. This triumph will always be considered a turning point in India's sporting history, yet it is merely one of the many ways Rajyavardhan has tried to contribute to the country. Unlike other Olympians, Rajyavardhan didn't start practising his sport at the age of five or seven. Rather, he began training at 28, just six years before Athens. Incidentally, this, he reveals, might make him one of the fastest ever to win a medal. Before that, he spent many years in the Indian army, primarily in Jammu & Kashmir where his unit was involved in counter-terrorist operations. He had a decorated military career spanning 23 years before he retired as a colonel in 2013 to make an unexpected plunge into politics.

Just like his shooting career, Rajyavardhan's political career was marked by a meteoric rise.

Attracted to Narendra Modi's leadership and the 'nationalistic' ideology of the Bharatiya Janata Party (BJP), he joined the party ahead of the 2014 elections. A few months later, he contested his first ever Lok Sabha election from Rural Jaipur and won with a thumping majority. Thereafter, he was inducted into Prime Minister Modi's council of ministers as Minister of State for Information & Broadcasting. In the cabinet reshuffle of 2018, he was given independent charge of the ministry and also over the more relevant Sports Ministry, with the important task of revamping India's sporting infrastructure. However, he has not yet found a spot in the new government despite convincingly winning his seat once again.

A soldier, a professional sportsperson, and an elected MP and minister, Rajyavardhan has witnessed life through many different prisms. As we approach his Delhi home to meet him, we are curious to learn more about his different avatars and how each interplays with the other. 'I am to my core, a soldier,' he says, revealing that the army has not only shaped his personality but also his approach to sports and now to politics and governance. Those who know Rajyavardhan well say that the soldier-figure is indeed intrinsic to his personality and he has a no-nonsense attitude to his work. In our interactions with him, we noticed that as well, although his serious pragmatism is masked by his congenial personality.

Rajyavardhan talks of his 'maverick decisions', first to take up professional shooting while being a well-settled army officer and then joining politics. The inspired choices stem from the love of the 'thrill'; he wants to take on new challenges and is not afraid to fail, making it easier for him to take such risks. He attributes his smooth entry into politics to a bit of luck, right timing, and the BJP's endorsement of new meritorious leaders from outside the system.

While his ingress into politics may have been uncomplicated, the adjustment was not. He talks about having to acclimatize to a system that is set in its old ways. He felt the pressure to adapt his management style and 'tone down a little bit'; the government and bureaucracy cannot be managed by a military approach, he realized. Yet, he reveals that he still feels the need to 'challenge the system' every single day. His rather diplomatic and measured answers seem to belie a deeper frustration with the bureaucracy.

Despite this, Rajyavardhan has not just survived but rather thrived since joining politics. His is a rare case of a person without any political background or abundant resources entering the political system from outside and achieving success in a short time. The question is, how long will he go before wanting to make another maverick decision?

Interview

Q. Most successful people enjoy success in only one inning in their career. You've been successful in the army, then as a professional sportsperson, and to some extent now in your limited time in politics as well. Can you tell us what made you choose to do each of those things? What made you first decide you want to join the army, and then go into professional shooting, and finally, after having those two successful careers, why did you decide to enter what people would call the 'muddy world of politics'?

I have never actually chased success, as such, but I have committed myself to my passion. Whatever I was really inclined towards, whatever I felt could give me happiness in the long run, I would commit myself to that. But I think the good part has been that I have been able to commit myself completely. I have tried to excel in it, tried to be my best in it. That resulted in my progressing ahead and achieving certain targets that we all set for ourselves. I have never sat back on my laurels because the thrill is in living your life, the thrill is in taking new challenges. What has gone by has gone by, whether it has been success or it has been failure, one just keeps moving ahead. To tell you the truth I don't fear failing, and I have failed a lot in my life, and I think that's a positive always. So all of these professional career choices that you mentioned came with god's grace and brought an opportunity to me, and I liked all of them. Be it serving in the army for 23 years, being decorated in the army and the military academy as well. Then becoming a sportsperson and playing for the country gave me different and wonderful experiences. I think the most expensive thing in life is experience. And so that way I am very rich with experience, and now I am getting to work with people who lead the country, so that is another treasure of experience that I am getting from them. And why politics? It is because our lives invariably get affected by the decisions our leaders take. We may not realize it, a lot of us don't realize it, but our lives do get affected. And to bring about a positive change in our society, around ourselves, and in the whole country, we have to be part of that leadership. Rather than leave the space and then complain about the poor quality of leadership, we all as citizens of our country need to commit ourselves to be that leadership or choosing the right leadership, and that's why I am here.

Q. Was it an easy decision to decide to join politics?

No, it wasn't an easy decision at all. You see typical politics in our country, I don't know about others, is that you need to have your godfathers and you need to have your family in it, you need to have large resources available to you or deep pockets, sort of unaccounted-for money which you don't mind spending. I think what one really requires in today's politics in India is not an abundance of resources, but an abundance of willpower and commitment to doing good for your country. Once that happens, whether we commit ourselves for a short duration of time or a longer one, to what extent we involve ourselves will vary from person to person, but we all must commit. So it wasn't easy. My family was surprised initially but they are used to my tendency to take maverick decisions. For example, when I was in the armed forces I was a well-settled army officer and then I suddenly jumped into the Olympics, so that was a sea change for them. And then from being a sportsperson to jumping into politics was also a massive change for them but they are used to it now. But I am grateful for their support. Without their support, I wouldn't have been able to succeed in any of the career paths that I chose for myself.

Q. And of course it could not have been easy joining politics and the system ...

No, let me tell you that there is no way to get into certain political parties in India without actually having your family members in it. You certainly cannot come up beyond a certain level, you can be at the grassroots but not beyond that. That is reserved for, or rather let's say that is a preserve of select few. I think the growth of the BJP was happening at this time, and the leadership like that of Prime Minister Modi was shaping up at a time when I was at a career point in my life where I was thinking that 'yes, this can be an option'. I think I was lucky in a way because this is the only party where people are selected on merit and a person like me, and there are, by the way many, more like me as ministers as well and as MPs in this party who had nothing to do with politics, but we have been meritorious in our own fields and were handpicked by the PM and his team.

Q. *What kinds of challenges have you faced? Can you talk about some of the frustrations and difficulties?*

To change the method of working of our country which has been accustomed to bureaucratic delays, corruption, nepotism, and to bring about a difference requires one to challenge the system on a daily basis. So, those have been the challenges. I wouldn't call them frustrations because we have been able to overcome them, so you don't get frustrated but it is an eye-opener certainly about how this country had been governed earlier and satisfying now that we are able to bring a change. It is challenging because we have to overcome the past practices, the past mindset of a '*chalta hai*' attitude, and so that is now changing.

Q. *What about you being a military man for 23 years being in the army, has that shaped your approach to politics, or even your out-look towards life in any way? Has it had an influence on you and on your politics?*

The army has built my personality, it has shaped me. I am to my core, a soldier. That has helped me in my sports and then helped me in delivering clean and efficient governance as part of the prime minister's team. The die-hard attitude of an army man, the talk-straight method of working, the ability to adapt to the environment and take people along, taking strong ownership of our mission are things that helped bring a difference to my ministries and to all the other work assigned to me.

Q. *You are known for being a straight shooter with your words, which is like a pun for you. Did that ever ruffle any feathers initially or did that rub people the wrong way in politics, in your ministries, or has it been a smooth ride for you?*

I think I've had to adapt a little bit, tone down a little bit because after all this is not military and there is a bureaucracy which is, like I said, accustomed to certain old habits. However, I must compliment the officer cadre as well. I have been one of them earlier not as a civil servant but in the army. In every organization, there are some very good officers. Every institution has its share of the very good people and they are the ones with whom it is a great pleasure to be working with. They drive the execution of projects, so it's fantastic. It is a great learning for me as well, meeting people with different ideas, and engaging with them. But yes, initially I did find that I had to settle in the not-so-military way of working.

Q. *You mentioned you've had failures in life and you look upon them as positives. Can you speak about any one or two of these that have profoundly impacted your life and your career?*

Well, during sports and military days, there were many occasions when we would be assigned tasks and we would assign tasks to ourselves or set goals for ourselves but be not be able to accomplish them. Also taking on new projects, getting out of the comfort zone, and then trying to excel in something that is completely new has been very challenging always but I have never shied away from it. I have also never shied away from accepting my failures and falls. One important thing is failing and not being afraid of it. Secondly, accepting that you failed because of yourself rather than the circumstances is also important. It is very easy to blame the circumstances but I feel that when you are willing to accept the blame it is a very strong step in ensuring that you become stronger. So we've had good mentoring in the army to do these things. In terms of examples, there are numerous examples, from my operations with the terrorists in Kashmir where on many occasions the operations didn't go as I would have expected them to go, but we emerged stronger from it and ultimate winners. Similarly, in training to face my own fears created by my mind, taking on opponents, taking on and excelling in an environment where I might not have been very comfortable. Quite late in my life, when I was 28, I saw a professional shooting range for the first time. At 28, people were already world champions. But at 34, I was an Olympic medalist. So six years. Six years is a very short time in the lifespan of any Olympic medalist. I would probably be one of the shortest, in terms of the time frame, to have won a medal. So not accepting any sort of excuses, like I come in late and I need more time to win. I have learnt from my opponents, I have learnt from my environment, but I have pushed myself to learn and keep moving ahead.

Q. *You mentioned that the BJP is probably one of the only parties where someone like you could get absorbed in and achieve this success in such a short time. Was this one of the major factors why you decided to join the BJP? At that point, if you spoke to other parties, given the decorated career you had, you may have had other opportunities. So what attracted you to the BJP? Was it the ideology? Was it Mr Modi's persona? Was it the feeling of the then imploding Congress party? What were the main factors?*

I think in everyone's lives there are various factors because of which you get opportunities. And again there are various factors because of which you move ahead on certain options. In terms of ideology as well, being nationalistic is the core ideology of BJP and every soldier is engrained and trained to be nationalistic. When you participate and play for your country as well, you play because you have very strong feelings for your country. So all of these things coincided and that's why I was able to move ahead.

Q. *One has never heard you say anything about religion, you stay away from debates on say Ram Mandir, issues that a lot of people in BJP would be addressing. Do you sometimes find it difficult to reconcile your own views and values with some that your party and party spokespersons are advocating on national television on a usual basis?*

I am glad you asked this question. You need to understand what the core message of the party is and what some fringe elements or a few members of our party are saying. What few members say cannot become the core message of the party. I don't shy away from the core message of my party because I believe in that message which is Hindutva. Hindus were everyone who lived from the geographical area of the Hindu Kush right up to the Indian Ocean. They were all Hindu. Hindu is not a religion, Hindu is a way of life. And we are the ones who have absorbed—and by the way, Hindu religion is a religion of seekers, it is very different from Islam. It is a way of life where we are seeking and that's why we are open to people. And that is why we have absorbed cultures and we have also accepted invaders. We have never invaded any country. There is no history of India ever invading any country. That doesn't make us weak, it makes us doubly strong. We are so comfortable in our culture, in our own beliefs and strength that we don't feel the need of really attacking any other country to feel comfortable about ourselves. We are rich in mineral resources, in finances, in intellect and in philosophical knowledge. In terms of Ram Mandir, my party's message is very clear. We are not talking of hundreds and hundreds of temples that may have been destroyed and mosques built over them. We are talking about the only place, one place, where *Bhagwan* Ram was born. If I draw a parallel, the parallel would be Mecca-Medina. Now imagine, what sort of importance Mecca-Medina has for their religion. So we're talking about something parallel to that and we are saying this place needs to have a temple, because it was the birthplace of *Bhagwan* Ram, this land belongs to *Bhagwan* Ram. If you look, our policies and execution of the policies are for all. A campaign is run against us, both in India and abroad, that we target a certain community or we neglect a certain community. Nothing could be further from the truth than this false campaign against us, because if you look at our policies, prime minister right from the beginning has been saying, '*sabka saath sabka vikaas*', which means 'development for all, taking everyone along'. Our policies are reaching every person from every religion. Be it the construction of houses for them, be it resources for the farmers, be it resources for women, be it loans for the youth to move ahead, it's for all. So it is incorrect. This whole campaign is to basically malign us because the opposition cannot accept the fact that here is a bunch of people who can run a country without corruption. There has been a massive amount of corruption in our country. We have stopped all that. We have stopped the leakages. India is now becoming stronger. So there are a lot of interest groups working against us. So if they can't find anything in terms of corruption for us, they manufacture this narrative that we are communal people.

Q. *We are the youngest country in the world with more than half of the country's population below 25. Different governments are of course performing at different degrees, but as a country, we are struggling to provide enough opportunities to the youth. Everyone says it that we have to somehow reap the demographic dividend and not allow it to become a demographic disaster. As a former Minister of Youth Affairs, what are your thoughts on it? Is it something that concerns you?*

One of the most important resources for our country is the human resource. If we are the youngest nation in the world and we will continue to be so for a decade or so, then we must be able to utilize that resource and add value to them so that they are then able to contribute to society, to the nation, and to the world and make it a better place to live in. Our government has worked in that direction tirelessly and will continue to work so that the huge population of the youth that is there in the country—if they were to make a country for themselves, it would be one of the top 10 countries in terms of population in the world. Now just imagine, that large a population, we are skilling them, we are providing them with resources, with infrastructure, with digital access, we are motivating them in their examinations by sort of mentoring them, the prime minister is sort of mentoring them as well as like their elder brother, like an icon. So we are creating an environment of positivity in our country and also making them ... you know *Saksham* is the right word in Hindi ... more capable. So the entire apparatus of the whole country is being used in a very synergetic way so as to bring the best value to our youth.

Sachin Pilot

s we get off at the Member of the Legislative Assembly
(MLA) quarters in Jaipur early one morning, we are
greeted with utter chaos and confusion. On the narrow
road outside Deputy Chief Minister Sachin Pilot's home, a couple
of hundred people have gathered holding up giant banners of the
Congress party and Pilot, the party's poster boy in Rajasthan.
Loud chants of 'Sachin Pilot *Zindabad*' reverberate as the police
rush to put up barricades to control the crowd. Within minutes,
the chants become deafening as Pilot himself emerges from his
guarded gates. He walks across the road and personally meets
each person in the thronging crowd. Some are there to show
their adulation, while others have come with specific requests and
grievances. He patiently listens to them and occasionally askes his
secretary to take note of their requests.

Inside the office attached to Pilot's house, about 20 people are
waiting to meet him, including two members of the Rajasthan
assembly. In the next hour or so, we watch quietly as Pilot expertly
switches back and forth between three different meetings, each
happening in a separate room. We wonder if there is a big event
we have missed that has drawn so many people to Pilot's home all

at once. 'This is nothing new, it's like this every day,' we are duly informed by his secretary.

We are intrigued by Sachin Pilot for two main reasons. The first is that at the relatively young age of 42, he has already had, as he puts it, 'the full flavour of Indian politics'. In his 15-odd years in active politics, he has been a two-time MP, a union cabinet minister, an MLA, the state president of the Congress party, and now, the deputy chief minister. Very few of the next generation political leaders in India can boast of similar credentials with handsome experience at the state and central levels. The second reason is that Pilot receives widespread admiration from across the board, including from Bharatiya Janata Party (BJP) politicians and many citizens we have come across—from taxi drivers to hotel staff, from local politicians to our friends and acquaintances.

Pilot's role in rebuilding the Congress party in Rajasthan has won him immense adulation. In 2013, the ruling Congress got wiped out by the BJP in the Rajasthan assembly elections with its tally dropping to just 21 seats, its worst ever in the state. Soon after, in the 2014 Lok Sabha elections, its seat tally plummeted to zero from the 20 seats it had won in 2009. Pilot lost his seat too. When most politicians of Pilot's age and profile lose an election, they use it as an opportunity to travel, spend time with families. and take a break from the travails of active politics. Pilot decided to drop everything else, move to Rajasthan and dedicate the next few years to rebuild the party in the state. 'I don't do things half-heartedly,' he says. He tells us about his strategy—starting from the very bottom, focusing on the *panchayat*, *zila parishad*, and even dairy elections, and then working his way to the top. He also discusses the many obstacles he faced, showing us pictures on his mobile phone of wounds that the police had left on his face and legs during his *dharnas*.

Our discussion with Pilot is wide-ranging, covering the adverse impact of politics on his personal life to the party's decision to not appoint him chief minister when they won back the state in 2018.

He comes across as intelligent and sincere. At times, however, we get the sense he is reticent, or possibly just repeating the party line: he knows what to say to whom. Despite the somewhat predictable responses to some of our questions, we notice a fiercely independent streak in him—a sense that he is willing to pull out all the stops once he has enough conviction about an idea. Maybe that explains how he was able to go and do what almost no other politician does, or even how he and his wife got married without his wife's family being present at the wedding. 'My life has not been all that easy,' he confesses to us.

'Good, young people like Sachin Pilot can never become prime minister while Rahul Gandhi is in the Congress,' laments one of our taxi drivers in Delhi. It seems to be a perception shared by many, and they often point to the fact that he lost out on the Rajasthan CM seat despite successfully reviving the party in the state. While Pilot launches a vigorous defence of his party and its leadership, it's anyone's guess as to how much the party will allow him to grow further. There is no doubt, however, that as the party aims to rebuild itself in the many states where it virtually no longer exists, it should exhort state leaders to follow the example set by Sachin Pilot.

Interview

Q. You studied at Wharton, did an MBA there, you have worked at General Motors and the British Broadcasting Corporation (BBC). You could have been in business or the armed forces. So what made you join politics, at the young age of 23?

Sometimes destiny makes a lot of decisions for you. I was doing my MBA programme at Wharton when my father met with an accident, but I came back and was working in the corporate world. It made me realize that, whatever I had seen growing up as a young person, my experiences, my surroundings, whatever I had learnt from my travel and my exposure, I thought I could best add value on a platform that was public in nature. It was a very conscious decision for me to join politics. I was 21–22 when my father passed away. I very consciously decided to take the plunge because I thought I could add something to this. I thought about the country, I believed in the party I was working, and I thought that I will be able to provide a lot more and bring about many more changes and effect those changes, which I did. Four years after my father had passed away, I decided to contest elections. And I think it is a good thing that people with good degrees and good educational background take up leadership challenges. It is a positive change.

Q. What qualities did you learn from your father, both on the personal front and on the political front?

You see, I have a last name that has certain goodwill and certain resonance. My father came from almost nowhere. He lost his own father (my grandfather) when he was only eight years old. He milked cows and sold milk in many households to earn a livelihood, sent his three sisters to school and arranged their marriages. He had a very tough upbringing and coming from that background, he qualified to be a fighter pilot in the air force and then left that job (which was a very well-paying job at the time) to take up public service. I saw how rooted he was and the fact that having a position in a high office did not alter his ethos, his connect to the ground, his affection and relationship with people. In Indian politics, you have to remain connected. One must not forget where you come from just because you attain a high office. So that is one thing I learnt—to be humane, to be humble, to be approachable. That sort of quality I think endures for a long time even when you are gone.

Q. *Do you approach and model your politics based on your father's ideals?*

I obviously learnt a lot from him. When I was younger I would try and emulate him in many ways. But I know that I am my own person. I have learnt a lot from his value systems. As a young person growing up in that house, I think I was able to imbibe my family values which I really cherish. But ultimately, I have to make my own decisions and my own career path. When caught at the crossroads of what I should do, I take inspiration from him. But I don't think I want to or have lived my life trying to be my father. I can't be him. He and I have different backgrounds, different circumstances. We're both different people. But yes, I have his name and in my own career of 19 years, if I have not been able to add anything to his name, I have at least tried my best not to let him down and keep it going.

Q. *How have you evolved both personally and politically over these 20 years? Politics at 23 and 42 must be very different?*

Initially, my focus was on my constituency and development work. I was very young, I wanted to bring changes and I would easily get frustrated with the bureaucracy, et cetera. But, over time I have learnt how to move around those things and realized that it takes time and patience to execute things in this country. We should try to make it better, but that is how it is for now. Over the years, I have been an MP, a member of the Union cabinet as minister of state looking after telecom, IT and postal services, and then holding independent charge of corporate affairs which was a whole different field for me to learn in. I moved back to Rajasthan in 2014 and the Congress was almost wiped out here, it was a tough time. But party organization, Parliament, state legislator—I have been very lucky to get a well-rounded experience, the full flavour of Indian politics. It has been a good journey. I have had ups and downs and I have tried to learn from where I have not succeeded, but I have not let it bog me down. That's one thing I have learnt, that one must persevere. And if you remain connected to the grassroots and the masses, positions and elections, victories and losses, opposition and government, these are all transitional. If you are principally clued in and attached to what you believe is your job at hand, then people will give you the strength to carry on whether you are in government or opposition.

Q. *You lost the 2014 election in your constituency, Ajmer, despite having such strong ties to the people. What did that teach you?*

In 2014 elections, I had worked really hard in my constituency, I got an airport made, got a university made, I got 46 trains running—thousands of crores of development work. But ultimately, people's will prevailed and I was very humbled with that loss, I was not expecting it. I thought despite all the anti-Congress sentiments, the *jumlas* and the slogans, I will still make that election. But I didn't. It was tough for the first few days to sink in. But then I thought that just because I am not an MP doesn't mean I stop working for the people. So all our work in that term actually helped me in 2018 to win the by-elections in the same constituency. I wasn't fighting as a candidate for that election but people remembered the work that we had done when I was an MP and I really got the full political dividend of my hard work there in these by-elections.

Q. In the last five years you did something that most politicians, particularly those with similar backgrounds like you, rarely do. You decided to stay away from Delhi, you stationed yourself in Rajasthan for almost five years to rebuild the party from the ground-up. How was that experience for you?

When I was tasked to revive the party in Rajasthan, I moved bag and baggage to Jaipur, I stationed myself not just in Jaipur but I made sure that I travelled across the state. Once I take up a responsibility, I don't do things half-heartedly. Rajasthan is geographically the largest state in India, it is bigger than Maharashtra and UP, so to connect with people who live in such far-flung areas one has to really reach out to them. I must have covered more than half a million kilometres in the last four-and-a-half years. I travelled a lot and stayed in Rajasthan because my workers had to see me sweat and bleed with them. You share not just political speeches but also your lives and that creates a bond that is really unbreakable. So that is something I invested myself in fully. And I think ultimately it paid off.

Q. What was your approach? When the party is so weak on the ground in a state so big and so dispersed, how do you go about it?

Once we lost the Parliament and assembly elections, I decided to focus on the local elections—*panchayat, zila parishad,* block, *sarpanch,* dairy elections, they are all cooperative elections but very grassroots. I started focusing on those elections and those are really the bedrock from where you can launch yourself onto the state elections. These local body elections—municipality, mayor elections, *nagar palikas*—which earlier perhaps the Congress party wasn't so focused on, are ones I really invested my time and effort in, to rebuild that part of my party. Once we had the base covered, we had the groundwork done to be able to take on the next level which was the assembly elections. And more than that, people should not see you work only during campaign time, or wait four years for the anti-incumbency to kick in. We lost in December 2013, in January 2014 I had my first mass agitation. So we started working in campaign mode from day one. People actually see this, they see that these people are not in power but they're still standing up for us. You have to win their hearts and minds right from the beginning as opposed to waiting until the election time.

Q. Did you run into any obstacles or challenges?

Plenty. I was beaten up by the police, while on the *dharnas* (shows scar). There is a lot of opposition, there are a lot of internal party problems too, but you have to make sure that you still go on and do your job. This (points to scar) is from a *lathi* charge on my arms and I was out of action for a few days. We were just surrounding the assembly and the police had *lathi*-charged and I got whacked in the middle. But that apart, we did our *dharnas, pradarshans, gheraos*, functions, rallies, and protests. Whenever we felt that the government of the day was acting against the people's wishes we stepped in and I think people remember those days when we fought for them.

Q. Do you think this is the model that Congress should follow in other states where it has become almost irrelevant and needs to rebuild itself?

I think it is important that there is a leadership in which the people believe, and you must lead from the front. You cannot expect your party workers to do all the hard work and you sit at home. So if you work 18 hours a day, your followers will be compelled to work 16 hours a day. There is no way that can't happen. But to think that all the hard work can be outsourced to other people, that doesn't work. You have to work hard yourself, be an example., be in the front and do a sustained consistent campaign as opposed to last-minute sporadic dashes. Those don't work anymore.

Q. *After the Rajasthan elections that you won, a lot of your supporters and a lot of the youth across the country were left disappointed. You made such a big sacrifice stationing yourself here, you rebuilt the party from the ground-up, yet you were overlooked for the CM's post in favour of somebody under whom the party actually reached that position five years ago. How did that make you feel?*

I have never asked anything from the party. At 26 I was an MP, then minister, at 35 I was party president, so my party gave me a lot of responsibility and ultimately we left the decision to the party and the party decided that Mr Gehlot should become CM and I become the Deputy CM. I was part of that decision and I accepted it and I want to discharge that responsibility to the best of my capacities. You don't work for positions, but from 21, we were able to get a 100. We have increased our number of seats five times. The swing was actually phenomenal despite all the money and the campaign that the BJP led. So I am satisfied with what we have done and I am still party president and I have got an important job in the government. I am a very optimistic person, there is nothing to feel disappointed about. You asked me how I felt, I felt that I have done my job. I felt that I have accomplished what I was asked to do and I was able to deliver to the party when it needed me the most. Because these three states are very important, the momentum changed because of them.

Q. A lot of critics of the Congress also argue that the bright and talented younger lot (whether it is you or Jyotiraditya Scindia in Madhya Pradesh) are overlooked for top posts because the party wants to avoid Mr Rahul Gandhi being overshadowed in any way.

It was Mr Gandhi who appointed me as his party's president. He has been quite fair in allocating work and responsibilities all across. I don't think there is any credence to these conspiracy theories. It is who is required at what time. Ahead of the 2019 campaign, Jyotiraditya Scindia was appointed the general secretary of Uttar Pradesh, the most crucial state in India for our elections. I am party president here and I am deputy chief minister. So I think enough has been given to people at the leadership roles. It is unfair to criticize people just because you didn't get a position.

Q. Another criticism of the Congress is that the president's position gets passed down from mother to the son, and now the daughter, Priyanka Gandhi, has joined as well. Is it a party that doesn't allow meritocracy or an equal chance to people?

That is very unfair. Nobody from the Gandhi family has become prime minister in the last 30 years. Narasimha Rao was not from the Gandhi family, Manmohan Singh was not from the Gandhi family. The Congress follows an election process where we all unanimously elect a leader. It was initially Mrs Gandhi and then Rahul Gandhi was the president. We have the choice to do that. How the BJP elects its presidents no one knows, other parties I don't want to comment on. But I am saying it is the choice of the Congress workers that here is a person who we believe can hold the party together and lead from the front. It is our party's choice, in a democracy we choose who we want to elect. And enough people have gotten enough positions in the Congress. Don't forget Mrs Gandhi led us to two victories back to back in 2004 and 2009. So that is the answer for that criticism. I know that I have been given this much by the party which is more than what I could have asked for. But one must not really barter for positions because people like that will get compromised on the way.

Q. *In an interview with Simi Garewal in 2006, you had spoken about the difficulty you faced around the time you were getting married. You got married without your wife's family taking part in it. Do you feel that being part of a political family has caused you to make a lot of personal sacrifices along the way?*

I have got a lot from people in this country and I think it is a bit rich to say that I have made all the sacrifices and that I should be given more empathy, et cetera. No. I think I got a lot from who I am, what my family is and I owe a lot to this country and people who I live with. Yes, my life has not been all that easy because although from the outside it looks very comfortable, silver spoon and born with all the privileges, et cetera. In reality, it has been a struggle. You have to prove yourself each time. It doesn't matter whose son, nephew, or granddaughter you are, you have to prove to the people who you are. To win people's hearts and minds takes a lot more than last names. You can get that perception, you can get your foot in the door, but you have to perform. It is not an easy life because you are being questioned, judged, and evaluated 24×7. Everybody loves only two things in this country, cricket and politics, and everybody has a suggestion to make. It is also difficult to satisfy all the aspirations and expectations people have. Especially if you are a well-known name then people expect you to perform as well as your father or mother if not more. So that way it is a bit challenging.

Q. *On the personal front, with the demands of politics, it must be difficult ...*

Yes, I have two young boys and I do wish that I get to spend more time with them. But whatever time I do spend with them I try and be their dad as opposed to anybody else. But yes, no regrets, it's all good.

Q. *As a political leader, a deputy chief minister running a state, there are people around you managing your time and running your day-to-day life. It is very easy to fall out of touch. How does a politician stay in touch?*

It is almost impossible not to be in touch. If you take your job seriously, if you are available to the people then you are answerable and accountable. This country is not like the US where you can just email and write postcards and kiss babies and things are okay. Here you have to be involved in people's daily lives, share good times and bad times with them. It is not a profession, it is a way of life, it's a 24×7 commitment to what you do. If you fall short of that people will put you by the wayside. In the Indian democratic systems, our electorate is brutal, to say the least. So if you think you are high and mighty and cut-off from people, the time will come when they will actually vote you out. You walk a tightrope every day of your life.

Q. *You have had many successes in the last 20 years. What would you count, if not as failures, then at least things that you wish you had done better?*

I don't regret anything. But I look back and say, 'Well, I'll do this better next time.' I think when I was part of the UPA-II government, we could have been better positioned to reflect what we have done. We lost a perception battle. What has happened in hindsight is that these so-called 'scams' have come to nought basically. But we have paid a political price for that because we didn't communicate as much or effectively. That is something, not as a person but as a government, we could have done better. I just hope that I learn from all of my experiences, both good and bad.

Smriti Irani

From arriving in Mumbai to take up acting with just 'three dollars' in her pocket to becoming the youngest cabinet minister in the Modi government at the age of 38, Smriti Irani's career has seen a stunning rise. The political journey, however, has not always been smooth sailing. Irani unsuccessfully contested the 2004 elections from Chandni Chowk in Delhi. Ten years later, she again suffered a defeat, losing to Rahul Gandhi in Amethi despite putting up a tough fight. But Irani is not the one to be bogged down by losses, nor is she afraid of more battles. 'A lamb can only be slaughtered but twice. The sheep shall not meekly go to the slaughter anymore,' she said to us ahead of the 2019 campaign, when pressed on the election losses. Inevitably, there was absolutely no meekness on display as she entered the Amethi battlefield once again, this time to serve the Congress a shocking defeat and wrest the seemingly impregnable Gandhi family bastion from its leader.

Smriti Irani is perhaps the most recognizable younger female leader of the Bharatiya Janata Party (BJP), not only because of her past as a popular television actor but because she is very forthright and not known to shy away from arguments. This is also apparent in our meeting, where she candidly expresses her views with conviction on a wide array of issues ranging from her election experiences to reforming India's education system, as well as the challenges she faces as a combative woman in politics. She has a sharp wit, loves banter, and does not hold back from making provocative statements.

We speak at length about the trials and tribulations of being an Indian woman, especially one in politics. 'It's not difficult to be a female in politics. It is difficult to be a female in power,' she declares. She feels that women need to stop being painted as victims and seeing themselves as victims. Self-confidence, in her view, can and should be built through the education system: women can do anything. They can even enter the fractious world of politics easily. But sometimes self-confidence is not enough. Unique challenges detrimental to women's political participation abound as women face double standards. For instance, an assertive woman is called arrogant, but an assertive man is not. The pushback from men is pervasive in all areas, but the resistance posed to powerful female politicians is most noticeable when women want to bring changes to how things are being done. Irani gives the example of one of India's foremost scientists asking her to lean on his understanding, confiding that officials like him presume they know it all and get deeply perturbed by a woman suggesting other recourses to a problem. In her trademark style, she then surprises us by naming the scientist as well.

Irani is acutely aware that she has a reputation of being controversy's child. But she is also least bothered by it. 'When you challenge the status quo, you are bound to ruffle feathers,' she says, insisting that she rejects the idea of playing by the basic rule of politics to 'let sleeping dogs lie' because Narendra Modi was not elected to maintain the status quo. She attributes a lot of the controversies to her 'no-nonsense attitude' and the difference in power equation with those taking orders from her. Confronting male egos and hypocrisy has been less than ideal for her, yet she has, over the years, learned how to navigate them and doggedly achieve her goals. Towards the end of our interview, we, in fact, get to see this in action. We are interrupted by a telephone call from the male head of a government institution. He was calling her back regarding the alleged sexual harassment of a female student by a teacher in the institution he headed. A fuming Irani pulls him up and tells him in no uncertain terms that she would hold him personally responsible if the harassment did not stop, with the teacher appropriately punished.

In more ways than one, Smriti Irani is unique. She has a wicked sense of humour; she is a modern politician who, perhaps because of her own life experiences, is a big believer in individual responsibility. She stresses the role of individuals in creating the change that they seek. As she took her oath while being sworn into Narendra Modi's new cabinet in May 2019, fresh from her historic victory in Amethi, she received the loudest cheer from the gathering at Rashtrapati Bhavan. That is just one of many signs that show that she has a very bright future in the BJP and in politics.

Irani tells us that when she retires, she hopes to be remembered for being 'audacious'. Whatever happens to her political career, the history books will definitely grant her this wish.

Interview

*Q. You had a very successful career as an actor. You won so many
awards. Why did you enter what people often call the 'muddy
world of politics'?*

One of the greatest injustices that we do to politics is calling
it murky and muddy. I think that adjective has been added to
politics so that good people stay out of it. The murkier you make
it sound, the worse off people feel they would be if they became
a part of the process of change. I was nominated as the United
States Agency for International Development (USAID) ambas-
sador to India for the World Health Organization (WHO) oral
rehydration salts (ORS) programme. I had worked significantly in
the health sector and the social sector before I came into electoral
politics. And while I was serving under the aegis of the WHO and
USAID, I recognized that when you are a part of a social activity
there is only so much that you could do. There is a limitation.
And real change comes when you become a part of policymaking
and implementation of that policy which is only possible through
two avenues. Either you join the administrative services, which I
was not a part of. Or you become a part of electoral politics. So
for me, that is why I gravitated from working in the social sector
to somebody who became a part of policymaking. I was extremely
fortunate that my media and political career grew simultaneously,
and never at the cost of each other. It was only when I became
a Member of the Parliament that I decided that I will reduce
my media load and concentrate on people's issues since I was an
elected representative. And the minute I became a minister, I
gave it up altogether because I did not want to be a minister who
is available for only a few hours of the day. It is a 24×7 service.
And for that you need to be free of any and all shenanigans and
be dedicated and focused only to that particular cause or office.

Q. *How has the journey been? Has it been easy for you? What have you found fulfiling, and what have been some of the challenges?*

Tumultuous (laughs) … I think the fact that you can apply yourself to solution every day and bring change every day is something that is not often celebrated about politics. The cacophony of politics sometimes overshadows the contribution of it. And for me what has been significant is the desire to change and be a part of change and be a part of somebody's solution. In a country which has such diversity, be it cultural, linguistic, or otherwise, that you could give a myriad of solutions is something that fascinates me. The fact that in my country I need to communicate with my citizenry in 1,600 dialects in itself may be a challenge for many, but for me, I look at it as an opportunity.

Q. *Has it been difficult for you being a combative, outspoken woman to join a party like the BJP and join a political system?*

I think women per se are combative because we are not subjugated easily, irrespective of our geographies. Especially in a day and age where more and more women are aware of due process, of law, especially in a day and age where women know that they are not alone in this battle, for equality or for security. And given that, does that make my combativeness a burden that I carry? No. It, in fact, arms me to help other women and other people in the system who need that added measure of support.

Q. *You led the BJP's women wing, the mahila morcha. Do you feel there is a glass ceiling for women in Indian politics?*

I feel that no accomplishment is big enough. When the sky is the limit why would I look at any ceiling? So for me, I think that this nomenclature of glass ceiling is a limited perspective of a capacity of a woman, that you presume that okay if you reach 'x' milestone that means that you have arrived.

Q. *Is the system structured in such a way that makes it more difficult for women to succeed?*

I don't wear the victim chip on my shoulder. I have come from very humble means. I barely had, if you look at it in dollar term, I had 200 rupees in my pocket, that's 3 dollars. So I began my career with 3 dollars. So for somebody who has come from that background, I feel that I will not look at myself as a victim and when you stop looking at yourself as a victim, much changes about your perspective towards life and how you lead it. If you thrust upon women the victim complex, then they get so burdened by the enormity of the discrimination that they view themselves only from that prism.

Q. *As a leader, what can you do to change this view?*

We are looking for holistic solutions but in a world which is so competitive we need to empower the individuals to pursue their own goals. So we have wallowed in this worry, that what can we do? And I think Swami Vivekananda said that if you educate a woman, she will look after herself. So when you say educate, is it in the literal sense of 'send her to school', because there are many in schools and colleges who genuinely don't apply themselves for their own better future. I think if you make women conscious of the fact that they control their own destinies, that is the biggest support you can give them.

Q. *The Indian society, especially the political world, is pretty male-dominated. How do you deal with it? As a female politician, do you find these things challenging?*

No, I don't. Why I don't is because the minute I put myself in that self-pity box that's where the purpose of this desire to be looked upon as an equal is defeated. I do myself a great disservice if I look at myself only from the prism of gender and not capacity. I don't tell people I am one of the best women around. I tell people I am one of the most capable persons around irrespective of whether I am competing with a man or a woman.

Q. *How do you spread this message across India?*

I think that's the message we need to spread—that women need to be judged on capacity and talent. And need an opportunity to complete equally. And that is true for women across the world. So when I sit at a table and let's say if I am in a negotiating position, I will ensure that I am the best possible negotiator for my particular department or my ministry. And, I don't get overwhelmed or underwhelmed because of the pure designation which is looked upon from a gender perspective. For instance, in the Ministry of Women and Child department, one of the Ministers of State was a man. But that's what a male prime minister has done. He has said that women's needs in this department need not be looked upon only by a woman politician. Put a man at the helm. That is a change. Because you will always find that woman politician approached by the media and asked what you will do for the women. Male politicians are never asked what they will do for men. That means you view the male politicians from the possibility that when male politicians work, they work for both genders. But when you look at a female politician, there is an expectation that she might do more for women. Now even male politicians can't afford to look only after men. Women in 2014 and even before that when Narendra Bhai was CM of Gujarat, we could qualitatively and from data establish, that women as a vote bank is the most effective vote bank because they have the propensity to support a politician who delivers on development. And that became one of the talking points of the 2014 and pre-2014 election scenarios in the country.

Q. *What were your findings about women voters? Is there something unique about women voters and politicians?*

If women voters and politicians are studied, then two aspects emerge. One—whenever women administrators or women politicians come in, the Human Development Index (HDI) goes up. Because they put more money in education, health services, infrastructure, and social ills are deftly dealt with. So there is enough data available in various pockets of the country, which has certified this. Second aspect—as a vote back, when women see people delivering on development, the stickiness factor of women is much more as compared to men.

Q. *Whether it is justified or not, you are looked as someone who has caused a lot of controversies. Why do you think that is?*

When you are assertive, when you challenge the status quo, you are bound to ruffle feathers. And there is no other adjective that can be given to somebody, which is less controversial. Because people assume that the basic ethics of politics is to let sleeping dogs lie. And here you are trying to rumble up things. And people say why? Why can't you be a ribbon-cutting politician who smiles well when the photographs are clicked? But then Narendra Modi was not voted into power to maintain status quo. So it is the resistance to change and the resistance to accountability. It's not difficult to be a female politician. It is difficult to be a female in power. When you are in a position of power and somebody has to take orders from you every day, that is where the power equation gives you a new understanding of human nature. As a female administrator, if I have a no-nonsense attitude, then I would be termed arrogant. If a male administrator does the same, he would be called assertive.

Q. *Do you think that is what has caused some push back? Have you managed to get all your decisions implemented?*

I have never had push backs. I have always had all my decisions implemented. And I think that is the problem. That I not only said something but also managed to do it. The idea of the attack is to break the spirit, so that she is not audacious enough to do it. But that audacity is something I have maintained in five years.

Q. *Does the resistance to your decisions come in largely from the male-centric bureaucracy, politicians?*

When I was in education, the resistance came from academicians. They said what can this woman do. I actually had one of the top-most scientists of the country say to me that why don't you lean on my understandings better. Anil Kakodkar said this. They were enraged because they presumed that they knew everything. And how can that chit of a woman tell them that no, there is another perspective or way of getting to a solution? So it's not about men in power. It is about men with ego.

Q. *So that must have been very difficult to deal with?*

No. Ego isn't difficult to deal with. Women deal with it every day (laughs).

Q. *But wasn't it upsetting to deal with this kind of behaviour?*

The hypocrisy of it was amusing. Because one is made to believe that if you are a learned man then you must have shed this disability to be so myopic in how you judge a woman. The hypocrisy of it all—of saying on the outside how much they support women but on the inside, when the chain is being driven by women, they'd be so upset by it.

Q. But did you get the required level of support from your colleagues?

I was picked by the prime minister to do my job. If the PM thought that I needed a crutch, then I wouldn't be given the job.

Q. Does it bother you that when people look back at your time as education minister, they talk about all the controversies instead of the achievements?

That's fine. I take it with a pinch of salt. The men who matter know …

Q. In spite of a spirited and good fight in Amethi, you lost that election in 2014 and the election in 2004. What were those experiences like for you?

I was not given seats to win. I was given seats to lose. That means that there was no man who had the quality to go and fight the tough fights.

Q. (Before 2019 election) You performed well in both the campaigns that you lost. What did you learn about electoral politics and the demands of it in the election losses?

I can only say this that a lamb can only be slaughtered but twice. The sheep shall not meekly go to slaughter anymore.

Q. There is no doubt that you have had a remarkable success and it has been a meteoric rise. Is there anything that you look back on?

In the middle of all those successes, do you wish you had done something differently?

No. The only regret that I have in my life is that I never wore a uniform. And never served. Because I think that is the greatest act of selfless service and honour. To go to the battlefront without a speck of fear in you. I think that is the greatest kind of service. Now that I am in the textiles ministry, I have found a way to be of service to the armed forces. Most of our armed forces personnel were buying uniforms and other items of need from outside the country. In my three years in as textile minister, that changed and now 80 per cent of the needs of the armed forces are met domestically. So that is my tribute to the Indian armed forces. But that's still different from wearing a uniform and standing on that border.

Q. *You married into a Parsi family. Your kids are raised as Parsis. Did it upset you when people were questioning your religion by asking you things like 'what's your gotra?'*

No. When you are a public person, you can't be mollycoddled into comfort. You can't sanitize the questions that are thrown at you. If you are so fragile, you have no business in being a public personality.

Q. *What about being part of a party that speaks about Hindutva so much, about religions that have originated in India? How do you reconcile that with this? Do you find people treating you differently?*

Why?! I feel you presume too much for my party. What matters for my party is nation-building. Not what my name or surname is. This is a party that elected Dr Kalam as President of India. Need I say more?

Q. *Would you say that BJP is a large coalition and the things that hold the coalition together is the understanding of development and the idea that the nation comes first? Within that you can have different points of view—it could be people from different religions or perspectives—is that the glue that holds the party together?*

Yes. The fulcrum is the group is bigger than the individual, and the nation is bigger than the group. Which means that your country's needs are supreme. So you are absolutely right. Nothing matters other than India's interest. You don't matter. Your politics doesn't matter. Your ideology doesn't matter. What matters for a BJP person is only and only India.

Q. *Do you think that these contradictions are easy to manage in a party that is trying to win the election?*

No, not at all. The party is dedicated to ideology building and people connect. The government is dedicated to nation-building. So there is a clear distinction between the two. And if ever, god forbid, one feels that the party and the government might come to a point where you have to choose between the one and the other, it is always the nation that we choose.

Q. *India faces a huge challenge reforming its education system. You have spoken about the work that you've done to be able to provide quality education to the children of this country. A lot of intellectuals and people in politics have said that the government is trying to have more focus on India and Indian culture, push for an education that is more rooted in India's culture …*

I think education is so politically looked at that it falls in fragments and gets lost in the gaps of conversations which are ideologically loaded. If you look at Manjul Bhargava who received the Fields

Medal of Honour in Mathematics. Manjul learned mathematics through Sanskrit and poetry from his grandfather in the city of Jaipur and today he teaches Mathematics for non-mathematicians at Princeton using those same instruments that he used as a child. As a minister, my ardent desire was to see how do I aid a student in need? If the student desires a degree, how do I make it administratively a fruitful journey? If a student desires knowledge then how do I give that student a plethora of divergent means to get knowledge? Because knowledge is best served by a curious child. That child might ask questions that are contradictory to the very basis of the knowledge, to the very basic systems that they getting it from. And I think India has thrived so well because we have always taught our students to question everything that has been given to them. And what I saw as minister was, that the rote system is killing that curiosity. But can you deny the parents the opportunity who want to stick to that rote system? You can't. So you have to serve those varied interests and desires as minister. That whatever you desire—free education, fine! If your desire is scientific education, fine! If your desire is Indian knowledge, fine! We are here to serve that every need and every desire.

Q. If tomorrow you were to retire, what would you like to be remembered for?

For being audacious. If I ever have a grave, that is what it should read. And little earthling saying, 'Thank god, she is dead. Now she is someone else's headache.'

Supriya Sule

S upriya Sule, MP from Baramati and a senior leader of the Nationalist Congress Party (NCP), hails from one of Maharashtra's most prominent political families. Her father Sharad Pawar, the president of the NCP, is an extremely senior leader in the state. Despite leading a small regional party he remains one of the most influential politicians in the country with great relations across the political spectrum, including with Prime Minister Modi. Had he not left the Congress in 1999, he may very well have become India's prime minister.

When we meet Supriya Sule at her home in Mumbai, our initial impression is of someone who has a lot on her plate. A politician in a rush, she has little time for niceties and urges us to start and consequently end the interview quickly. Early into our conversation, however, she begins to open up, eventually giving us a lot more time than she initially had planned to. We find her to be a pragmatic, enterprising, and hardworking politician who prides herself on getting things done for people. She keeps an almost punishing schedule, travelling 20 days a month, mostly to her constituency which involves a six-hour car or train journey from Mumbai. She refuses to fly there, despite the convenience, because it doesn't allow her to interact with as many people on her way. She finds it imperative to listen to and address her constituents' daily concerns.

Raised by a Christian mother and a Hindu father, Supriya celebrates both Christmas and Diwali at home with equal fervour. These shared religious traditions in which she was brought up probably inform her secular ideology—she is comfortable with pluralism in faith. Despite this, and somewhat surprisingly, Supriya has a more cautious approach to social change. When the discussion turns to the questions of women's entry into Sabarimala and the building of a Hindu temple at Ayodhya, she firmly maintains that with deeply precarious issues which evoke such sentiment and emotion, such as religion and dogma, people should make their own decisions. Changing people's minds is a slow process and she feels it should chart its own course—social norms of all kinds, not only religious matters but also gender roles, are remarkably sticky. The state, she implies, should not be in the business of changing belief systems, particularly for incendiary social concerns. Education cannot engineer social change alone either. Yet, this doesn't stop her from trying. From constantly throwing statistics at her young friends to get them to stop smoking to walking around Mumbai's crowded Crawford Market to talk to Muslim women about Triple Talaq, Supriya is always trying to better understand complex social issues.

Her opinions on the role of the state vis-à-vis social matters mirror the classic centrist position adopted by the Congress Party, that electoral politics should not intervene in the social norms of communities. This ideological similarity is not surprising because, as she avers, there is no ideological difference between the NCP and the Congress. This ideological similarity between the Congress and the NCP also poses complications for Supriya's own political future. If a small regional party is not ideologically distinct from a behemoth that competes in the same region, its future growth only seems limited. A party like the NCP survives because of the charisma of the leaders and the affection of the constituents towards its founding family. This may constrain her political career.

Supriya has a confident outlook, a legacy of her modern, urban Mumbaikar identity—'Don't forget that I am a Bombay girl,' she quips, when asked of the challenges one faces as a female in a political system dominated by men. While she was raised in an environment supportive of women, she acknowledges with acute mindfulness that not every female is privileged like her. Despite the party's middling prospects, Supriya seems unperturbed and is focusing entirely on solving her constituents' problems. 'Everything touches me,' she says as we get ready to leave, explaining that her desire to work for people stems from the pain she feels when she sees them suffer. 'And I hope I never lose my sensitivity.'

Interview

Q. What are things that you are most passionate about, the ones that truly drive you?

What drives me is the ability to create legislation that touches people's lives and can change their lives. Hence I am in Parliament because that's where we make legislation for the country which can change people's lives for the better. I want to touch every life to make it better, in whatever way I can. It could be one life, a thousand lives, as long we can make somebody smile and happy.

Q. You have done a lot of work on female foeticide. Recent research has shown that the more educated women are giving birth to fewer girl children, whereas the less educated women have more girl children being born, but they die after birth. What are your thoughts on this?

Social issues are very hard to address. First of all, it is a mindset issue. Urban people have this issue because everybody wants only one child and they'd rather have a boy. So education is not something that drives social change; the mindset does. Secondly, in rural India, the Indian numbers are not that bad as they used to be, even a decade ago. India's malnutrition numbers have gone down; most pregnancies are institutionalized; most women are going to nearby hospitals to have babies. Clearly the biggest challenge in women's healthcare is none of the above, but anaemia. And that is what generates several pregnancies into malnutrition. So it is really anaemia that we need to tackle. The minute the mother is not anaemic, she will have a healthier child.

Q. If education does not drive social change, then what does?

Clearly, education does not drive change alone. You have to keep working on it. You have to change an entire generation. We have rules for dowry. Has dowry stopped in India? No. In wealthy families it is not called dowry, it is called 'gifts'. Even if we expect, it is a form of dowry. So, dowry, child marriage, female versus male. In bigger homes, if there is a decent amount of money, the boy is sent to English-medium schools and girl is kept back at home. India, with all its diversity in languages and culture is a very complex country. So it's not really 'one size fits all'.

Q. *Are there social issues that you wanted to work on but because of the system, you couldn't make enough of an impact?*

It happens. It is part of the game. No job is easy. That's what leadership is all about. You have to find a solution around it, that's why you are a leader! There are several examples, like making social change in female foeticide. You have to just keep working at it … keep working at it! When we worked on it, we saw that the number of foeticides in Maharashtra was going down, which is wonderful. Girls' numbers have gone down substantially. It is not where we need it to be but it is a big change. Because mindset is not something that changes overnight. We are not machines that we all will produce the same outputs. We come from different cultures. I come from an exceptionally modern background but that doesn't mean everybody else thinks like me. The beauty is to work with people. Another example is tobacco control—another big challenge. My young friends, who I keep throwing data at, still don't give up smoking. They throw it back at me and say, 'that's for the next generation. I'm not in it.' But I don't give up. You have to keep working to bring awareness.

Q. *Your father is one of the tallest figures in Indian politics. He has a larger than life presence in Maharashtra politics. Have you modelled your approach to politics based on him?*

I don't model anything that I do on anybody. I lead my own life on my own terms. I don't even use my family name. I am married and I use my married name. Each one has to find their own path. I don't compete with anybody. I compete with myself and that's so much fun. I don't worry about what he has achieved and what I have not. Of course, you always learn something from your parents. I was brought up in a culture where every elder person knows something more than you.

Q. *India has the highest level of electoral volatility in the world and re-election rates of MPs are very low compared to other countries. You've been re-elected twice now. How do you figure out what your constituents want?*

These are two different things—what constituents want and politics being volatile. My voters are my stakeholders. If I do not know what my stakeholders want, then I should not represent them. I travel 20 days a month because it gives me a pulse on what's going on. If I sit in this house and think that I am going to run something then it is not going to work out. I am a legislator who represents 23 lakh voters. I have to be a good listener and hear them out. My voice in Parliament is not about what my party wants but about what the people want. So if that reflects in my speeches in Parliament, then this is what policymaking is all about. It's what I believe in. The more I travel the more I know. And I travel by car or train, I don't take aircrafts to my constituency so that I can talk to more people. To give you an example, I have spoken on Triple Talaq twice and I was feeling cheated myself because I do understand that Triple Talaq must be banned but I was completely against the idea of criminalizing it. First of all, Muslim marriage is a contract. So if it is a civil issue, where is the question of putting the man in jail? There is domestic violence law anyway in India. We really didn't need to get this. So if you want to call it unconstitutional, let's just finish Triple Talaq so that even if you say it a thousand times, it just doesn't make a difference. So, to understand these complexities, I met a lot of people, it was weighing on my mind. I was coming back from my constituency. I got down at Crawford market. I walked the streets and talked to women. They told me what they felt. I quoted a woman in my speech in Parliament. When the channels asked who that woman was, I gave them the contact and told them to meet her. So when you are making policy, you have to have stakeholder's interest.

Q. *Being a woman in Parliament, do you feel a special responsibility to raise women's issues?*

Not at all. I think every parliamentarian represents men and women. And please don't underestimate the men in Parliament. Even men in Parliament are very sensitive to these issues. Don't think that just because we are discussing women's issues only women speak. Not at all. There are many men who I take great pride in and they stand up for women's issues. We represent everyone.

Q. *But our political system is somewhat dominated by men. Have you ever found that to be a challenge?*

It is. Which field is not dominated by men? But I never found it to be a challenge. Don't forget, I am a Bombay girl. And I am too educated and exposed to think about what gender I am in. I represent modern India. But every woman does not get the opportunity. My home, my in-laws, my education, everything makes a huge difference.

Q. *You have spoken recently about reservations for Dhangars. Reservations is a big debate in India. Is reservation the way to look after a community's interests? Do you see any downsides to it, or do you only see positives?*

This government which is in power today had committed to reservation. So they've brought it to the table. So they really need to answer this—if you promised something then why didn't you deliver it? The community of Dhangars was first given reservation by Mr Pawar. And one can see a big change in the community, it has benefited from it. There are a lot of lawyers and engineers from the community because of reservation. Reservation helps in getting the first foot inside the door. So the child does get admission in an engineering college. But eventually you have to perform and deliver to yourself. If today Marathas have got reservation, that is not for me. Clearly it is not. I mean it will be a shame for me if I took it. It is for thousands of Maratha or Dhangar kids who don't have access to the quality education that I do. They come from communities which don't have access to good education. They may be a hundred times brighter than me. But I have access to good schools, I have access to tutors, I have access to parents who are educated. So it is more for parents like them who really need this. If you don't have reservation then you miss out on education just because you can't afford it. So it's a very complex issue to comment to. But honestly, I feel these kids need reservation only for a lot of social barriers that they go through.

Q. *What are your thoughts on the debate of religious practices versus the rights of women that recently erupted in the Sabrimala case?*

I think it should be each one to their own. You follow your religion. You'll follow what you like. Nobody can force things on you. I am a Hindu, in that sense of the word, but my mother is a Christian. So we do celebrate Diwali and we do celebrate Christmas. And I think that's the beauty of India—the diversity is just phenomenal. And that's what makes this country so vibrant and beautiful. So, I think it's each to their own. I won't say what is right and what is wrong. But at the same time, if there is access to everybody, men or women, I think it should be a non-issue in the twenty-first century. It's always about sentiments and most families will follow sentiments. These are emotional issues.

Q. How's your party, the NCP, different from the Congress?

We are not different. We are two brothers from the same family. We are not different from Congress at all. We are different from Bharatiya Janata Party (BJP) and Shiv Sena because clearly, we are a far more modern, liberal, free-thinking party. They are completely outdated. We are completely for women's rights. RSS doesn't think women should have all the rights. I mean if I was in power and I had the kind of power Mr Modi has today, the first thing I would have done is get the women's reservation bill. That's the message India would have gotten, that we are serious about our commitment today. Nothing happens through consensus here. With this kind of power, so many legislations can happen through consensus. They are all trapped and very happy if the Mandir is built. That's not our core. Mandir issue is again about faith. Let the local people there build the temple. Nothing right or wrong about it. But that's not what parties should fight for. That's for people to do. What we should do, is once the temple is built, we must give the full infrastructure—safety, security, drinking water, sanitation. That is our job. That is what government is supposed to do. I mean if I had the power, first thing I would do is eradicate poverty from this country. Make sure 100 per cent education should reach everyone. No child left out of school or school; work on skill development; talk about population control. There are so many issues in this country. Nobody is talking about them. Even though people might say that our public education system has failed us, I have big faith in it. Most people who study in India do exceptionally well when going abroad. They are so used to working hard that they do very well, better than most kids anywhere in the world. I kept my kids in Indian school because I have full faith in them. There are government schools which do good jobs and there are government schools that do bad jobs. I still have a lot of faith in government systems. In education, we may have disparity, plusses, and minuses. If you read the Annual Status of Education Report (ASER) made by Pratham, you will find that there are challenges. That's because there is a need to impart skills to teachers. Access is also required. India's economy would have not done so well if the education was so bad.

Q. If the Congress and NCP are aligned in terms of ideology, why have separate parties?

We had an issue … We have had 15 years of a coalition government here in state, plus 10 years at the centre. And we have done quite well. You will say, in Boston why do you need five colleges?

Q. An article in The Economist *framed the choice for Indian voter in 2019 an interesting way. It implied that when you vote for the BJP, what you get, even if they underperformed economically, is a hard-lined, right-wing social agenda. Or you vote for the opposition and you risk moving back to corrupt ways of doing business and running the country. There is a perception that parties like Congress and NCP are stuck in these old ways of doing business, sometimes not very transparent. How do you respond to that?*

That is a perception. I agree with what you are saying but at the same time what different transparency has this government shown? They don't walk the talk. They only talk. But they don't walk it. What big changes have they made in the five years of their government? Nothing. Zero. Look at the kind of allegation 18 ministers had in Maharashtra and the CM (former chief minister, Devendra Fadnavis) gave them clean chit every time. In the five years that they have been in power who have they been able to hang? Nobody. Or even prove any allegation that has been made. So these are all political vendettas because they have all the power in the world.

Q. *Have you learnt anything unique about India and its democracy, through your experience with fighting elections? Has there been anything that surprised you?*

Every day teaches you something. It's a very exciting job. There is nothing you can predict in it. That's the beauty of it. Something that has surprised me has been extreme conflict management. How to manage it. We deal with people. Conflict management is something that you have to keep doing. Every time you do there is something more complex. Unexpected things keep coming up. So you have to keep managing it. It gives so much amount of information, which no data manual in the world can give you. You always keep learning because it is people you are working with.

Q. *Today for a Muslim or a Christian, the Congress party, which stood by them for a long time, has suddenly taken a new garb. It is being alleged that they are playing a soft Hindutva card by talking about cows, going to temples ...*

Not at all, it is better than lynching people. I mean, on a scale of one-to-ten if the BJP is at ten, the Congress is at two. This government is talking about churches and all the bad things happening in churches. The party that stood up for them is Congress. BJP talks about it all the time. Look at their MPs, how they talk. Look at Yogi Adityanath, how he talks. I think lynching cases are just horrible. They don't even know what they are talking about. That is a shame! Now that's clearly not the Hindu agenda. It is completely extreme. And Hindu religion is not about extremism. No religion is. It is about how we interpret it as. I don't think any religion is as harsh as it is made out to be. They all are more or less the same if you read their books and need to share an understanding about it. And all this takes away from the core issues, which is the sad part of it—issues like unemployment, healthcare. Not lynching. Not whether the meat is mutton or beef.

Q. *Are you still moved by some of the social and developmental issues you used to work on before joining politics?*

Everything touches me, fortunately even today. I still get hurt when I see a widow, when I see poverty, when I see pain, when I see disaster. And I hope I never lose my sensitivity. I hope not.

Sushmita Dev

S ushmita Dev's family has a long history of public service. Her grandfather was a freedom fighter and minister in the Assam government, her mother a Member of the Legislative Assembly (MLA) in the Assam assembly, and her father a cabinet minister and Congress stalwart. While her legacy is not dissimilar from those of other prominent young politicians we've met, Sushmita's political journey is far from formulaic— she did not join politics in her early twenties, unlike others, and become a career politician. The roots of her unique journey are quite personal: despite being a veteran politician and seven-term Lok Sabha Member of Parliament (MP), her father, Santosh Mohan Dev, always stressed that whatever it may be, politics is not a profession. He insisted that Sushmita first find a way to put food on the table, before joining politics. As a result, she spent over a decade practising law before taking the political plunge.

In 2011, Sushmita was elected to the Assam assembly from her hometown, Silchar. Three years later, she wrested the Silchar Lok Sabha seat from Bharatiya Janata Party (BJP) stalwart, Kabindra Purkayastha, who had won the same constituency from her late father five years earlier. While Sushmita participated actively in

Parliament, taking charge of key issues and raising a wide range of important questions, she was, like many of her party colleagues, swept away by the BJP wave in the 2019 elections. Despite the loss, she is keeping her head high, and keeps herself with busy with work. She remains the president of the All India Mahila Congress, the Congress party's women's wing, and frequently travels across the country for meetings and engagements, often with the Gandhi siblings to whom she is considered to be very close.

Sushmita doesn't have a romanticized view of Indian politics. She rues the unpredictability of it—in politics, one's 'input does not equal to output' and even after doing years of great work in Parliament and in their constituency, MPs lose elections because of factors outside their control. She candidly tells us that politics is an extremely tough profession with a 'heavy personal cost' to it. 'There is no mercy in this field,' she laments. She does not, however, show any sign of regret. She didn't join politics to keep the family legacy alive (in fact, her three older sisters all decided to stay away from public life) but because she sees it as a great platform to make and influence policy decisions. She hopes to eventually be remembered as a good policymaker rather than as a great politician.

What's striking about Sushmita is that she has a nuanced understanding of political and legal issues and is willing to brave the elements by advocating for unpopular or contrarian positions. She talks to us at length about why her opposition to the Modi government's Triple Talaq bill doesn't betray her fervent advocacy for women empowerment, what needs to be done to increase the cultural integration of people from the Northeast, and why the National Register of Citizens (NRC) is not a workable solution.

Given her involvement with the Mahila Congress, we spend a good amount of time discussing the challenges faced by women in politics and what can be done to increase their representation. She is acutely aware of these challenges, arguing that the journey of a woman in politics is more difficult than that of a man at every step of the way. Yet, she rejects a lot of measures aimed at women empowerment as pure 'tokenism'. She gives the example of the Maternity Benefit Act, which was recently amended to increase the paid maternity leave to women from 12 weeks to 26 weeks and was touted as a significant step towards women empowerment. Yet the Act, in her experience, has only made women less employable. She firmly believes that the key to empowering women is gender sensitization of men because any attempts to empower women without having men involved will be a futile exercise.

Given her experience leading the Mahila Congress and her proximity to the Gandhis, Sushmita Dev is likely to play an important role in rebuilding the party, particularly in the North-east where the Congress has ceded a lot of ground to the BJP. Hopefully, she will also get more opportunities to influence policy decisions through Parliament or otherwise.

Interview

Q. Let us talk about women in politics. There is a massive under-representation of women in politics. Is it difficult to be a woman in a system that is very male-dominant?

Gender insensitivity exists across the country, across professions, across situations. Thus, the challenges that a woman faces in politics are not any different from the ones she faces in any other profession or calling. It is just that the extent varies. For example, a woman may not make it to the Board of Directors of a company because of gender discrimination or a different kind of discrimination at her workplace. However, in politics, especially in India, the electoral process itself is not perceived as a safe place for women. Electorally a woman is not in a safe place because news about the amount of violence that happens, the abuse of money and the use of muscle power is rampant. I am not saying that it is an admission of what I do or what somebody else does, but it happens in India. These are some of the factors that make it tougher for a woman to be in politics than in any other profession or other walks of life.

Q. We interviewed Ms Smriti Irani and she said that it is not tough to be a woman in politics, but it is tough to be a woman in power. She also talked to us about bureaucrats not wanting to take instructions from her and other people in politics responding differently to her because she is a woman. Would you agree with that statement?

But politics *is* perceived as a power play, isn't it? There are fewer women entering politics, in the first place, which is then followed by fewer women reaching and attaining powerful positions. So, it starts right from scratch. First, how do you enter politics; second, how do you survive in politics; and third, how do you rise in politics. This journey for a woman is completely different compared to a man who goes through the same processes. The bias of gender roles in predominant and I think that's what Smriti Irani is talking about. She essentially cannot exercise authority despite the fact that she has the jurisdiction and the power, because she is not taken seriously. This happens across the board and it is because they haven't seen many women make it to powerful positions.

Q. *As the head of the All India Mahila Congress, an organization that deals with these questions every day, what are some of the solutions you have come up with to make this situation better for women? How do you increase representation in politics?*

There is absolutely no way one can empower a person belonging to a certain sex, caste, gender, creed, or language unless others in the system facilitate said empowerment. For instance, if men are opposed to me because I am a woman, empowerment will just turn into tokenism. Hence, gender sensitization of men is the key to empowerment of women. Keeping women in isolation is not going to work either. There has to be an integration of both men and women who together have to understand that women empowerment is important. What generally happens is that a whole lot of women get into a room and have a seminar on women empowerment discussing about greater political participation of women, more jobs for women, et cetera. There is no point. What is essentially standing in the way of empowerment? One, social norms, and two, a fight for space with men. Thus, it is men who must discuss women empowerment because all women agree that we should be empowered.

Q. *In the political system, do you find opposition to that by male colleagues?*

I keep thinking of ways to initiate integration. For instance, I run the Frontal Organization—there is one for the youth, one for students and one for women. I try to encourage integration in the programmes held by the Frontal Organization and other bodies as well. I suggest the Youth Congress to conduct women empower-ment programmes such that we can join them. I tell the parent body that we are hosting a programme and we want our top male leaders to attend it. Sometimes by creating different compartments one tends to isolate women and it becomes that much easy to perpetuate gender discrimination. The idea is to put everybody in one pool and say 'now work it out for yourselves'. If somebody has worked in my Frontal Organization, I make sure that if they have worked diligently they get promoted to the parent body. So, they see the organization as a stepping stone, a softer platform to get into the mainstream party. Unless we change the perception of women's organizations, we will just end up being a separate compartment that has nothing to do with the rest of the party. We don't work in that way.

Q. *Are you finding the required level of support from male MPs across different parties in the parliament? Or are you and other women still finding resistance?*

Of course, women still find resistance, and there are two reasons for that. Firstly, politics is a place where input is not equal to out-put. It is not as predictable as any other job, and it is competitive. So in order to compete with a man, you will have to be as good and privileged as a man. The second thing that stands in their way is the fact that they are women so it is easier to sideline them and push them around in an intense environment.

Q. *Are there some issues in politics that you, over your time and career in politics, hope to be able to address? Any issues that you have a particularly deep interest in, a particular passion for?*

The worst thing that happens to the empowerment of women is when it turns into tokenism. For example, we have a law called the Maternity Benefit Act. This Act gives 26 weeks of paid leave to a woman or lactating mother. In India, the implementation of this Act has made women more unemployable. If you look at some of the other countries where this law exists, the government contributes as well which ensures that she is not such a big liability to the company. Going back to the question—I am consistently focused on trying to alter the really skewed view of women empowerment that exists in India. In the name of women empowerment you can't actually, one, isolate the women from the mainstream, or two, give them so many benefits that they are seen as a burden. Although our constitution does not permit discrimination and the law of this country has to treat everyone equally (Article 14), women and children are an exception and are seen as a special case because they need that added advantage. Having said that, we can't keep making laws that actually isolate them. Hence, I am constantly focusing within the party, inside the parliament on making sure that we don't go in the wrong direction when it comes to women empowerment.

Q. *What is the most fulfilling thing about being in politics? And what are some of the biggest challenges that you have faced?*

I think you cannot come into politics and survive unless you are crystal clear that the motive is to serve the people. You need to understand that you are a policymaker. Whatever you do, say, agree, disagree, debate, amend in the legislature actually shapes the nation. I am also a lawyer and I have a bar at law from the UK. So what I find most fulfilling about what I do is the fact that I can discuss policies. I was an opposition MP, so I can't say that I formulate them. But I definitely had a say in them. Being a politician or being a political representative is not just about building roads, bridges, and railway lines. It is also about representing the people of your constituency effectively in Parliament. It is about raising their issues, finding solutions to their problems, and giving them a political voice. Some governments build more roads while some build more railway lines—that's a matter of degree. But your real job as a politically elected representative is to make sure that the voice of the people is heard. Thus, sometimes when you ask a question of the government, it doesn't always materialize into a solution for your people. Your people back in the constituency feel proud and hopeful that their problem was raised in the highest forum. That is also something that I find most fulfilling. The biggest difficulty that I have faced in politics is I feel that sometimes what one does over five years can get washed out in the five months before elections. Such is the nature of Indian politics. I feel this is because public recall is very short. Elections in India are sometimes fought on sentiment. So you may have done all the right things, but some unwanted unforeseen trigger in the last five months can make it all go against you. So, what I don't like about Indian politics is that it is very unpredictable. Another thing that I don't like is that good parliamentarians don't always win. If you look at the data of Lok Sabha, more than 50 per cent of MPs don't get elected in the next parliament. Thus, the fact that you are an effective parliamentarian doesn't necessarily translate into electoral victory. The factors are very different. That's the unpredictable part which makes me uncomfortable.

Q. *Incumbency rates in India are very low compared to the US and the UK where the re-election rate is over 90 per cent. Why do you think it is so low in India? Do you think it is partly because the parties aren't giving them tickets again? Or is it that the parties are giving them tickets again but these people are failing to win the second time?*

Generally, you get a ticket if you have won the first time unless your performance has been outrageously bad or you have done something that was very controversial. Most of the people help you, the party will give you a ticket, but people don't re-elect you half the time.

Q. This issue is unique to India. Do you find that despite your efforts you are unable to convince your voters that you have done the work? Or is it that their expectations are so outrageous that it is something that you just cannot deliver how much ever you try?

Apart from the fact that there are some people who underperform or don't perform, I feel the biggest problem with our system is that the demand is more than the supply when it comes to roads, railways, and the like. Since the resources are limited, is there an objective way of selecting who is going to get what? I am consistently asking for a railway line but they have given me a stadium. So there should actually be a constituency-wise study or a state-wise study to understand the allocation of funds and resources to every state. There should be a way of objectively identifying the need of each constituency so that it is not left to the whim and fancy of the authorities, or the capability of that minister to identify the issues properly. Currently, there is no such objective measure. For instance, if the authorities favour you, you will be granted funds for five roads, whereas your constituency might be much better off than someone else's constituency. Thus, this is problematic. Like for instance, there is data that that is made available for malnutrition, for maternal mortality rate, et cetera, which the government then uses to base its expenditure on. So, connecting it back to why MPs win and lose—everything is not in their hands. In a parliamentary system, it is the council of ministers and the set of officers who decide what the budget and the new policies in the scheme are going to be. There is no impact that a normal MP can have on them. Thus, if I suddenly see a bill in Parliament which is totally detrimental to my constituency or to my state, there is nothing that I can do about it because the government has already bought it. All that can happen is that it can go to a standing committee. However, recommendations of the standing committee are not mandatory. The problem with our parliamentary system is that we are elected but the lack of the kind of decision-making power that we should have in the government hampers the rate of re-election.

The last five years have been completely disastrous. Several bills have come and not gone to the standing committee. So, there is no legislative scrutiny. There is only a simple debate and then whatever the government wants will be passed.

Q. *Since you are a role model for a lot of young women across the country as the head of the Congress's women's wing, people were disappointed about your statement of reversing the Triple Talaq decision if you came back to power. People look at the decision as giving women across the country their due, giving them their individual freedoms, freeing them from oppression and injustice. What are your thoughts on the issue?*

The biggest problem with this country is that we blindly believe what we are told on a TV screen without actually investigating who is saying what. I am the MP from Congress who debated the Triple Talaq bill on two occasions because it was brought to Parliament twice. First, they passed it, it went to the Rajya Sabha and then it came back with amendments. What I said inside the parliament is exactly what I said outside the parliament. I started by saying that the Supreme Court has done justice by banning instant Triple Talaq as being wrong in theology and therefore, being wrong in law. But what I said that this bill is doing is it is criminalizing it. In the bill, the Supreme Court already says it is banned. So, if you were to say 'Talaq! Talaq! Talaq!' to your wife, it is of no consequence. However, all that the bill has done is that it has criminalized it. What I said in that function was that the bill is pitching a woman against a man in a criminal procedure where it is a civil judiciary and that we will undo this law, this bill, and not the Supreme Court judgement. None of the Acts that govern marriages whether you are Hindu Christian, Parsi, Buddhist, et cetera, criminalize desertion. So why is this government so keen to criminalize it when it comes to Muslim women? There are two reasons for it. One is that Narendra Modi has a desperate need to get rid of his anti-minority image, and the other is the desperate need to keep demonizing Muslim men. Why do they not give the same right to the women of other religions? Why not make it an offence for every religion? Why are you so keen on Muslims?

Q. *So you are in support of the Supreme Court judgement. You want to do away with this social evil.*

I said that Narendra Modi ji has got a bill that has pitched a Muslim woman against a Muslim man and that we will not allow this bill to go through and we will make sure this bill is revoked. I never said that the Supreme Court judgement should be revoked. I also said Congress has always stood by anything that empowers women, and we will not stand by this bill. The funny part is, they kept saying that 100 or 200 odd women have been a victim of Triple Talaq and this needs an ordinance, that despite the Supreme Court judgement this evil continues to exist. So, according to that logic murders and rapes continue to happen despite the fact that under 302, murder, rape, et cetera, are offences. If they want to do it, then they should give the same right to a woman who has been deserted under any other religion. They'll not do it. Why? It is very clear to my mind. The rhetoric of women empowerment is the worst thing that happens in this country.

Q. *As an MP from Assam, you are also representing the Northeast. Can you elaborate on some of the tensions that you see in the Northeast? Are the problems faced by people there different from the rest of India in your opinion?*

The Northeast is very sensitive vis-à-vis its ethnicities and ethnic identity. The RSS doesn't understand that. It will take them another 25–30 years to understand or begin to even decipher the names of different tribes. They want a *Hindu rashtra*, which means there is no space for any other religion, ideology, or practice. This thought process is completely contrary to what Vivekananda's Hinduism is. *Hindutva* is a political concept, Hinduism is a philosophy, religion, whatever you want to call it. The RSS tried to impose things on the anti-Muslim narrative which didn't work in the Northeast. Just because you win an election doesn't mean what you are doing vis-à-vis governance is correct. Especially not in this country. Even if the common man doesn't understand the nuances of what is happening, given that Arunachal has the longest border with China, Meghalaya has the longest border with Bangladesh, you cannot afford to have disturbance in these areas. The biggest disservice that RSS has done to the nation is disturbing these areas. This is not just a Northeast problem.

Q. What steps can be taken to increase the cultural integration of people from the Northeast with the rest of India? What about the youth of the Northeast? You don't have many industries, so how do we give them the level of opportunities that they need?

Integration is a two-way road. Some things, like higher education, have to be brought to the people of Northeast while other things that cannot be made available in the area have to be sought out by them. We are geographically disconnected. Except for the chicken's neck we are not connected to the rest of India and we have to go through Bangladesh in between. I feel that we are still struggling for connectivity to the mainland by way of flights and trains. We have to find a way of making it cheaper for people to travel because our economy in the Northeast is a smaller and less rich economy. Despite the Ude Desh ka Aam Nagrik (UDAN) scheme, it hasn't worked. The Ministry of Development of North Eastern Region used to subsidize airlines, but now they have stopped that. The most important way to increase integration is connectivity. Kids in mainland north India are not used to seeing people who don't look like them, who don't think like them. What's the reason for this? It is because they don't come here that often, they come in very small numbers. So, they have preconceived notions about them.

Q. *You disagree with what the BJP is trying to do with NRC and their approach to the whole issue of immigrants from Bangladesh and other areas, and there has been some polarization as well that has led to a lot of people resonating with their stance on immigrants. What is your solution? How do you resolve those kinds of issues?*

I come from a part of Assam which is dominated by Bengalis, and we were a part of Sylhet before partition. So I am a Bengali from Assam. The problem of migration has to be faced by India as a country. Most Northeastern people do not want immigrants to encroach on their land because six schedule states treat their land differently. So essentially, there are two issues before the country—one is preserving the identity of the Northeastern people, and two is dealing with the issue of illegal migration. Bangladesh is not taking them back and that is pretty clear. So firstly, nobody knows the extent of illegal migration. That's where NRC started and it has not ended since. Secondly, we have no idea what to do with them because Bangladesh is not taking them back. Thirdly, India as a nation has an excellent record of giving asylum and refuge to people except for one or two instances. So, there is a question of international law also. I know we are not signatories of the 1951 convention, yet, India has never been known to push back people through the border. Hence, we have to look at it from the regional, national, and an international perspective and find a solution because these people can't be sent back. So eventually when NRC is over and you know how many foreigners are there, India as a nation will have to solve this problem.

See, what is NRC? It is like a self-assessment. You go to the government and say, 'These are my papers and I am a citizen.' Entire Assam has applied for it claiming they are citizens. Now Narendra Modi's bill is saying that if you are a foreigner and you have come for religious persecution, if you belong to a certain religion and if you come from some other country, you can come and stay here. So now you have to prove you are from the other country. You spent the last five years proving you are an Indian, now you have to prove that you have come from one of these three countries. It is not a workable solution either way. But yes, there are two problems. One is not hurting the cultural identity of Northeast, and two, India as a nation has to deal with this. The United Nations is watching us what we are doing with the foreigners' problem eventually. We can't walk away from our international obligations. Let's see. Only time will tell what will happen.

Q. *Why did you decide to join politics? You have had members of your family in politics. Was that the main reason? What were some of the drivers that made you decide to get into politics?*

See, because you come from a political family is not the reason you join politics, because I have three other sisters who have no interest in politics.

Q. *Why were you one of the four sisters who decided to join politics?*

My dad was very clear that politics is not a profession and that you can't expect to put food on your table if you get into politics. My grandfather was a minister in the Assam legislature, my dad was an MP, my mother was an MLA. So, it was very clear to me that I should come into politics only if I am interested in policymaking, in being an effective representative for the people of my area and go on to also serve the interests of the people of my area. If you have any faux reason, you can come in politics but it is unlikely that you will last. It'll be like a shoot and scoot kind of a situation. However, I always wanted to do representative politics, because to serve the people you can always just run an NGO. You don't have to come into politics. As an NGO you can serve the people, you can serve the country, but you can't make policy decisions unless you are in the legislature or you are in the parliament. You just end up as a pressure group, and I wanted to exercise a direct impact.

Q. *Outside of politics can you talk about some things that you are very passionate about? What do you take interest in?*

I used to play golf, for which I don't have time any more, and apart from my political career I think I would love to do organizational work. And if I were to say that I am not doing my work, then I would definitely become a professional golfer.

Q. *If the US President makes time for golf, you can make time for golf…*

Because he is the president! He can tell someone that I don't have two hours now, I am going to play. I am not! If I make it to that level then I would be able to say that I'll be busy for two hours playing golf. But I know what you mean. That is no excuse, you are probably right. I am just lazy.

Q. *Being in electoral politics and being as active as yourself comes at a big personal cost. Have you faced that?*

There are absolutely no timings in this profession, there is no mercy in this field. It is like no other profession. You have to be completely committed and obsessed with what you do. Anything short of that and you can't survive in this. Because there are no working hours, there are no holidays. If there is a fire then you have to get up and go at 1 am in the morning. If someone is in an accident and they call you, you have to make sure that you take that call and make sure they're alright because it is serving the people. It is a very tough profession and I think there's a very heavy personal cost to it. There is no doubt about that aspect and anybody who wants to be in politics should gear up for that.

Q. *You had the election loss in Silchar in 2019. What were the take-aways for you after this surprising defeat and what kind of impact does a loss have personally? Did it surprise you? How do you think about that?*

I think my election was a tough one. I always knew that. I think I lost to polarization. Basically, I feel the BJP completely polarized my election. Personally, victory and defeat are part of a political career. You have to take it in your stride. It will start working in the end. The challenge for the Congress is to have a narrative to develop the economy, address the unemployment. Our challenge is to bring the narrative back on these issues, rather than religious profiling of people.

Q. *The performance of Congress was unexpectedly poor. The party finds itself in a very weak position today. As you said you are not in that position to speak for the party. In your personal view, is there any steps that you hope that Congress would take to revive itself?*

We have to work harder at the grassroots—that is what I person-ally think. Basically, we lost to a machinery: a machinery that takes a lot of things which are not factual, created a narrative. We didn't have a mechanism or machinery to counter that.

What India is going through is cult politics and every opposition party has to find a counter-narrative to depolarize it. There is no way to measure what impacted who and to what extent. Absolutely no way to scientifically measuring that. But one thing is crystal clear that the tilt of the prime minister's campaign in this last election was clearly towards polarizing India. He took huge advantage of the army, despite us going to Supreme Court about the inaction of Election Commission. The Election Commission basically did nothing. The Election Commission did not so much reprimand or even caution the prime minister. You are up against not just the party but against an entire system that is not working for you. Look at the state of media. The media in India is such that whenever an issue of national importance comes up, the media turns around and does not question the government but questions the opposition.

Q. *It seems Congress knows it has to find a solution. But nobody is really belling the cat. Why don't you come up with at least internally, some sort of framework or solutions and push the party towards the implementation of some of those?*

I cannot do it on my own. Everybody has been focusing on the leadership question. As far as I am concerned, the question is what is it that we are going to do. We have to put together a strategy. It is more important to focus on the way forward. What can one president do until all of us put our heads together? It is as easy as that. It will happen. You started by saying that the Congress is in a weak position. There is no doubt it is a setback, I am not denying that. This election is definitely a setback. But it is not the end of the road. Crores of people have voted for Congress party. There is enough data out there to say that Rahul Gandhi's USP has gone up in the last five years from what it was in 2014. Because he fought for the issue. It is not the end of the road. Even if they don't vote for us, they want to see Congress revived. Even then there are a lot people who voted for us. We just have to build from where we are, It is not the end of the world. Obviously, It is going to take a lot of hard work, a lot of micromanagement of voters. Because we have to take our message and politics to the lowest denominator. That is what we have to do. Everybody has to and so do I.

Q. *If you look back on your life when you are, say, 80, what are some of the things that you would like to be remembered for?*

I would like to be remembered as a good parliamentarian and a good orator. I feel I am still too young to say what I could be remembered for because I was just a first-time parliamentarian. Nevertheless, I would like people to remember me for my speeches and making sense and saying the right things. I want to be remembered as a good policymaker.

Varun Gandhi

Pilibhit Member of Parliament (MP) Feroze Varun Gandhi's unique journey, both personal and political, makes him one of the most enigmatic next-generation politicians in India today. As the scion of the Nehru-Gandhi dynasty, he carries both the privilege and burden of being the nephew, grandson, and great-grandson of Indian prime ministers. This legacy made him a household name across the country and gave him a ready political base. Yet it is also a burden; his party, the Bharatiya Janata Party (BJP), has made the Nehru-Gandhi dynasty the focal point of its attack on the Congress and repeatedly calls into question its contributions to the country. In his turbulent career, there have been enormous personal costs as well. Varun lost his father, grandmother, and uncle when he was very young. The consequent security risks meant that much like his cousins he had a very sheltered upbringing, surrounded permanently by armed guards, even having to switch between countries to complete his schooling.

His political journey has been equally tumultuous, with a meteoric rise followed by a sudden fall. He joined politics in his twenties, something he seems to regret, and soon got embroiled in a massive controversy over a hate speech that he was accused of making, for which he was later acquitted by the courts. He subsequently rose to become the youngest ever general-secretary of the BJP. This feat, however, was short-lived as he soon fell out of favour with the new Modi–Shah dispensation, allegedly for refusing to toe the line. One of the reasons often cited for this dispute is his apparent refusal to campaign against his cousin Rahul Gandhi, with whom (he reveals to us after the interview) he shares a very good personal relationship.

Since the Modi government took office in 2014, Varun has mostly stayed away from party politics. Instead, he has focused on remaining connected with the public through writing and speaking engagements. He delivered 284 lectures in two years, most of them on college campuses across the country. His syndicated column reaches a subscriber base of over 200 million through 17 newspapers, covering many different languages. In early 2019, he released a densely researched book on rural distress in India, which became a bestseller within days of its release. He was back on the campaign trail during the 2019 elections, but his focus was limited to his seat and that of his mother's. He repeatedly made national headlines for controversial and divisive remarks—from calling the Samajwadi Party(SP)-Bahujan Samaj Party(BSP) candidates 'representatives of Pakistan,' alleging that Mulayam Singh Yadav has the blood of the Ram *bhakts* on his hands, and that people like the BSP candidates are fit to 'untie his shoelaces'.

Meeting Varun, one is surprised that he is the same person making these statements on the campaign trail, or that he could be even accused of being a firebrand leader delivering hate speeches. He is exceptionally soft-spoken and gentle, and also 'cerebral', as another BJP leader whom we interviewed describes him. Our conversation with Varun covers everything from the deaths in his family to his awkward dynamic within the BJP to the hate speech fiasco and more. His answers are detailed and thoughtful, even candid, for the most part. We leave the interview intrigued by the contradictions that characterize his personal and political life.

Varun attributes his shift in focus away from party politics to a profound realization that occurred after the extremely painful death of his four-month-old daughter, who suffered from a rare metabolic disorder. Her death made him rethink his choices and priorities, pushing him to expand the focus of his work in politics to no longer 'play the game', but instead to try and change it. This, he says, resulted in his single-minded emphasis on policy, research, and writing. He insists that he is 'not a votary of party politics' and that his time is better served through thought leadership than through conventional politics. In fact, he claims that he had himself requested Prime Minister Modi in 2014 to let him cut back on party work.

What stands out most about Varun, however, is not his dissociation from his work for the BJP but the fact that he has chosen to join and stick with the party despite having a completely different ideological outlook on many issues. While the BJP has always been a right-of-centre party, Varun openly and proudly identifies as a progressive left-liberal. His economic outlook is particularly divergent from that of his party. He goes so far to call Bernie Sanders and Jeremy Corbyn, both known for advocating far-left economic and social policies, as his political inspirations. He even jokes that the communists call him the 'communist in the BJP'. It is evident that his allegiance to the BJP is less an ideological allegiance, but rather one determined by his social and familial ties to the party.

So, is the real Varun Gandhi a liberal intellectual or a firebrand politician, or both? Could it be that he feels compelled to behave a certain way on the campaign trail due to political compulsions? While we sense that the latter may be the case, the real answers to these questions remain unclear.

What is clear, however, is that even if Varun decides to take on a more active role in the BJP, his ideological dissonance with the party, coupled with what appears to be strained relations with Modi–Shah, means that he may not be able to play a significant role in the party or government in the foreseeable future. However, his successful policy outreach, repeated electoral successes, and deeply entrenched family legacy would likely ensure that he remains a distinctive contributor to India's public discourse for many more years to come.

Interview

Q. You lost your father when you were just a few months old. You lost your grandmother, too, at a very young age. How did these family crises impact your upbringing, your outlook on life, or your approach to politics?

I didn't really know my father, I was 100 days old when he passed away. So having not really known what it means to have a father, I suppose, mitigates the severity of not having one. I got married in 2010. In 2011, I had my first child and we lost her. She died about four months after birth. She had a metabolic disorder. That really shattered me because I was unprepared for it, but also that, when you have a child it's like your heart is beating out of your chest, and the unconditional love that you feel is unprecedented. When I saw my child struggling to survive, and after she died in my arms, there was a long period of silence within me. And I felt that I needed to rethink who I was as a person, what was important to me. I felt that all our lives we prioritize things that are really unimportant to the larger scheme of things. I felt if I were to continue in public life, I must expand the focus of what I am to do. And that laid the foundation for my policy writing, my larger outreach, and a lot of things which started after that. I felt a greater sense of responsibility, and I felt that there is no point being in politics to play the game, the only reason to be in politics is to change the game. When I look at people like Gandhi, Tilak, Madan Mohan Malviya, or even Maulana Azad, all of them wrote indefatigably, they wrote tirelessly, and they wrote to establish a deeper relationship with the Indian people. People like Jagjeevan Ram used to write in Hindi '*saare niyam shithil karte hue yeh nirnay liya jaaye*' which is that 'all rules should be completely set aside for this decision to be taken'. Today does any politician have the courage of his convictions to write that? They don't even want to sign on a file. And the reason is that then people had not only a deeper sense of passion towards governance, but they had a knowledge of governance. People who had been in jail, in adversity, had taken the time to be autodidacts, to be self-taught and to increase their self-awareness, and to be agents and vehicles of greater change which came through a process of knowledge because empathy, love, and kindness can only arise from a state of greater self-awareness. So when my daughter passed away, I feel that it led to a very deep sense of loss within me, but it also led to a deep sense of being free of all the baggage that perhaps I would have held on to had such a horrific tragedy not happened to me.

Q. *Why are you in politics? If it is about changing and impacting people's lives, there are many ways that one can do it.*

I am not seen as a conventional politician. I do a lot of things that are outside the box. I have the largest syndicated column in India. I write for 17 newspapers. I write for the two largest Marathi newspapers *Lokmat* and *Sakaal*. I write for the largest Gujarati newspaper. And I write solely on policy. I don't write on politics in an adversarial manner. A lot of them are solution-oriented and the syntax is not meant to be polemical, it is not meant to be an us versus them, me versus you, because in policy terms there is no me and you, there is only us. So for instance, because of my recent book, *A Rural Manifesto*, I was able to travel the country widely. And my next book is on urbanization, it will be out by the end of next year. I am also starting something called the Hunger, Nutrition and Climate Justice Collective, where we are going to work in five districts in India to eliminate hunger completely and we're looking at sustainable means of nutrition. We have already started this in my constituency, which is probably the only hunger-free constituency in rural India. We did the 'roti bank', we feed about 30,000 people a day sustainably. It's just civic society. We don't put money into it now, we only did that in the first year. But I also want to look at the way climate change has affected the Indian farmer and people living in riparian communities. The fact that 100 million hectares of land is now not arable anymore, it's important to conduct climate trials where we get the farmers and people from rural communities to come and talk to bureaucrats and politicians and policymakers, and think tanks and tell them how they have been affected, so we can evolve a document very quickly where we go to states all over India and tell them specifically how we can help them deal with climate change for their own people with simple solutions. I am also a poet and I am invested in literature, so the other thing I want to do is to start a poetry collective where we get young poets writing in various Indian languages from all over the country, from rural backgrounds, get together on one platform. So I am interested in different things.

Q. How has this unconventional approach helped you in politics?

I'll be honest with you, I have fought three elections and I have won with pretty large margins. The act of winning an election is to me a means to an end. I don't believe in the status quo-ism of party politics or conventional politics because I find that very bureaucratic and I also find it a complete waste of one's life. I feel that if you have been given a voice, if you have been given an opportunity, put your all into it to see how you can be a vehicle for larger transformation. And the voice that I have been given, with all due respect, is larger than the voice that most others have been given. I want to use that voice for good. I never took a parliamentary salary in the last 10 years.

Q. We know that you have donated your salary to different causes, mainly to the farmers ...

Yes. And then we ran a movement where we helped raise about 30 crore rupees. I am an economist by training, so we made an economic model where farmers who fall within those criteria are four times more likely to commit suicide. We went across UP and we crowdfunded. I put in a crore of my own money and we didn't take more than 10,000 from any person. So it was truly a large venture. But it then dawned on me that whether you help one person, or you help 5,000 people, it comes down to the same thing. The only way to help 40–50 crore people is through policy.

Q. For someone who has so many academic interests and who thinks of policy solutions, how do you fit into the party system that functions on a war footing, running from one election to another? Why do you find it necessary to be in politics?

The thing is that when I joined politics I was very young and I didn't know even the kind of person that I really was. In a way, it has been a very strange journey because I have had to grow up, since I was born, in the eye of almost a billion people. When people ask me what it feels like to always travel with a lot of security, etc., I tell them that I haven't known any other life. It appears absolutely normal to me. But when I go abroad and I am absolutely by myself going to a bookstore or a records store or taking my daughter for ice-cream, I am at my happiest, because it is very liberating for me. Were I to do it all over again, I would probably think of joining politics in my forties, because that's the time I feel that I will be truly comfortable in my own skin and I will know exactly what I need to do going forward. The twenties are often a blur in your mind, hormonally, in between adolescence and adulthood, the transition is very awkward, and you are supposed to behave in a way in which you may not perhaps emotionally subscribe to.

You have used a very right word which is 'necessary' and I see politics as necessary. I don't see politics as that something that addresses my core because I am quite spiritually inclined. I see the addressal of my core as a deeper journey. But politics is the realization or the actualization of that journey, it is an important tool. And the process when done with the right reasons in mind can help a tremendous amount of people. But like I said, I am not in it to play the game as it is played. I have done a lot of conventional politician things. It is exciting and heady, in a way. But it doesn't mean anything to me anymore. The only thing that now means something to me is to use the time that I have on this planet to do bigger things. I have done 284 lectures in the last two years. That is a very punishing pace. The reason I do that so that I can create a larger connection, a larger movement.

Q. *Do you feel that because you are not playing the political game, you are not getting your fair share in the BJP? You were the general-secretary and then were removed, you were not a part of the BJP's UP campaign or the 2019 campaign ...*

In 2014, I met the prime minister, and I said to him that I want some time off and I want to write, I want to travel, I want to do new things. And he said but you are a general-secretary and in charge of West Bengal and Assam and you have to be here. To be honest, I had done party work for six years, and I had done it to the best of my ability, but I was tired of all that. I wanted to do something that I felt radiated the kind of energy that I felt within me. And I felt that had I clung on to some responsibility, it would have taken up a huge amount of my time (because I believe in doing things well) which at that point in time I wasn't really ready to give. I didn't feel that I should ask for a responsibility only to do it half-heartedly. So I voluntarily stepped back. The thing is, I can step back into that overt political role any time because I am very much a person of the people.

Q. *And you've had this experience at a young age, you have won elections ...*

Yes. My mother has won eight elections, I have won three, and I shall God willing, win 10 more. But the fact is that the politicians that inspire me: *the* Bernie Sanders and *the* Jeremy Corbyn, all these politicians are full of a different kind of energy. I am driven by issues of economic inequality, of environmental justice, progressive issues of disadvantaged communities. I have taken many stands that are divergent from the party. And to be fair to my party, nobody has ever said anything to me. I came to thought leadership from mass leadership. I became a general-secretary at a very young age because, to be fair, in Uttar Pradesh, I helped restructure and resurrect the party from a very marginal position. We had about, if I am not mistaken, 47 legislators. I was at that point given 30 tickets, out of which 27 candidates won. That part of politics is not something that I find difficult. It is very much intrinsic to my character because I feel that if you are not comfortable with people-to-people contact then you should not be in politics. I love campaigning, I love going out and talking to people, I like learning from people, I like listening to their experiences. But what I am talking about now is taking that engagement to the next level, by seeing what you can really do for them as a person. It is not enough to shake hands and kiss babies and all that because that is a way of showing affection. Unless you have a real path that can deliver him economic and social justice, you have no business pretending to him that you care. So thought leadership, or whatever word you would like to use, is in a way me investing my time in things that I feel will tomorrow be good for the country. Because if I don't know anything then what do I have to give? The day I have nothing to give anymore will be my last day in politics.

Q. *We keep reading things like you are not happy with the party leadership or the party leadership is not happy with you, and you might want to move to the Congress, et cetera. Or are you and the party leadership in equilibrium in terms of your role in the party?*

My sense is, if one were to look at it in terms of ideology or policy, then I am a centre-left thinking person. I am not a right-wing person by nature. If you have read all my writings, for the last 10 years I have had a consistently progressive liberal record. As a person, I have grown into this voice which is what's inside me. But I do find the BJP over a longer period of time (because when you look at political history you can't look at it in a three–five year dimension, you have to look at it in a 25–30 year dimension) in a way quite tolerant of different intellectual disciplines within the larger political framework. So it is true that there are strident right-wing voices within the BJP. But it is also true that there was a Vajpayee, who for a large part of his life talked about Gandhian Socialism. In terms of religion I am a believer, I am an *aastik*, so I pray I believe in God, et cetera. So I am not an irreligious atheist, and I derive my strength from a spiritual centre. A spiritual centre and religious centre are two vastly different things. And I do feel that there are some very good structural things within the BJP. When I joined the BJP, after a few years I realized one very good thing about it was that there was a decentralization of power. I think that centralized power in any form is never a great thing. So what I felt was here was a party where even if you fell out with one leader you could survive and succeed because there would be four other people to see goodness and talent and worth in you. That is one thing that encouraged me as a young person.

Q. *Being someone with progressive liberal views, being centre-left, what really draws you to the BJP? Why are you sticking with the party? Why not move to a party that is more in line with your values and your outlook on so many issues?*

I feel that there is a path in life which is individual and then there is a path in life which is political and public. I have been in this party for 15 years almost, I have built relationships within it,

I have got friends here. I feel that in the medium-to-long term, the workers of the BJP, I feel, are very committed, hardworking, middle class, humble, salt of the earth people who mean well for this country. I am not a huge votary of party politics, to be honest, so that's not what I think about at all.

Q. *Your grandmother, great grandfather were associated with the Congress. A lot of people would say that your views align more with the Congress.*

I have good relationships with many leaders across the board. On Twitter, Facebook, and on general public opinion, nobody from the other parties hardly ever knocks me. Even (Asaduddin) Owaisi is a dear friend of mine. Or the communists who always joke with me that you are a communist in the BJP. But what I mean is that at the end of the day, I feel that I am more bi-partisan by approach, definitely by thinking. But I have made a home here in the BJP, I have made relationships and I feel very secure here.

Q. *People have this perception that you are a firebrand leader and a right-wing leader. The origins of that lie in the alleged hate speech controversy in 2009. Do you still feel you are carrying baggage from that time?*

I don't think, to be honest, that anybody thinks any more that I am a firebrand person or a strident person. If you look at any of the public platforms, I don't think anybody would mention that. The thing is it was a very bizarre thing, this so-called speech, because when I fought my case and won, they apologized to me. The case was almost a complete mockery of justice and had it not happened during election time, it would have really been casti-gated. There were 40 witnesses against me out of which 22 were found not to exist on this planet. The voice match has 0 per cent match. If you talk to me I have a very soft voice, but if you hear that person shouting and screaming he has a voice like Amitabh Bachhan or Danny Denzongpa, not like me. The CD was spliced in 70 places. In one place I was supposed to be saying that '*Katuo ko* vote *mat do*' which is an insult against Muslims. But what am I saying? I am saying '*Ram Narayan Singh* CPM *se chunaav ladta hai aur who humesha* 5/10/15,000 *vote Lok Sabha mei paate hai aur aapke gaaon ke hi log* vote *dete hai. Toh aap jo jeetne waala aadmi hai usko* vote *deke uske upar ehsaan karo taaki use baadmei kaam lo.* Vote *katuo ko* vote *mat do jo keval vote kaatne ke liye ladh rahe hai aur jeetne ke liye nahi ladh rahe.*' (Ram Narayan Singh runs for the election from Communist Party of India (Marxist) (CPM) and he always gets 5 to 15,000 votes. You must vote for someone who is there to win, so that you can get work done by him. Don't vote for someone who is there only to divide the votes.) There was no original CD. I am known to almost everybody in this country, so if I really said something like that supposedly once in my career (which I find in any case very bananas because why would anyone be one way over a period of 15 years and then, one day just go off?) Why is it that the so-called CD came out nine weeks after I supposedly gave the speech? If I gave a speech in India it would be on TV in 10 minutes. So what were they doing for nine weeks? Obviously somebody was just cutting and pasting the wretched thing. When I went to court and we presented everything, then not only did I get exonerated, but the UP government had to apologize to me, which they did and then the matter ended over there.

Q. It must have been a difficult phase for you, especially because you were only in your late twenties then.

Of course, it was a terrible phase for me and the reason it was terrible was because it was very far from what I was as a person and that is why I made a commitment to myself that till I don't get exonerated in court, I will not do anything else. It took me two years and I went to court 63 times. I was my own advocate and I fought my own case and I learnt the law to fight the case and I got exonerated. The district court was five hours away from my house. I would get up and go there, argue my case, and come back, and people just felt that it was a fool's errand but it was very important to me morally. That's why I don't agree that anybody sees me as a firebrand anymore because it has been a very long time and there have been a hundred things I have done since then. I was the only MP in Parliament that supported Anna Hazare; I was the only MP that went and sat at his *dharna* and I spoke about him in Parliament supporting the Lokpal Bill. So I have always taken stands that are symptomatic of some desire for progressive change. The kind of support and love that I get from a variety of audiences, I get about 10 times more support from the liberals than I get from the right-wingers. In fact, I get knocked by the right-wingers many times but I never get knocked by the liberals ever.

Conclusion

As we embarked on this journey, we weren't quite sure what to expect, given the nature of the exercise itself. From very real concerns of access, approach, and logistics, we were also preoccupied with the big picture—who will we get to meet, what we might learn, whether we will learn anything at all, and what might the interview process be like? Ultimately, these interviews proved to be a rewarding experience and gave us great insights into not only the ideals, passions, and personalities of the next-generation of India's political leaders but also the issues and tensions that lie at the heart of contemporary Indian politics.

There is a persistent myth in India that the younger politicians, especially those with dynastic lineages, are living off the fruits of the labour of their elders and hence lead easy lives. A nepotistic privilege often bestows economic, educational and political resources, and readymade traditional constituencies. What we discovered is that all of these politicians are more thoughtful, hardworking, and incisive than they are given credit for. Contrary to the common imagination that it is all smooth sailing, many of the leaders we interviewed have borne substantial personal costs from being active in Indian political life. This is true even for the dynasts. For many of them, it has not been an easy undertaking, and either they or their family has made big sacrifices. Six of the 20 political leaders we interviewed lost their fathers, all of whom were in politics, at a very young age. Rajiv Gandhi was assassinated and Pramod Mahajan murdered by a family member, both at the peak of their political power. Three others, Sanjay Gandhi, Madhavrao Scindia, and Rajesh Pilot died in accidents early on in their lives. The Gandhi cousins, Rahul, Priyanka, and Varun also witnessed the assassination of their grandmother, Indira Gandhi.

Politics in India is a full-time job. Almost all of the leaders we met said they struggle with maintaining a healthy work-life balance and more often than not have very little time for themselves. Across the board, a common wish is to be able to spend more time with their families and children but the precarious demands of the job make it challenging to have even the semblance of a wholesome personal life. On a day-to-day basis, their schedules are packed: we witness this firsthand. Almost all the politicians we interviewed had lines of people waiting to meet them. This was true across party lines, and even for Jignesh Mevani, the one independent politician we met. There were throngs of people outside the offices of Sachin Pilot, K.T. Rama Rao, Supriya Sule, and Akhilesh Yadav. Those who met us in more private settings, either in their homes or their offices, were running tight schedules; we often had to either wait for long or reschedule the interview altogether. The vast number of individuals that these leaders interact with daily affords them little space and time to themselves. Those who have a security cover feel the constraints of being surrounded by people at all times. Rahul Gandhi tells us that the only time he gets some privacy is when he travels abroad.

All the leaders we met are insightful and have a keen understanding of political and in some cases, legal issues. Regional politicians like Kalikesh Singh Deo and K.T. Rama Rao have in-depth knowledge of political institutions and the role of the various levels of government—local, state, and national, as well as the interaction between them. They speak openly of the sometimes limited power of state governments. Assaduddin Owaisi is a sharp legal mind who has mastered the interpretation of the Constitution of India. He can make quick references to arcane legal materials to support any argument. Most importantly, however, all of the politicians we meet are deeply aware, depending on their political positions, of the limits of their influence. Mewani speaks of the powers of dominant castes and classes on Indian society, economy, and politics. He also knows that as an independent and unaffiliated elected MLA, he has little direct influence on the actions of the government.

A fact that cannot be underlined enough is the willingness on part of the politicians to answer any questions we posed to them. After our first interview with Rahul Gandhi in Berkeley in 2017, many people asked us if the conversation had been scripted. We still get the question quite often. As we noted in our profile, Rahul had indicated in no uncertain terms that he was an open book; we could ask him anything. In fact, none of the 20 interviewees laid any preconditions before us. They did not ask us to tell them what questions or topics we would discuss with them, in order to vet the questions or prepare ahead. Neither they nor their offices intervened in the interviews—the politicians gave us carte blanche to ask them anything. We did. Furthermore, they answered the questions ex tempore. We perhaps benefitted from the fact that the interviews would appear in print and that too in an academic book. Smriti Irani encapsulated the common sentiment quite succinctly by remarking that if she could not answer tough questions we posed to her, she did not deserve to be in her line of work!

Not only did they answer any and every question, but many of the leaders were also refreshingly candid. Priyanka Gandhi had no hesitation discussing the allegations against her husband Robert Vadra and the impact of the investigation and news coverage on her family. She spoke openly about how she dealt with it personally and explained it to her children. Milind Deora was frank about the challenges the Congress faces, his relationship with the party leadership, and his occasional ideological differences with the Congress. Jignesh Mevani spoke openly about his limitations in how he may have treated his female partners. Devendra Fadnavis was upfront about the influence of the RSS in his upbringing and how the BJP's central leadership helped ensure that he didn't face factionalism. Assaduddin Owaisi had no qualms discussing issues ranging from the business of making and drafting laws in Parliament to the problems facing India's youth. Omar Abdullah's convictions—earnest, and given the recent developments in Jammu and Kashmir, possibly polarizing for the undiscerning reader—were front and centre in our conversation with him. Aaditya Thackeray, anticipating a transformational moment for Shiv Sena, addressed the need to change his party with the times and how he is trying to walk the talk.

While all of India's next-generation leaders face some common challenges, there are some deep ideological differences among them. Some of these differences are par for the course and along party lines. The Bharatiya Janata Party politicians we interviewed spoke of the importance of nationalism and strong kinship with the party cadre to them. On the other hand, Congress politicians tried to emphasize that they represent the diversity which is emblematic of India. Their vision of the party, it emerged, was one which focused on a coalition of disparate social and economic interests. Leaders from regional parties spoke openly of fiscal and political centre-state disputes and the need to protect state interests. Interviewees affiliated to caste or religious parties were explicit in their identity-based politics, stressing the primacy of the needs of the caste and religious groups their parties stood for.

Certain dissimilarities between our respondents, however, do not follow partisan affiliations. We found that the parties are rarely ideologically homogeneous. There are many instances of dissonance between the party and the person. Varun Gandhi, a member of the BJP, proudly proclaims that he is a progressive liberal whose economic and social ideology is modelled on that of Jeremy Corbyn or Bernie Sanders. Aaditya Thackeray is advocating for policies like Mumbai 24×7, which one would hardly associate with the Shiv Sena. As the interviews make clear, Varun Gandhi, Rahul Gandhi, and even Aaditya Thackeray are far more ideologically similar than one would ever imagine.

There is one area where ideology cuts across party lines, and that is the position of women, both within the pluralistic societies and cultures all over India, as well as in political life. All the female politicians we interviewed, from the NCP, BJP, and the Congress, reported similar gender-based challenges. These ranged from problems of perception, the idea of feminine labour, and meritocratic difficulties where, as it is aptly quipped, women have to work twice as hard to be considered half as good as the men in their profession. It was observed across the board that women had difficulty in political life because of the multiple tasks which had to be dealt with simultaneously, from the home to be a full-time politician. Some like Smriti Irani were explicit about the tribulations they faced in getting men to understand and accept that they were in charge, and that their views had to be heard and followed. None of them was in favour of a tokenist approach to encourage women's political participation, that is, giving women positions just because they were women. All of them seek a fundamental transformation of gender relations in India.

In the 'Introduction' to this book, we observed that all of the next-generation leaders of India have grown up and come of age in an era of factionalism, identity politics, social and political conflict, and a deep polarization of the society along the lines of difference. None of those challenges and conflicts have yet gone away, and are in fact likely to become only intensified. Populations across the country are still driven by religious, caste, class, and linguistic divisions. Some of these problems are only getting murkier as India urbanizes rapidly, with heavy migration, deeper digital linkages, and an assimilationist push towards nationalism and identity-consolidation, something that is also happening elsewhere, from Europe to the Americas. India's behemoth of a youth-force also faces an unpredictable future, with difficult economic conditions, sclerotic job growth, agricultural distress, declining living quality across cities, and more and more frequent extreme disaster events stemming from climate change. Will this generation of leaders be able to comprehend and deal with the plethora of upcoming challenges? We entered this project somewhat unsure of the answer to that question. But, as we completed these interviews, we are far more hopeful than before about the capability of these political leaders to address these issues effectively and bring meaningful change to not just their constituents' lives, but the face of Indian politics itself.